D1474814

International Order
and Foreign Policy

Westview Replica Editions

This book is a Westview Replica Edition. The concept of Replica Editions is a response to the crisis in academic and informational publishing. Library budgets for books have been severely curtailed; economic pressures on the university presses and the few private publishing companies primarily interested in scholarly manuscripts have severely limited the capacity of the industry to properly serve the academic and research communities. Many manuscripts dealing with important subjects, often representing the highest level of scholarship, are today not economically viable publishing projects. Or, if they are accepted for publication, they are often subject to lead times ranging from one to three years. Scholars are understandably frustrated when they realize that their first-class research cannot be published within a reasonable time frame, if at all.

Westview Replica Editions seem to us one feasible and practical solution to the crisis. The concept is simple. We accept a manuscript in camera-ready form and move it immediately into the production process. The responsibility for textual and copy editing lies with the author or sponsoring organization. If necessary we will advise the author on proper preparation of footnotes and bibliography. The manuscript is acceptable as typed for a thesis or dissertation or prepared in any other clearly organized and readable way, though we prefer it typed according to our specifications. The end result is a book produced by lithography and bound in hard covers. Edition sizes range from 200 to 600 copies. We will include among Westview Replica Editions only works of outstanding scholarly quality or of great informational value and we will exercise our usual editorial standards and quality control.

International Order and Foreign Policy:
A Theoretical Sketch of Post-War International Politics
Friedrich V. Kratochwil

The author develops a new perspective for the study of problems of international order by drawing on and integrating insights from game theory, social psychology, hermeneutics, and language philosophy. His case study is the rise and demise of the Cold War. This newly developed approach not only allows a critical evaluation of the contending arguments of revisionist and traditionalist historiography, but also facilitates the raising of more normatively oriented questions and enhances our understanding of conflict in connection with the investigation of the present international order.

Friedrich V. Kratochwil, assistant professor of political science at the University of Maryland, Baltimore County, received his Ph.D. in international relations from Princeton University. The present work was written under the auspices of the former University Consortium of World Order Studies and was furthered by a fellowship grant from the Konrad Adenauer Foundation of Germany.

δεμένοι. ἐχθίστη δὲ ὀδύνη τῶν ἐν ἀνθρώποισι
αὕτη, πολλὰ φρονέοντα μηδενὸς κρατέειν.

It is the most hateful of sorrows afflicting mankind to
have knowledge of so much and power over nothing.

Herodotus. Histories. Bk. IX. 16.

International Order and Foreign Policy

A Theoretical Sketch of Post-War International Politics

Friedrich V. Kratochwil
Preface by Richard Falk

Westview Press
Boulder, Colorado

A Westview Replica Edition

Published in 1978 in the United States of America by
  Westview Press, Inc.
  5500 Central Avenue
  Boulder, Colorado 80301
Frederick A. Praeger, Publisher and Editorial Director

Library of Congress card number: 77-94107
ISBN: 0-89158-065-4

Printed and bound in the United States of America

TO MY FATHER †
AND MOTHER

CONTENTS

PREFACE
by Richard Falk

It is surprising how little literature in international relations withstands the test of time. Sometimes it seems not only as if Thucydides, Machiavelli, and Hobbes established a dominant tradition of inquiry, but long ago managed to write virtually everything that it is possible to know about the subject. This dominant tradition of speculation has emphasized "the realities" of a world in which political actors engage in rivalries that are resolved by diplomatic manipulation if possible, by open warfare if necessary. There is no pretention that a system of humane governance is possible on a global scale. Appearance to the contrary, the League of Nations and the United Nations are extensions of the state system rather than alternatives to it, providing a convenient forum for discussion without posing any threat to the predominance of the sovereign state. The outcome of international conflict remains ultimately a test of statist wills and capabilities. Might makes right. Peace treaties sanctify the fruits of aggression. Prudence and self-restraint are as close as diplomacy comes to morality.

The Marxist analysis of international relations, especially through its interpretation of imperialism, has added a dimension to this "realist" tradition. The revolutionary outlook of Marxist thought is, indeed, the one optimistic view of global reform that continues to be taken seriously. In many parts of the world, Marxism rests its internal case on the conviction that the socialist transformation of national societies will automatically produce a harmonious global society constituted by a community of socialist states. So far, historical experience defies theoretical expectations. In practice, national interests have proven more decisive than ideological affinity, as strained relations within the socialist sector of world society suggest. And so, except for the most dogmatic adherents of the faith, Marxism-Leninism does not provide a credible path to a peaceful world system.

Among non-Marxists, those who insist that drastic global reform is possible and necessary are scorned or simply ignored, dismissed as "idealists," or utopians, treated as victims of illusion who would actually be dangerous if ever given access to power because of their failure to grasp the play of forces at work in international life. This cynical consensus has not been dissipated in the nuclear age. It is generally accurate even for those heads of state who constantly proclaim their aspirations for peace and justice. It includes even those leaders who announce that the time has come to supplant balance of power politics by world order politics, yet act as if geopolitics as usual were the only viable option.

The value-laden rhetoric used by statesmen may express the sentiments of a given leader with sincerity. Such leaders are, however, without much freedom of action. A political consciousness shaped by centuries of thought and practice is distrustful of all efforts to premise foreign policy upon the hypothetical values of peace and justice for all. The bureaucratic framework of the modern state, as well as highly entrenched domestic pressure groups, place strict limits on what it is possible for a head of state to do. Usually, also, long before such a leader emerges, whether by election or selection, his reliability as a custodian of traditional attitudes has been established. Occasionally, a popular leader can ignore these constraints to a slight degree by mobilizing mass opinion behind his policies, but in the modern state, at least, the space for innovation is highly restricted. As a consequence, the system of states seems rigid, resistant to reform through the voluntary adjustment of existing policymakers and powerwielders.

What seems evident is that sovereign states continue to be preoccupied with increasing their power, wealth, and prestige to the extent possible, even as they acknowledge the new vulnerability of such a logic of acquisition in a global setting of scarcity, severe inequality and deprivation, and a spreading capability to engage in disruptive violence, whether it be randomized terrorism of dispossessed groups or the highly cerebral terrorism of national security specialists. Such a dynamic in a complex world of 150 states, at least six of which already possess nuclear weapons capabilities, has caused considerable anxiety about whether the human species is likely to endure very much longer. Throughout this era of geopolitics, the United States and the Soviet Union have dominated the international scene and by their prowess, by their intense conflict with one another, and by their managerial efforts to avoid direct warfare. For many people the relationship between these two superpowers has been until very recently virtually tantamount to the whole history of international relations since World War II.

This bipolar configuration of power began to disintegrate at the start of the 1970's in response to a series of developments: OPEC's oil embargo and pricing policy, India's nuclear explosion, Vietnam's victory on the battlefield, Third World solidarity on global economic policy, and China's emergence as a junior superpower. These factors have temporarily, at least, supplanted the Cold War and for a while shifted the attention of most statesmen away from East-West issues and toward a focus upon the North-South axis of conflict.

For the North the principal question was how to respond to a variety of Third World demands for redistribution of power, wealth, and economic advantages. In the United States a controversy emerged as to whether to accommodate or confront "the barbarians at the gates." This period reached its climax, at least in the current phase of North-South relations, with the Sixth and Seventh Special Sessions of the United Nations General Assembly in 1974-75. Since then pressure from the South has ebbed and renewed concern with Soviet-American relations has taken shape.

Part of this revival has resulted from a change in administration in Washington. Jimmy Carter arrived at the White House in 1977 with the conviction that the United States had given more than it received in the context of detente diplomacy and that American statecraft should strive for the high moral ground calling for, among other things, an exposure of Soviet failures in the areas of human rights. As well, a new series of claims are being made in American policy circles that the Soviet Union is on its way to a position of military superiority unless the United States steps up its own efforts at weapons innovation and deployment. For the Soviet Union, there never was "a threat from the Third World" (except in the sense that its antagonism with China represented a threat). Soviet foreign policy has consistently aimed, it seems, since World War II at catching up so as to become an equal superpower with the United States, and to either share fully in the work of global management or to play an equivalent geopolitical role. Having caught up on the military dimension, the possibilities of primacy may be now intriguing Moscow policymakers, for Soviet leaders have never abandoned their preoccupation with East-West relations. However, within Soviet ruling circles there has been since Stalin's death in 1953 an evident split between hard-liners and soft-liners. It is difficult to construe the causal chain, but there is recently discernible in Moscow, as well as in Washington, a hardening of outlook, a relatively greater priority accorded the conflictual side of the relationship. In this new period superpowers' tensions are higher and a fundamental uncertainty exists about the character of the relationship, which seems to waver somewhere between a full-fledged renewal of the Cold War and further extensions of superpower detente.

Against this specific historical background, an adequate conception of international order—that is, the order appropriate and possible for a system of sovereign states—is difficult to specify. A few general attributes can be noted. First of all, to be credible such a conception must exhibit an understanding of the centrality of power in the interaction of states. Secondly, the ordering logic must not be derived by analogy to the domestic structures of governance that have emerged within states. Thirdly, due note must be taken of the elaborate efforts by principal rival states, to almost always limit conflict to mutually acceptable forms. In a significant sense the study of international order is the study of the conflict-limiting mechanisms operative within a particular historical context. That is, international order reflects the interplay between a statist structure and specific historical circumstances.

At present, the interpretation of these historical circumstances seems unusually difficult. An underlying condition of flux is especially pronounced. As a consequence, most formal political discourse seems confused, often almost irrelevant. It is a time when it is difficult to know what to expect, what to hope for, and what to do. At such a moment occasionally a book comes along that penetrates several levels of bewilderment and leaves a reader with an excited sense of a deeper understanding of what is going on in the political realm. Friedrich Kratochwil has written such a book. It combines a theoretically innovative approach to international order with a detailed inquiry into Soviet-American relations that is illuminating on the level of practical politics. Kratochwil substitutes a process model of interaction for the traditional model of governance to get at the distinctive character of international order. This substitution enables Kratochwil to avoid the artificial choice between claiming that international order is somehow analogous to domestic order or to allege that international order is a contradiction in terms given underlying conditions of "anarchy."

What Kratochwil argues, and to great effect, is that the form and quality of international order depends predominantly (although not exclusively) on horizontal interactions on the level of state-to-state relations. Following from this line of interpretation is the marginal relevance of vertical institutional structures (i.e., international institutions) for an understanding of international order. Such a conception of international order could also embrace vertical geopolitical (e.g., imperialism, spheres of influence) and transnational (e.g., MNC's) relations, although this dimension of control is not especially pertinent to Kratochwil's main concern about ordering relations among autonomous states. Kratochwil addresses the basic question of international order—how can there be order without government? His response is a sophisticated one, premised on the reasonableness of regarding the process by which governments interact as capable of generating varying degrees of order (in the sense of stable expectations). Such a process does not function automatically. Its success depends on the sensitivities and prudence of critical policymakers in the key governments of the world.

Kratochwil argues normatively that the prospects for managing international conflict—preventing unnecessary tension and warfare—depend on making policymakers as conversant as possible with the signaling, bargaining, interactive process that is the essence of international relations. In essence, Kratochwil maintains that "rule-governed" behavior is a characteristic of all human interaction, although the signaling system and rule-making procedures vary with the setting. By applying this ap-

proach to the history of the Cold War, Kratochwil shows that
the heightening of tensions after World War II can be explained
in part by the failure of policymakers in the Kremlin and White
House to have the requisite "background knowledge" to
discharge their new superpower roles. Kratochwil shows very
persuasively that perceptions are shaped by such elements of
background knowledge as myth and metaphor, drawing on what
was dangerous in the past to construe the present. He also
argues that unless the experience of the adversary is taken into
account diplomatic behavior might stimulate a destructive
spiral of misperception that heightens the war-proneness of interstate relations. A principal conclusion of Kratochwil's book
is that the Cold War evolved out of such a spiral, each side finding abundant justification for its worst suspicions about the
other. Partly, this outcome was a predictable consequence of the
fact that both the Soviet Union and the United States had until
1945 been relative "outsiders" in international relations for
several centuries during which time the ordering of statecraft
was the almost exclusive preserve of the leading European
states. Others have argued to similar effect at times, but
without achieving Kratochwil's analytical clarity and historical
depth.

As Kratochwil realizes, understanding the potentialities for
managing conflict by establishing a shared experience of the
rules of the game does not assure (nor does it preclude) the quest
for international justice, nor can it meet the allegation that the
ordering capacities of the state system are unable to deal successfully with the pressures mounted by ecological and
economic forms of interdependence. Nevertheless, we are likely
to be dependent on the state system for a long time to come. To
make leading actors less prone to miscalculation is to make war,
including nuclear war, less likely. In this respect even those who
like myself are dedicated to transforming the state system must
still, in the long interim, somewhat paradoxically support those
who seek to make the state system work better. For these
reasons, Kratochwil's book is a path-breaking contribution to
international relations, enabling us to understand what is hap-
pening better, as well as encouraging leaders to act more wisely.

Of course, not every specific recourse to "background
knowledge" is a contribution to world peace. "Outsiders" may
not have the background knowledge to interpret the intentions

of their adversaries in a realistic fashion. The diversity of outlooks active in world society engenders some rather peculiar diplomatic stances. What are we to make, for instance, of current warnings to the West from Peking that "detente" is appeasement, building toward a new Munich? The new Chinese leader, Hua Kuo-feng sounds like a reincarnation in parody of Dean Rusk or Lyndon Johnson when he warns that "the fate of the British Prime Minister Neville Chamberlain" awaits those who "cherish the illusion" that peace with the Soviet Union can be achieved by "compromises and concessions." Does the Chinese Prime Minister know something we don't know or is he misusing historical metaphors to mobilize fears about the Soviet Union? I believe that the Chinese are repeating American errrors of earlier decades by overstating Soviet expansionist ambitions, although their role in the ideological competition for leadership of the world revolutionary movement and the long disputed border create a natural, and perhaps quite rational, Chinese obsession with Soviet behavior, including an appropriate tendency to assume the worst about Kremlin intentions. Kratochwil's book gives us a way of perceiving about such patterns of diplomatic maneuver that is neglected or handled vaguely in most treatments of international relations, both by describing how governments communicate (including acts and symbols) and how they might communicate better.

As with any perspective on order there are dangers here, dangers about which Kratochwil is sensitive. European states with a wealth of background knowledge and an evolved sense of the rules of the game still managed to stumble into mutually destructive warfare on a grand scale twice in this century. Irrationalities, desperate strategies and psychopathic leaders can foil even the most perfected communications net. There is no assurance that making a statecraft function better will make it work well enough to avert catastrophe. War may come anyway. All that we can claim is that understanding the interactive dynamic creates opportunities to manage conflict more successfully if the actors are so disposed.

How far can we go with conflict management among sovereign states? It is one thing to stablize expectations in Soviet-American relations where territorial and resource conflicts seem reasonably well resolved. But what of emergent Great Powers acting on the basis of different cultural and

ideological assumptions? There is no doubt that we are moving
into a period of multipolarity in international relations. This
suggests greater uncertainty and, perhaps, greater difficulty in
achieving international order by establishing a shared
background knowledge. Indeed, in this new era, efforts to exert
control, that other dimension of international order, may largely
supplant efforts to negotiate. In this event, the quality of international order would become a changing mixture of imperial
patterns of domination and cybernetic patterns of interactive
signaling. Such an evolution of international relations seems
probable in a period of growing anxiety about the economic and
ecological viability of planetary patterns of industrial growth,
aggravated by continuing population expansion. Kratochwil's
important book could help us cope more effectively with these
disturbing prospects.

Richard Falk

ACKNOWLEDGEMENTS

It is almost embarrassing to be indebted to so many people considering the modest size of this book. Nevertheless, I am glad to give my sincerest thanks to Profs. Richard Falk and Ronald Rogowski of Princeton (and now Duke) University respectively, who have supervised this study from its inception and who provided valuable criticism and encouragement throughout, I also owe a great debt of gratitude to Robert Gilpin, one of my former teachers and to my colleagues and friends, Nicholas Onuf, Frank Burd, Nicholas Miller, Patrick Dobel, Melissa Bailey and Andrew Krieger, who read and discussed part of the manuscript and made helpful comments. Helen Pasquale, Cheryl Reed and Susan Griiser cheerfully and competently helped with the typescript and Naomi Schwiesow and Tina Kimes did an excellent job in transforming my rough prose into readable English.

I am also grateful to the former University Consortium for World Order Studies and the Konrad Adenauer Foundation of Germany which provided research fellowships.

Errors of fact or judgement are of course exclusively mine.

INTRODUCTION

Purpose

This book has two objectives: first, to develop an approach to the problem of international order (Part I, Chaps. I-II), and second, to demonstrate the heuristic fruitfulness of this approach when it is applied to the analysis of concrete international interactions. For this latter purpose the period from 1945 to 1972 (Part II, Chaps. IV-VI) is chosen as a case study.[1] The investigation of the difficulties that arose after the collapse of the European state system in 1945, and of how those difficulties were gradually overcome by establishing a new international system, is meant to throw some light on the general problem of the establishment, the maintenance, and the transformation of international order.

Fundamental to my approach is the conviction that critical thinking about problems of the international order cannot limit itself to an enumeration of mere desiderata or a speculation which presupposes far-reaching changes in man's definition of social and international reality. Rather than basing my analysis on the assumption of a radical transformation of man and society, I maintain that the investigation of contemporary problems in the management of power need neither be uninspiring nor status quo oriented, since it it only through cautious and wise management of these power relationships that the visions of an international order which minimizes the outbreak of large scale violence and which, through changes, would allow for the more equal sharing of the world's wealth, can become a reality. To that extent, my work, although informed by normative concerns, is closer to the work of Inis Claude[2], who combines an interest in normative questions with rigorous international relations analysis, than it is either to the "world order through world law school"[3] or the more reformist oriented works of Warren Wagar,[4] Richard Falk,[5] Buckmister Fuller,[6] et al.

This perspective has important repercussions upon the treatment of our particular concerns, as it is one of my basic assumptions that the analysis of international order requires a study of the process by which particular conventions—or "rules of the game," as we also call them—arise, persist, change, and decay. Also crucial to this approach is the belief that human action is "rule-governed"[7] and that in the process of interaction, the meaning of the various moves on each side becomes intelligible to the participants when they start to acquire a common "background knowledge,"[8] i.e., a set of conventions by means of which they can in most cases correctly predict the actions of other actors. Such "background knowledge," it will be argued, comes into existence through the usage of particular "inference guidance devices" and through repeated interactions when various interpretations of the opponents' moves are advanced and "tested" until one frame of reference becomes socially dominant and is selected as the "correct" interpretation of social reality. It will be the task of the first Part of this book (Chapters I through III) to give more theoretical precision to the ideas outlined here in a cursory fashion.

For the reader familiar with the literature on "symbolic" and "strategic" interaction it will be obvious that this approach is heavily indebted to the works of George Herbert Mead,[9] Erving Goffman,[10] Herbert Blumer,[11] Peter Berger and Thomas Luckmann[12] on the sociological side. On the side of international relations, analysis was stimulated by the works of Arthur Lee Burns,[13] Oran Young,[14] Thomas Schelling[15] and Robert Jervis,[16] who all in one way or another focused upon how policy choices are constrained in iterative bargaining relationships.

From these general remarks the plan of this book can be derived.

Chapter I elaborates the implications of this approach by criticizing some of the conventional world order literature. This literature seems implicitly or explicitly based upon the hobbesian notion that order is created by the imposition of superior force. By contrast, Hume's observations concerning the problem of order[17] opens the way to an investigation of order-problems in terms of a system of constraints arising out of iterative bargaining relationships. A conceptual clarification of some of the crucial terms employed in our discussion follows. To deal with the confusion and the proliferation of terms like "international order," "world order," "peace studies," I propose some criteria for a meaningful discourse on the problem of "order."[18] When "order" is defined in a general fashion, specific distinctions can be introduced to separate "world order" from "international order" and similar concepts.

As I am mainly concerned with the problem of *international order,* I submit that an especially vital part in the establishment and maintenance of this order was and is played by the "super-powers,"[19] i.e. those powers that have world-wide aspirations and the politcal and military means to pursue such extensive foreign policy goals. Consequently, I further submit that the study of Soviet-American interactions between the breakdown of the European state system in 1945 and the demise of the bipolar pattern of postwar international politics in 1972 is an appropriate case study for the problem of international order.

The second chapter deals more explicitly with international conflict and the role that conventions or rules play in conflict resolution. I do not see conflict in terms of structure[20] but rather as an escalation in the interaction process among political actors: therefore, I attempt a further theoretical elaboration of the origin of conflict and its resolution by de-escalation or settlement.[21] Again, I try to clarify my position by first criticizing some of the current theories on the "determinants of behavior" in conflict situations, especially Richardson processes and structural-functional and psychological interpretations of conflict escalation.

Fundamental to my own explanation of escalation—is the idea that defections from normal and expected behavior are common and usually ignored. They can be well modelled in terms of a "mild chicken game" in which one of the protagonists prefers to be "exploited"[22] by the defection of the other and thus to avoid conflict escalation. Such an escalation process begins, however, when through the engagement of new values, defections are no longer interpreted as a "chicken game" but in terms of a prisoner's dilemma game. The upping of stakes on both sides can then be described in terms of an extended game that reverts from a prisoner's dilemma to a more and more daring chicken game.[23] Having dealt with the escalation process I try to investigate de-escalation procedures, an area largely ignored by conventional bagaining literature due to its emphasis on "commitment" by the foreclosure of options. Using the more behaviorally oriented problem-solving approach,[24] important insights can be gained about "crisis management," which finds ways of de-fusing the issues and de-escalating the process.

Chapter III tries to clarify the way in which rules impinge upon behavior. It begins with the observation that rules work like "signals" rather than "labels." The crucial idea is that rules serve as *inference guidance devices* by helping to define situations and by providing justifications for particular inferences. Having given the comon characteristic of all "rules," I distinguish five sets of rules that seem of particular importance for political decision-making, as they determine the space within which choices have to be made. These five sets of rules or rule-like inference guidance devices which form the crucially important "background knowledge" are "laws" or legal rules, "doctrines," "historical analogies," "metaphors" and "myths."

As a great deal of research is done lately about the nature of legal rules and their influence on the policy process,[25] I consider in this work only the other four rather neglected sets of inference warrants. Under such circumstances it seems useful to establish an adequate criterion for distinguishing between a rule of law and other more informal constraints. The recent tendency to grant legal status to every constraint impinging upon political decision-making[26] is unhelpful because it blurs the distinction between the "validity" of a rule of law and the "private reasons"[27] for obeying a rule, and because it equates the policy process with that of "law creation." At the same time, this crucial distinction between "reasons" and "rules" also helps in general to illuminate the difference between subjective and intersubjective definitions of the situation, a problem which is usually not fully elaborated in the literature. Although decision-makers normally explain their moves in terms of having followed a particular rule (unilateral or subjective definition of the situation), we can only speak of rule-governed behavior in the

strict sense if this unilateral definition of the situation is accepted
by the other players and thereby affects the decision premises of
other participants (intersubjective definition of the situation)
when responding to the original move. In utilizing this
distinction it is hoped to gain more insight into the rule
generation process which is of great importance to our task.

Furthermore, by providing a clear criterion for distinguishing
a rule of law from other inference warrants, I hope to gain not
only some new theoretical insights into the function of law in the
international arena, but also a clearer view of the differential
impact of various types of rules upon the decision-making
process.

Having shown the commonality and difference between a rule
of law and "doctrines" in terms of the discretion allowed for the
implementation of a particular purpose, our interest focuses in
the following sections upon inference guidance devices that help
to define situations in which choices have to be made. Here the
role of historical analogies, metaphors and myths is investigated.
Historical analogies, it is pointed out, make a bewildering new
situation comprehensible and establish criteria for the choice of
an appropriate strategy by pointing to "similar cases" in the
past. Metaphors work in a similar fashion by identifying features
of the new situation with images taken from familiar contexts,
thereby suggesting particular courses of action. Thus, the
metaphorical description of the Watergate affair as a "cancer on
the presidency" not only presents reality in terms of a pathology
but also counsels radical and painful remedial action. Myths, on
the other hand, provide an encompassing frame of reference into
which particular experiences described in a metaphorical fashion
or by means of an analogy can be meaningfully and consistently
collected. Myths as "dramatic stories" not only make the
present understandable, by establishing through the narrative a
clearer link with the past and by informing us about the reasons
why things came to pass in a particular way, but also provide an
image of the future consistent with the ideals and the self-image
of the group adhering to a myth.

Part II of the book begins with the empirical investigation of
Soviet-American relations after the Second World War, which
serves as a case study for the approach outlined in Chapters I
through III.

Chapter IV is devoted to assessing the role historical analogies played in creating a set of conventions that served as "background knowledge" for each side's interpretation of the opponent's moves. The hypothesis of this chapter is that the explanations of the origins of the Cold War advanced by traditionalists and revisionists are largely misleading because they are based upon a spurious selection of facts. What seems to be required for making a more convincing case is not so much the addition of new facts as the discovery of a way to assess the meaning of particular actions. Only within such a frame of reference can we answer questions like what was a "reasonable" response to a challenge, what was an "offensive" move, or what was "responsible" or "irresponsible" behavior—issues so crucial to the arguments of both traditionalists and revisionists.

An additional thesis of this chapter is that the breakdown of the European state system, and the rejection of its conventions by both the Soviet Union and the United States, left decision-makers on both sides without reliable guides as to the other's motives. Under such circumstances the most useful inference guidance devices seemed to be the lessons of history. The influence of historical analogies is investigated in three short studies dealing with postwar planning, the establishment of the United Nations, and the fear of the "Ghost of Munich" and of "capitalist encirclement."

Chapter V, dealing with myths and metaphors, focuses particularly on the period 1946-1947 when the reassessment of foreign policy in both the United States and the Soviet Union led to the announcement of the Truman Doctrine and Zhdanov's reiteration of the "Two Camp" view of international politics. It is the hypothesis of this chapter that the construction of "test cases" on both sides had convinced American and Soviet decision-makers that the continuous misunderstandings were not the result of negotiable conflicts of interest but were of a much more fundamental nature. Thus, differences were increasingly interpreted in terms of a prisoner's dilemma degenerating into a chicken game. The process of escalation heightened anxieties, but it was not international difficulties alone but very much the perceived threat to domestic institutions that persuaded each protagonist that its "way of life" was at stake. Thus the fear of subversion on both sides—the parallel between the Red Scare and the "Zhdanovchina" has not been sufficiently analyzed—made it plausible to dramatize conflict between the United States and the Soviet Union in mythical terms.

The link between domestic considerations and the inability to achieve an international diplomatic settlement is further investigated in probing the metaphor of "containment," the decision-premise for American foreign policy from Truman to Nixon. It is argued that an imaginative blending of domestic and foreign policy concerns endowed containment with its special persuasiveness. American policy-makers favoring diplomatic adjustment could point to the "holding action" program as a step toward some future negotiations. On the other hand, those convinced that only a radically changed Soviet regime would be willing to negotiate outstanding issues, could suggest that the "adroit application of counterforce" would eventually lead to a mellowing of Soviet power and a more conciliatory foreign policy. The policies of the Truman-Acheson and Eisenhower-Dulles teams are discussed in this context and treated as variations of this theme.

Analysis of Soviet policy during this time stresses the problems that surfaced after Stalin's death and the revision of his policies that led to serious differences of opinion within the CPSU. Failure to reach a diplomatic settlement despite greatly changed circumstances is thus explained as the result of the inability of both blocs to define a mutually agreeable role for a reunited Germany, which was the key to an all-European settlement. Conciliatory moves were interpreted as signs of weakness that justified raising the stakes, and as Germany was considered essential to the stability of each bloc, the German reunification problem was not negotiable along the lines of Austrian neutrality.

Thus, the "normalized" situation that emerged in Europe in the 1960's, in spite of several serious probes against Berlin, was not based upon either an explicit diplomatic adjustment or the transformation of the adversary; instead, it came about through default and acquiescence to the stalemate that developed after the war. Meanwhile, new issues had developed whose resolution promised to break the deadlock in Europe. The stalemate, cemented by an increasingly ominous nuclear force-structure on both sides, it seemed, could only be broken by shifting competition to areas where quick moves and the non-existence of clearly defined spheres of interest promised decisive advantages.

These newer developments are analyzed in Chapter VI, which discusses Soviet-American interaction in the sixties and early seventies in terms of the strategic debate in both countries about the importance of nuclear weapons and the role of the developing countries. The focus of these two factors as the crucial variables in bringing about the change from a "mythical" perspective on world politics to a more open-ended approach is derived from the theoretical arguments presented in the first chapters. As it was argued there, the nature of a bi-polar international game changes when common norms emerge which serve as "implicit third parties" or when actual new players enter the arena. Thus the choice of a doctrinal focus here is by no means accidental, for the advent of total mutual nuclear vulnerability as well as the addition of other parties compelled a reassessment of the means employed for the advancement of one's foreign policy goals. Avoidance of nuclear war, whose catastrophic implications became more and more obvious, presupposed at least a rudimentary understanding of the requirements of deterrence. The ensuing debate, carried out within both countries between military groups, defense intellectuals, and party bosses but always with an eye on the "audience" on the other side, is dealt with in terms of the various strategic doctrines that competed for adoption and translation into actual military posture.

The superpowers' attempts to preserve their nuclear monopoly are studied for their effects on the cohesion of the respective blocs, and these effects are seen to be a transformation of the international system to a more loosely structured set of "polarities." A good deal of light can then be thrown upon such important phenomena as the Sino-Soviet rift, disintegrative tendencies in NATO, and an emergent common interest between the superpowers to arrange bilateral deals outside the U.N. or their respective alliances.

The turn to the underveloped world as a new arena of competition between the two social systems is investigated in terms of the Soviet doctrine of "national democracy" and American "developmental" doctrines, which led to painful and rather sobering experiences on both sides by the end of the sixties. Attempts by both sides to come to terms with the contradictory implications of the new "adversary relationship," which includes common interests as well as the retention of a good deal of enmity, and both sides' wish to retain influence over events in the rest of the world where the East-West conflict no longer serves as an organizing principle, are then dealth with in terms of such "doctrinal" crystallizations as the Nixon and Brezhnev doctrines, the agreement concerning peaceful relations of states, the SALT talks, and Soviet interest in new forms of "collective security" in areas from which they have been traditionally barred.

I On Order, Symbols And Preferred Worlds

1. *Introduction*

Despite the considerable interest the problem of world order has generated, there seems to be a good deal of confusion about what this term actually designates. In order to clarify it, we could perhaps look at some programs of recently introduced "world order studies." But these international-law-cum-international-relations-plus-some-esoteric-subject-agglomerations lack a proper organizing concept themselves. True, nowadays there is less talk about revamping the United Nations Charter, or about "legislating" war out of existence, but the decline of a utopianism that formerly clearly distinguished students of such problems has not enhanced their conceptual clarity or revealed a distinctive perspective on such issues. Concepts like world order and international order are sometimes used interchangeably; sometimes the latter is the means for the former or vice versa. Myres McDougal[2] essentially identifies them with the flow of authoritative and effective decision-making that constitutes international law. Some authors focus more narrowly on the conditions that prevent unauthorized violence, whereas others use a broader definition that tends to shade into mere description. Richard Falk, for example, maintains:

> World order intends only to describe the characteristic forms of behavior by which security and change are pursued by states and other international actors. As such the study of world order is concerned with the structure of authority, types of conflict, the

role of violence and methods of settlement that are relied upon by
international actors in pursuit of their goals. [3]

A study by the World Order Studies Consortium, however, has
more normative overtones; it refers to "efforts of creating a more
dependable international environment which would lead to a
significant reduction of international violence and to an
improvement of the quality of life everywhere."[4] The last
element in this definition shows how the narrow description of
world order problems, as concerned with war and peace or with
the strengthening of the authority structure of the international
system, has lately been replaced by a more encompassing view
of the world political process as an allocator not only of security
but also of welfare, skills and other values.

To make sense out of this confusion we will have to ask some
radical questions. First, what concretely do we mean by world
order and what is the relationship between this concept and the
term international order? Second, what does "order" in this
context refer to? Third, as a result of one and two, is the study of
world order a separate field, or is it coextensive with or even
equivalent to the discipline of international relations? The key
question is obviously the second one, as we can hope to answer
the two others after sharpening the strategic concept of order.

But how shall we proceed? A strategy that seems quite useful
for our purposes is to begin with a discussion of our
common-sense notions of political order, which are grounded in
particular traditions. This naturally does not guarantee analytical
clarity, but it allows us to bring out, through subsequent
conceptual refinement, those half-conscious assumptions which
are a crucial part of conventional arguments and which are
seldom properly reflected upon. A critical illumination of these
silent assumptions can provide an invaluable guide for our
discussion of world order problems.

The next section, therefore, opens with a short recapitulation
of some conventional order conceptions. An attempt follows to
identify the minimum requirements of any social order, and to
distinguish international order from world order. Having
answered some of our preliminary questions concerning the
status of world order studies, and having pointed out that the
main emphasis of this study will be on *international order,*
we turn to a closer examination of some of the assumptions

underlying international order.

The third section aims to deepen our understanding of international order by bringing to bear some aspects of the bargaining approach. Two thoughts are of special importance here. First is the idea that in iterative bargains precedents, customs and traditions can serve as guide posts for structuring expectations, thus making the coordination of choices possible. The Hobbesian dilemma, which originated from uncertainty as to the intentions of the other party in a bargaining situation, can therefore be avoided. Second, the availability of commonly shared symbols allows an assessment of the moves of the other party, and may therefore allow for the development of interactions without major disappointments.

But if the structure of expectations is usually the most decisive variable in the creation and maintenance of order, then force is only one of several ways to structure expectations. Another way to maintain order is to manipulate the symbolic universe and shape perceptions. It is exactly because of the importance of symbols for the creation of social order that the role of a "political entrepreneur" is decisive. Through the invocation of shared symbols, groups form: human action can be patterned, and a "public space" common to all is defined. The general and special conditions for social order can now be given more precision, and it becomes clear why the international system is sometimes called a "primitive" political system: on the most fundamental level, any order depends upon a structure of expectations, communicated and induced by shared symbols. But the process of structuring these expectations in the international arena is markedly different form what occurs domestically. Internationally, we said, the structure of expectations depends on historical experience and on norms that evolve out of iterative bargains. But such a structure is prone to periodic breakdowns, because no overarching loyalties or interests can be invoked. Domestic political systems, on the other hand, have political entrepreneurs or leaders who can manipulate diffuse symbols, which invoke loyalty and stress the symbiotic character of the social order.

Here the importance of overarching symbols, including a shift of attitudes from purely ethnocentric to more global concerns and their connection with the goals of the "reformist" school of world order studies, becomes obvious. Although this book has a narrower focus, these problems will be touched upon in the final chapter. For the moment such a cursory treatment must suffice, and we turn our attention now to three traditional order speculations.

2. *International Order and World Order*

Since social order among men is not a natural condition but an artifact, it has to be created and explained. Basically, we can distinguish three major traditions of order speculation according to their respective basis for social order. Thus, "classical" political theory from Plato to Thomas Aquinas derives social order not only from biological needs but mainly from man's participation in (divine) reason, making the "insight" of the soul attuned to the "order of being" the fundamental source of human social order. Another school, identified with Hobbes and "realism" in general, maintains that order is the result of particular institutional arrangements. Order is therefore created by imposition and the threat of superior force. Finally, a third tradition which could be called the "Humean" perspective derives "order" from the growth of a common perception of mutual benefit and the growth of conventions which set limits to socially disruptive behavior. Naturally, these three explanations of order are not necessarily mutually exclusive and can be found in various "mixes" in actual theorizing. Nevertheless, the emphasis of one tradition over elements stemming from another has important repercussions upon a subsequent "theory of order." Considering our special interest in developing an approach to the study of international order we are more than justified in asking which of the three "ideal types" of order speculation shows sufficient "isomorphism" with international reality so as to serve as a useful starting point for our investigation.

Starting with the classical conception of order, we notice that the scholastic definition of peace as *ordinata quies* is not very helpful for our purposes, as it presupposes some common knowledge about the natural order of things in a stable position. Modern experience cuts against this tenet in two ways. First, the decline of a metaphysically based human order, which dominated the Middle Ages, for example, and served as a meeting-ground for heretics as well as orthodox thinkers, led to a variety of rather exclusive idologies that have very little in common [5] with each other. Second, the precarious elements of world order exemplified in the *"regles du jeu"* of international interaction do not grow out of a static conception of human order but are the results of man's historical experience. For better or for worse, the concept of order in international relations seems to be heavily imbued with evolutionary overtones.

For the same reason a definition of order in terms of the "distribution of values" [6] seems to be deficient. Besides, world order, while it implies more than simply any "discernible arrangement" of values, cannot go so far as to specify the conditions for "the good life," [7] for the simple reason that international disorder results partly from competing attempts to impose one's idea of the good life on others.

Furthermore, the classical political tradition, aside from some stoic speculations and medieval treatises on a universal monarchy, never developed a coherent theory of inter-societal affairs. Plato as well as Aristotle, concerned with the "best" order of a body politic, take war and disorder in inter-poleis relations as given. After all, Plato's Republic [8] is to a large extent determined in its make-up by the conviction that war is an ever latent possibility, resulting from the impossibility of imposing a rational order upon inter-poleis interactions.

It was exactly this image of constant belligerence between states that served centuries later as the starting point for another major order speculation. Thomas Hobbes justifies his emphasis on the peaceless "state of nature" as the natural human condition by pointing out in his Leviathan:

> But though there had never been any time wherein particular men were in a condition of warre one against another; yet at all times, Kings and Persons of Soveraigne authority, because of their independency are in continuall jealousies and in the state and posture of Gladiators; having their weapons pointing and their eyes fixed on one another; that is, their Forts, Garrisons, and Guns upon the Frontiers of their Kingdomes; and continuel Spyes upon their neighbours; which is a posture of war.
> . . . For Warre consisteth not in Battel onely or the act of fighting; but in a tract of time wherein the Will to contend by Battel is sufficiently known: and therefore the notion of Time is to be considered in the nature of Warre. . . . So the nature of War consisteth not in actual fighting, but in the known disposition thereto, during all the time there is no assurance to the contrary.

All other time is peace.

To this Warre of every man against every man this is also consequent: that nothing can be Unjust. The notions of Right and Wrong, Justice and Injustice have there no place. Where there is no common power there is not law: where no law no Injustice. . . . Justice and Injustice are none of the faculties neither of the Body not Mind. . . . They are Qualities that relate to men in Society, not in Solitude. [9]

Hobbes' solution to this dilemma is well known. The absolute sovereign has to insure that compacts are kept at home, but states themselves do not create a Leviathan. Despite the fact that Hobbes seems to have understood the decisive difference between states and natural persons, which explains why he objected to a super-Leviathan,[10] his perspective—that sanctions explain compliance and the establishment of justice—dominated the thinking of statemen as well as scholars up to the most recent times. This is borne out by their preoccupation with sanctions, international "police-force" plans, collective security arrangements,[11] and proposals to make the Covenant or the Charter "work," as well as by the predominance of the "command theory"[12] of law up to the middle of this century.

Opposition to Hobbes' conceptualization nevertheless eventually came to the fore as his emphasis on compelling force resulted from an extremely pessimistic view of human nature:

If a covenant be made wherein neither of the parties perform presently but trust one another it is the condition of meer Nature . . . upon any reasonable suspicion it is Voyd. But if there be a common Power to stay over them both with right and force sufficient to compell performance it is not Voyd. For he that performed first has no assurance the other will perform after, because the bonds of words are too weak to bridle mens' ambition anger and other Passions without the fear of some coercive Power. . . . But in a civill estate where there is a power set up to constrain those that would otherwise violate their faith that fear is no more reasonable; and for that cause he which by the Covenant is to perform first is obliged to do so.[13]

This leads to the famous dilemma that, if in the state of nature contracts without sanctions are only words, no contract can come about in the first place. Apparently Hobbes' exclusive reliance on force is logically untenable and, as modern research into primitive law shows, empirically inaccurate. Emphasis on the "legitimate" use of force, even on the part of convinced "command theorists," also demonstrates that the instrumentalities of coercion cannot serve as the sole criterion of law. Norms, structuring expectations, operate even in cases where no need for reinforcement arises; as a matter of fact, we usually speak of "anomie" [14] when enforcement action surpasses a limit considered normal. Norms work via socialization and ideally define certain alternatives in a given situation as "illegal," thereby limiting the set of possible choices of an actor. Thus, in the search for an equivalent of force which would explain not only the continued existence of a political order but its very establishment, David Hume advances the argument that conventions arising out of interactions that prove mutually beneficial can structure expectations and thus allow the participants to overcome the posed dilemma.

> This convention is not of the nature of a promise; for even promises themselves arise from human conventions. It is only a general sense of common interest. . . . When this common sense of interest is mutually expressed and known to both, it produces a suitable resolution and behavior. And this may properly enough be called a convention or agreement betwixt us though without the interposition of a promise, since the actions of each of us have a reference to those of the other and are performed upon the supposition that something is to be performed on the other part . . . this experience assures us . . . that the sense of interest has become common to all our fellows and gives us a confidence of the future regularity of their conduct; and it is only on the expectation of this that our moderation and abstinence are founded. In like manner are languages gradually established by human convention, without any promise. In like manner do gold and silver become the common measure of exchange and are esteemed sufficient payment for what is of a hundred times their value. [15]

It is obvious that this perspective on order is of particular interest for international politics as it allows for a "theory" of order in a decentralized authority structure instead of making the centralization of effective and accepted power the prerequisite for order. Hume himself reminds us that "rules of justice" are not "entirely suspended among. political societies" and that "alliances and treaties are every day made . . . which would only be so much waste of parchment if they were not found by experience to have some influence and authority." 16

The advantage of choosing this Humean order model as a starting point for our investigation is not confined however to its greater "isomorphism" with international reality. Another point which is seldom reflected upon but which is of tremendous methodological significance deserves mentioning: the logic required for the construction of a model concerned with interdependent decision making, i.e. the "normal" case in a decentralized authority structure, is different from that of a "one power world" where decision making and authority structure are centralized. Arthur Lee Burns reminds us in this context that:

> Whereas the theory of a one-power system can afford to be positivistic (e.g., a Parsonian sociological model would be rich enough) that of systems of two or more members must employ logical resources of more complex order—at least as intersubjective as those of game theory. . . . Another way of making this point is that game theoretical models can often include many sociological models as special cases (e.g., as "games against nature") but not vice versa. 17

The same is naturally true of a change from a two power to a three power world, and this process seems to go on until there are so many players that the system itself becomes "dominant," to use Kaplan's 18 phrase. If this is true, then most of our conventional thinking about world order problems asks the wrong questions, because the "one power world" is our implicit model. But given the fact that the "imperial" or "one power" model of order has dominated our speculation, what would "order" refer to in a multi-power world?

To bring out the special features of order in such an arena, it might be best to start out with a general definition of order delineating crucial requirements which *any* regime of order in any arena has to meet, and introduce subsequently special characteristics which will allow further distinctions between such terms as world order and international order. Let us therefore agree that we mean by "order" on a general level the minimum conditions of social coexistence or, in the words of Hedley Bull:

> By order in social life I mean a pattern or structure of human relationships that sustain not the special purposes of this or that sort of society but the primary or elementary goals of social

coexistence, goals that are common to social life at all places. Social life requires, for example, some restriction on the liberty of members of the society to resort to violence, a presumption that promises will be kept, and a means of securing stability of possession. [19]

Now it becomes possible to give the terms "international order" and world order a bit more precision. Whereas international order means a pattern of relations that sustains the elementary requirements of social co-existence among states, world order comprises besides international order, transnational phenomena and influences of the domestic order upon the international environment. Although it is clear that the study of world order is a much more encompassing perspective on international reality than the narrower concern with international order, as indicated by the largely "reformist" tendencies of world order students, our main concern in this book will be the investigation of *international* order.

3. *Bargaining and International Order*
These considerations now make it possible to locate the central problem of this investigation more precisely within the field of study created by our particular perspective. Having shown that the one-power model is inadequate in its Hobbesian as well as "world government" variety, we move on to the assumption that international politics is best characterized in terms of bargaining relationships which are iterative.

> The iterative aspects of international politics make it necessary for participants in any given situation to consider the effects of their immediate actions on their future relationships. The multiplicity of actors in the system causes the bargaining relationship of any two to be constrained by their interest in later dealing profitably with the others. Moreover, while the international political system is highly decentralized and non-institutionalized, certain basic elements of society in the sense of a normative substructure setting up at least minimal rules of the game, support international politics. [20]

Important corollaries follow from this: a mix between cooperative and antagonistic interests is assumed for the normal case, whereas pure collaboration and pure competition are the two extremes. Furthermore, bargaining does not necessarily

refer to coercive relationships, as the strategic literature seems
to suggest, nor should it be seen as an alternative to coercion.

Let us start with the common observation that very often
bargains fail to reflect accurately the relative bargaining
strengths of the parties to a dispute. Labor negotiations as well
as international examples seem to bear this out. Besides,
especially in situations where conflict is rather intense, a solution
is often modeled after precedents, which may or may not be
analogous to the dispute at hand. A resort to precedent to resolve
a dispute changes a bilateral conflict to one where norms,
precedents, analogies and so forth serve as an implied "third
party." "Finding the key," writes Thomas Schelling "or rather
finding a key—any key that is mutually recognized as the key,
becomes the key—may depend on imagination more than on
logic; it may depend on analogy, precedent, accidental
arrangement, symmetric aesthetic or geometric configurations,
causistic reasoning and who the parties are and what they know
about each other."[21] Again we are back to the problem of
changing expectations, which Hobbes thought required the use
of threat of force, whereas Hume believed that by trial and error
people could coordinate their choices and thereby find a way out
of the "prisoner's dilemma" most conflictual situations
resemble.

At a deeper level we found that Humean "conventions" come
into being through shared perceptions and images of the other
party and of the situation. Here we move into the area of
"symbolizations" and their impact upon human choice behavior,
an area that has been grossly neglected by political science
despite the fact that classical political philosophers saw a close
connection between man as a political animal (zoon politikon)
and man as a symbol-creating animal (zoon logon echon).[22]
Whereas signs are unequivocally interpreted by the sense
organs, symbols create meaning by structuring our universe,
building up images far removed from the immediacy of sense
perceptions.[23] Because symbolic structures cannot be
unequivocally tested against reality—reality itself being a
cretion of the symbolizing activity that endows perceptions with
certain meanings—deception but also persuasion are possible.
Symbols, writes Kenneth Boulding,

remove the human organization from the prison of the immediate here and now in which all lower forms of life are trapped. . . . It is because of this symbolic nature of the image of man that conflict in the animal kingdom where images are only built up by signs and hence conflict is always face to face.[24]

The error in reducing social conflict to "aggression" or drives is now obvious. Two important issues appear. First, there seems to be a place in this system for an "entrepreneur" who offers a solution to the uncertainty created by the generalized prisoner's dilemma. Second, the context of political leadership and symbolic action becomes transparent, as it is the task of the "political entrepreneur" to provide schemes that structure expectations in ways that make the attainment of shared goals possible. Significantly, this role was absent from both the Hobbesian and Humean discourse. Hobbes therefore mistook "force" for the effective manipulation of expectations. But, as we have seen, this pathological picture of obedience cannot account for the phenomenon of legitimacy. It is exactly through the addition of legitimizing symbols that we acquire access to the most important function of political leadership. Through symbolic manipulation, groups are held together and choices are defined and made "on behalf" of these groups. "Political symbols," writes Murray Edelman, "bring out in concentrated form those particular meanings and emotions which the members of a group create and reinforce in each other."[25] But saying that politics involves symbols is not saying very much, as this is true of nearly all human activity, be it play or scientific discourse. It is rather a specific *type* of symbol that is peculiar to politics and induces action.

Political activity therefore has to deal with what Edelman calls "condensation symbols."

Condensation symbols evoke the emotions associated with the situation. They condense into one symbolic event, sign, or act patriotic pride, anxieties, remembrances of past glories or humiliations, promises of future greatness: some one of these or all of them. Where condensation symbols are involved the constant check of the immediate environment is lacking.[26]

But what are the implications of this particular perspective for international politics? In answering this question let us start with the observation that we commonly talk about an increase or decrease in "tensions" in international affairs. But very seldom does this term refer to changes in the physical distribution of forces, materials, money, etc. As a matter of fact, we speak of a "crisis" when effective communication "among the protagonists concerning such matters as attitudes, expectations, intentions and resolve" is based "increasingly on physical actions in contrast to verbalized statements through diplomatic channels."[27] The issuance of commands that result in a different distribution of physical resources is therefore only a special case of the general international "game," which consists of communicating with other statesmen. Different from the domestic sphere, where institutions translate social tension into public issues and where "structural certainties"[28] like elections and redress procedures are provided by the constitution, the international game is much less structured. It uses diplomatic channels, news leaks, international organizations and even table tennis teams to "get the message across."

But if the term tension, as used in political discourse about international affairs, refers to the prevailing image of what the whole game is about, then interpreting the players' moves requires an account of their respective models of the whole.

On the one hand, this disposes of the old debate about whether decision makers are acting "according to" the systems or models that international relations theorists have developed. It seems that statesmen are bound to have such "models," although they are often implicit and more akin to "hunches" than to the laborious explications of theorists. In this view, explicit models of world politics are merely elaborations of these implicit hunches. (This is naturally not to say that some models may serve different purposes than illuminating present reality; they might, for example, be used exclusively to think out the implications of the assumptions made, as Kaplan's unit veto system shows.)[29] On the other hand, clearly conflict is most likely to be managed when the various actors have congruent images of the world political process, its rules of the game and goals. This need not mean that the images are "alike"—for example, in an organization like a university, Boulding reminds us, the image the president has of himself will be different from the image the faculty and the staff of the physical plant have of him. But a minimum agreement must exist upon certain "roles" different actors are supposed to play.[30] In addition, the description of a given "world image" contains value preferences, historical experiences and "precepts" for action and therefore always transcends "data" in terms of factual knowledge, exactly because it is this horizon that gives meaning to the "facts." Schelling's idea that "focal point" solutions depend more upon shared meaning than upon logic seems to back this assertion.[31] The problem of international order, focused on identifying the minimum conditions for coexistence, therefore reduces itself to the question of how cooperative solutions can be discovered in bargaining situations and how they can acquire such prominence that conflict resolution becomes possible. This naturally does not thereby guarantee that the opponents will finally choose the "prominent" alternative, but it quite adequately circumscribes the *minimum conditions for probable solutions.*

"Prominence" in turn depends as we saw upon previous historical experiences, "lessons" learned from them, analogies which liken the situation to familiar circumstances, and preferences which inform particular strategies and which, unlike the "offers" in bargaining negotiations, do not consist of units of utility which are indefinitely substitutable.

If this is so, then the importance of perceptions is obvious and the classical theory of games provides—and does not intend to provide—little guidance for actual decision-making, as politics is more than the skill of maximizing certain values in a game whose rules have been created by fiat. It becomes a creative activity of risk-taking and transforming the game one is playing. To that extent, game theory is applicable only to situations in which the possibility of radical surprise can be discounted.

Given these uncertainties, how can we then talk about the importance of "rules of the game" for the international order? What does the term "game" refer to and how are rules supposed to impinge upon behavior?

It will be the task of the task of the next two chapters to clarify these questions.

II "Rules" and Conflict Resolution

1. Introduction

Having outlined the scope and purpose of our inquiry, it now seems appropriate to fill in the sketch with the details necessary for an orderly investigation.

Our main concern, as already stated, is the problem of how "rules of the game" develop and what their connection is with conflict resolution and the problem of international order. Departing from the Hobbesian perspective on order — a perspective that has informed most thinking on international politics, whether viewed as "power politics" or as a problem in the "world government" approach — our aim is to establish how rules develop through interaction, or, as Charles Lindblom, an adherent of the Humean perspective put it, through "partisan mutual adjustment.' [1]

> Although one can draw a distinction between ordinary decisions and coordinating decisions in central coordination, in partisan mutual adjustment one cannot. There are no coordinators in partisan mutual adjustment; such coordination as is achieved is a by-product of ordinary decisions, that is of decisions not specifically intended to coordinate. . . . A simple idea is elaborated . . .: that people can coordinate with each other without a common purpose and without rules that fully prescribe their relations to each other. [2]

One may reasonably doubt whether this adequately describes the domestic realm, where all decision-making is regulated by

25

the overarching goal of national unity and survival, where citizens' interdependence is extensive, where cross-cutting cleavages limit potential conflicts, and where loyalty to the nation sets limits to antagonistic differences.[3] But the passage quoted seems to describe quite aptly the international decision-making process.

An important corollary follows from this: in order to discover the rules of interstate behavior, we must focus on states' interactions and not on a "system" whose "maintenance" is at stake. Although this may seem to be of little importance, it will be argued below that the system perspective does not allow for an adequate conceptualization of social conflict. In order not to bias our inquiry from the outset by endowing a system with goal-seeking attributes (equilibrium maintenance), we adopt Herbert Blumer's position:

> People—that is acting units—do not act toward culture, social structure or the like; they act towards situations. Social organization enters into action only to the extent to which it shapes situations in which people act and to the extent to which it supplies fixed sets of symbols which people use in interpreting their situations. [4]

What then is the status of rules in regulating political behavior? Does conflict ensue in the absence of such rules, is it of anomic nature? Furthermore, to what extent do rules contribute to explaining and predicting behavior? What is their logical form, are they "descriptive" (rules of behavior) or "prescriptive" (rules for behavior)? Answers to these questions will begin to emerge in the subsequent sections as we deal with other attempts to find "determinants" of behavior, before attacking those central problems themselves.

From these remarks, the plan of the present chapter can be derived rather easily. In the next section we will examine some prominent conceptualizations of "determinants of behavior" and test them to see how far they can provide a satisfactory explanation. As our object of analysis is not the international or social system, since we are interested instead in political interactions and in the contribution "rules" make to conflict resolution, a better understanding of social conflict is vital. Section three will therefore be devoted to that topic and in the fourth section a decision-making framework will be devloped to show the roles rules play in the dynamics of conflict and its resolution.

2. *Determinants of Behavior*

The search· for determinants of political action is, as the age-old preoccupation with geographical factors shows, as old as recorded speculation about history and politics.

In modern times, the type of ''explanation'' which relies on determinants of political action that ''operate independently of anyone's rationally designed actions or consciously perceived goals''[5] usually focuses quite narrowly on one factor and is reformulated in terms of a mathematico-deductive model. Lewis Richardson's[6] attempts to formalize arms races is perhaps the best known example of this type of theorizing. Richardson uses a set of differential equations to characterize stability or instability of the international system. Applying his equations to the arms races that occurred before World War I, Richardson obtained a relatively good fit and virtually predicted World War II.

Nevertheless, not even Richardson sees the fate of man as so inexorably determined. Like a good liberal, he was convinced that increased trade could have moved the destabilized system into a peaceful equilibrium. ''In effect Richardson concluded, that if interbloc yearly trade had just been five million pounds greater (or equivalently, had the armament expenditures been smaller by the same amount), the whole process might have gone in reverse toward a United Europe.''[7] But such ''explanations'' hardly deserve their name, despite the close ''fit'' of differential equations with actual expenditures. Fitting curves to data does not mean that an underlying ''law'' has been discovered. At best it suggests possible directions for further exploration, but it does not dispense with the need to supply a fuller account, for example, by means of an explanation-sketch in terms of motives and interests.[8] Thus, Richardson's observation that the occurrence of wars can be described in terms of a ''Poisson'' distribution might stimulate our curiosity but does not mean anything until some frame of reference puts such ''data'' into perspective.· Richardson seems to be somehow aware of this problem when he points out that his equations are merely a description of what people would do if ''they did not stop to think.'' Although here the problem of intentions is recognized as a crucial addition to ''objective factors,''

Richardson's prescription to substitute trade for the folly of arms races falls prey to the same fallacy.

In this context it is important to remember that Richardson's work is not merely an unusual "derailment" of social science research, or a convenient straw man that can be beaten *ad libitum* but glossed over in serious discussion; on the contrary, it typifies a vast number of analyses that obfuscate rather than illuminate matters by employing "independent variables" in their search for "determinants" of behavior.[9] Such analyses must assume that unequivocal "givens" characterize human affairs, as phenomena like "Mass" do in Newtonian physics, and that those given serve as independent variables with little or no regard for a specific context, thereby dispensing with the need of a motivational account.

Nevertheless, Douglas Hunter[10] showed that even in deterrence theory where one can assume that a substantive consensus exists about the logical as well as the psychological requirements of various moves, data, e.g., about the force structure, are *not* unequivocal and need further elaboration through communications which are not part of the model.

This has important consequences for explanation in the social sciences in general. As Hanna F. Pitkin writes in making the crucial distinction between "competitive games" and "moral" discourse:

> It is part of what we call "moral" that rules and umpires cannot settle questions in that definite way; it is part of what we call "competitive" games that apologies and excuses and other such elaboratives cannot affect the description or the evaluation of what was done. If you swung at three pitches and failed to touch the ball on the third swing then you struck out. To know you struck out all you need to know are the rules of the game and to have seen what you did. There is no gap between intention and action which counts. But outside the area of defined practices, in the moral world, what we are doing has no such defined descriptions and our intentions often fail, one way or another, in execution. There knowing what you are doing . . . cannot fully be told by looking at what in fact, in the world you do . . . Knowing what you are doing involves being able to "elaborate" it, in somewhat the same way that knowing what you meant by something you said involves being able to elaborate that—put it in other words, explain why you said it, justify it.[11]

Now it is clear why Richardson's "explanation" was only valid when people acted blindly and did "not stop to think." The same is true of "strategic analysis" in general, which, as Rapaport reminds us, cannot by itself, "lead to the merging of interest . . . Interests of players are often merged for strategic reasons but this can happen only if the parties recognize their commonality of interest and suspend strategic thinking at least long enough to accomplish the merging."[12] In all such cases a "super game" is constructed whose rules are supposedly known and unequivocal or else are imposed by fiat. Then either underlying "laws of history" are suddenly discovered or determining factors (for Richardson) or "reasons" (in strategic thinking) can be seen as causing the actors to behave in a certain way. "We ask and give 'casual explanations,' " writes Hanna Pitkin, "in a whole variety of contexts where the actor's choice and responsibility are either at a minimum or do not interest us."[13]

Another attempt to find determinants of behavior in the explanation of social order or disorder is the "theory of action" that explains action in terms of the actor's value orientations and norms. "Norms," say Broom and Selznick,[14] "are patterns for behavior that set limits to the sphere within which individuals can search for alternatives in order to gain their goals. Norms thus limit individual goal maximization, differentiate situations for action, mediate a cultural tradition, serve as indicators for sanctions, in short they are points of reference towards which action is oriented. "Social action" comes about when "ego" and "alter" have the same image of the rules applicable in a given situation. Alter "expects" ego to act in accordance with a certain norm and "ego," knowing this, expects the same of himself. To that extent, norm and expectation are two sides of the same phenomenon.[15] Expectations are demands for rule-governed behavior in accordance with a commonly accepted norm, and roles are stabilized bundles of expectations[16] that define the relationship of role bearers to given objects.

To what extent then can we say that norms or rules determine behavior?

Judith Blake and Kingsley Davis[17] maintain that it is fallacious to think of them as causal influences and criticize the idea of a "blueprint society," where culture patterns are laid out in advance and determine the behavior of properly socialized members. Here language analysis helps us to clarify this point further, "A rule," writes Wittgenstein, "stands there like a sign-post. Does the sign-post leave no doubt open about the way I have to go?" [18]

Rules therefore are not "labels" for underlying facts (although one can treat them so for certain purposes), they do *not* refer to mental states of the actor: rather they are *"signals"* for a social practice. These remarks have important implications for explanation or prediction in social science.

> The identification of actions, knowledge of actions, are significantly different from the identification and knowledge of events. It is not that actions are by nature difficult to identify, like species of butterfly; but that a great deal more goes on in saying "what was done" than a mere descriptive identification. The identification of actions is problematic because action concepts are not merely labels for referring but are compounded out of a variety of complex signaling language games in a variety of circumstances. Or putting the same point another way, the identification of actions is problematic because the grammar of action words is significantly shaped in moral discourse, and in moral discourse we must take the other participant's views into account, since our relationship is what is at stake. [19]

According to this account, the underdeveloped theoretical structure of foreign policy analysis, for example, cannot be attributed simply to the lack of suitable "pre-theories"[20] that would transform "events" into "data" as building blocs for general theories, exactly because the lack of pre-theories is itself the direct result of the difficulty of classifying events—a difficulty that cannot be overcome simply by more and more elaborate taxonomies or coding agreements. Conversely, as no rule determines, by itself, its application, discord in international affairs results not from the lack of rules or norms but rather from disagreement about the usage of even elementary terms for appraising concrete events.

These remarks show perhaps more clearly what rules and norms can and cannot do. First, they correct the view that conflict is due to the "lack of common norms." As Richard Falk[21] remarked, *ex parte* contentions that differ widely in their rule applications and that cannot be reconciled under any overarching norm are part of every legal and political order. But the domestic framework offers an additional signaling system that allows contending parties to assess their respective power positions. Thus "a good citizen" has to obey the law. Large corporations that oppose governmental regulations can be charged by the President with acting against the "national interest." Hence a different set of very diffuse symbols can be invoked; it triggers action by creating a relevant "public." Contending parties can thereby be brought to "reason" as informal pressure mounts. This means that in most cases violent conflict is avoided.[22] Seen from this perspective the complaint of political scientists that such concepts as "national interest," "liberty," even "due process," have no clearly definable content is totally beside the point.

Second, the *process* of rule application seems to require study in its own right, as it is not deducible from the issues at hand. Third, the definition of the situation seems to be of critical importance. This latter point is of particular significance for us. Although much attention has lately focused on the termination of conflict, the *genesis* of conflict through various *definitions of a situation* has received little attention. This is all the more astonishing because experiments show that players of a game with the structure of prisoner's dilemma respond differently when various definitions of the situation are given, depending upon whether the opponent is introduced as antagonistic, competitive or cooperative. Rather than looking for the sources of conflict, or its underlying causes, like race, class structure, or stratification of the international system, we would do better to address ourselves to questions like this: Under what circumstances do decision-makers decide that all viable alternatives are exhausted save one: resort to violence:

> Is it possible to identify a point of no return in a conflict relationship progressing toward war? What effect do the nature, flow and interpretation of information have on the foreclosure of alternatives? Analyzing war decisions along these lines represents a much more fundamental approach than the listing of causes of war or the attribution of single overpowering motives to nations.[24]

As the definition of the situation is of paramount importance, norms or rules must be construed not as the dynamic aspect of an underlying social structure but primarily as articulations of subjective interests in a situation. To that extent, "status" positions must then be explained in terms of recurrent and similar definitions of the situation; that is, instead of deriving the dynamics of a social system from its statics, we explain its statics as a special case of its dynamics. The question whether a "system" in terms of structures exists is then an empirical question rather than an initial postulate.

In order to investigate these problems further we will turn in the next section to a discussion of social conflict.

3. Social Conflict

Anyone who is familiar with the literature on conflict will agree with Raymond Mack and Richard Snyder[25] that the concept of "conflict" is for the most part a rubber concept. First of all, many tend to see conflict as "a bad thing" that should and can be eliminated, given good will on both sides. But theorists from Georg Simmel[26] to Lewis Coser,[27] Ralf Dahrendorf[28], and Morton Deutsch[29] have stressed the usefulness of conflict in many aspects of social life, from preserving group cohesion to stimulating social change and solving problems. But, beyond agreement on the pervasiveness of social conflict and rejection of the dichotomy between conflictual and cooperative relationships as too simple, few concur about the scope and domain of the term.

In contrast to Dahrendorf, who uses the term for all types of contests, disputes, tensions, and competitions, I argue that it would make good sense to distinguish between possible sources of conflict and conflict itself, because "antagonistic psychological relations are not the same sort of phenoma as antagonistic interactions."[30] Besides, such a wide definition blurs an important distinction between "conflict" and "competition."

> Competition is from con (together) and petere (to seek). Conflict derives from con (together) plus fligere (to strike). The distinction between the quest and the blow . . . seems precisely the pertinent one for clarity and efficiency in social science . . . Competition involves striving for scarce objects according to established rules which limit what the competitors can do to each other in the course of striving. The chief objective is the scarce object, not the injury or destruction of the opponent . . . (In the case of conflict) the nature of interaction has changed . . . We can use a distinction between competition and conflict to sharpen our focus upon the point at which men abandon institutionalized norms.[31]

This distinction seems to be quite valuable even though reality is a seamless web and such distinctions might be difficult to make in a concrete case. One point is, however, overstated: that conflict is an interaction without rules. Snyder and Mack themselves recognize that "a conflict relation does not represent a breakdown in regulated conduct but rather a shift in the governing norms and expectations."[32] Nevertheless, it is probably fruitful to distinguish opposing claims pursued according to previously agreed rules from an interaction process where influence is used on the opponent in violation of the established rules. As Timasheff aptly remarks:

> In extreme, violent conflict . . . there is a temporary relegation of the original goal to a secondary position and substitution of force itself in its place. The elimination or substantial weakening of the opponent, the breaking of his resistance becomes the immediate goal. It should also be clear that in violent conflict the goal substitution is much more complete than in other forms of conflict.[33]

Having made those distinctions, we can list certain conditions that are, according to Snyder and Mack, present in all social conflicts:

1) Two (or more) distinctive parties must exist and have contact with each other.

2) They must pursue mutually exclusive, and/or mutually incompatible, scarce values.

3) This gives rise to mutually opposed actions and reactions.

4) Those actions exhibit behavior aiming at the destruction, injury, impediment or control of the other party or parties.

5) Attempts are made to acquire power by acquiring scarce resources used to pressure the opposed parties.[34]

It is therefore of great importance to understand social conflict as a *process* of escalation in which fewer and fewer alternatives are available. The situation thus becomes increasingly defined by the participants as a "game", be it "prisoner's dilemma" or "chicken."[35] Actions then take the form of unequivocal "moves" felt to be entirely predictable given the situation. Historical examples come easily to our mind: the outbreak of World War I, for example, seems to fit very well a prisoner's dilemma model: Austria, Russia and Germany mobilized their forces in quick sequence because technological developments seemed to argue that a delay in mobilization would inevitably result in defeat, due to the long lead-time required. Furthermore, the equilibrium between the two alliances was thought to be so unstable that each major power felt bound to aid its ally even at the cost of war, as an ally's defection would be even worse. Nevertheless, such a situation is a special case rather than an adequate description of international relations in general. As states have to play many rounds of such "dilemmas," the attribution of intentions, and attempts to shift the opponents away from perceiving a situation as a prisoner's dilemma in which noncooperative strategies have to be chosen, represent utility functions that do not show up in the game matrix, and are, consequently, of no concern to classical game theorists, despite their saliency for the actual decision-maker. Basically this means that the "objective" content of the matrix attaching utilities to each move is less important than the way in which players make sense out of each other's actions. The "strategies" then depend upon the motivational imputations of each player rather than upon the utilities represented in the matrix.

This theoretical point is all the more important as we can see that different strategies recommend themselves when the prisoner's dilemma is decomposed into its incentives. As Snyder observed, prisoner's dilemma situations result from two incentives, one "offensive" and one "defensive."[36] The "offensive" incentive is given by the fact that gains from noncooperation outweigh those attainable by cooperation, while the "defensive" incentive results from knowing this fact and wishing to limit one's own losses by a preemptive "double cross."

Theories of "misperceptions" or mirror image, and oddly enough, the "realist's" theory of the security dilemma see the decisive reason for choosing non-cooperative moves in the "defensive" incentive. But deterrence theory focuses on the given incompatibilities and the offensive gains.[37] Strategies for the solution of this dilemma will therefore vary considerably, depending upon which motivation one thinks is predominant in the adversary. The mirror image theory as well as realism would recommend measures intended to ease tensions, reduce insecurity and instill trust, while deterrence theory relies upon creating fear by raising the cost of defection. In the latter case the prisoner's dilemma is transformed into a chicken game. Henry Hamburger[38] has shown that a continuum can be constructed that captures some of these dynamics of social conflict. Consider for a moment the matrix of Figure I, which is an expanded chicken game whose upper left corner satisfies the conditions of a prisoner's dilemma.[39]

	I	II	III	IV	V	VI
I	3 3	-1 4	-3 5	-6 6	-9 7	-12 8
II	4 -1	½ ½	-3 0	-6½ 1½	-10 2	-13½ 2½
III	5 -3	0 -3	-3 -3	-7 -3½	-11 -3	-15 -3
IV	6 -6	1 -6½	-3½ -7	-7½ -7½	-12 -8	-16½ -8½
V	7 -9	2 -10	-3½ -11	-8 -12	-13 -13	18 -14
VI	8 -12	2½ -13½	-3¼ -15	-8½ -16½	-14 -18	-19½ -19½

Figure I

Assume further that both parties start with perceptions of a prisoner's dilemma. It would follow that both parties get locked in the "worst outcome" cell II,II. This outcome could only be avoided, under normal circumstances, when communication is allowed and both players "trust" each other to play I, I. As we assumed, however, that for the moment the offensive incentive dominates, it is clear that either player can now threaten to play III or IV and thus escalate the conflict. This looks all the more promising because such a threat entails only slight additional costs to the threatener but promises larger gains if the threatened is "impressed" and moves back to I, trying to minimize his losses. The threatened can, however, also decide to counterescalate: then the burden is on the originally threatening player to submit or move down the diagonal until disaster becomes unavoidable. From IV, IV on, the "irrationality" of the conflict becomes evident as moves are no longer made for expected immediate gains but to prevail over the other, not only threatening to inflict more and more losses but by showing resolve in accepting more and more punishment. At the end (VI,VI) the only rationale for escalation is the wish to "take the other along" on the way down when defeat is unavoidable.[40] By the same token it is also clear why most conflicts end long before this ultimate frenzy develops. As Coser remarked:

For all except absolute conflict, termination involves a reciprocal activity and cannot be understood simply as an unilateral imposition of the will of the stronger on the weaker. Therefore, contrary to what common sense might suggest not only the potential victor but also the potential vanquished makes a crucial contribution to the termination. How then is the loser moved to decide that he has, in fact, lost? Not only the objective situation but the perception of the situation is crucially important since only the latter will bring forth the requisite admission of defeat. Different contenders might arrive at variant estimates as to the degree of oppressiveness of a situation and of the value of the sacrifice demanded. Since such assessments are difficult to make and do not depend on rational calculations alone they are greatly facilitated by the availability of symbolic signposts.[41]

The importance of symbols is again apparent. Thus, for most Frenchmen the German capture of Paris in 1871 signaled the end of the war, whereas the Russian people's identification with the open land rather than with the capital meant that Napoleon's capture of Moscow (or for that matter the British capture of Washington in 1812) was not taken as a final blow. If such common symbols are lacking—which unfortunately is the usual case—peace-making is much more difficult, as no common definition of the situation unites the various subgroups of the opposing camps. In such a case negotiations, like military campaigns, can be effectively waged only when one group wins out over others and makes its definition "stick" (or when the unlikely event happens that a compromise satisfying all parties is reached).

The matter is, however, still more complicated. As Coser shows, sometimes the will to make peace is present but without that to accept defeat: the parties may be willing to stop short of "victory" but the exact point at which an agreement should be made may still be a bone of contention. Under such circumstances the search for a compromise will begin.[42]

> The willingness to negotiate a compromise . . . will of course depend on correct assessment of the situation and such assessment . . . will be facilitated by the availability of indices of relative standing in the battle. It is one of the key functions of the mediator to make such indices readily available to both parties. Symbols of defeat and victory thus turn out to be of relevance in order to stop short of either.[43]

This description certainly captures most of the salient features of such a situation, such as its assessment in terms of mutually complementary roles. But it is doubtful whether "mediators," especially in international relations, are (or even can or should be) such "disinterested" third parties, and consequently, whether one should abstract from their "interest" to make a definition stick.[44] Furthermore, the common definition of the situation seems not to depend exclusively upon the availability of indices of strength because strength is itself a problematic concept. Other factors, like Schelling's concept of "promin ence," and perceptions in general, seem to be of particula. importance here.[45]

This leads back to our initial problem, how conflicts become interpreted in terms of a prisoner's dilemma game in the first place, and how decisions are made in crisis situations when decision-makers have to attend to choices that have consequences along various dimensions, so that a single utility scale cannot be established. In other words, some of the strong assumptions of game models will have to be dropped, so that a clearer picture of the actual decision-process can be gained. We will try to deal with this problem in two steps. First, we will focus on the dynamic aspect of the interaction by expanding the matrix to the other side (top left side) and analyzing the stages before the prisoner's dilemma is recognized by both parties. In a second step, we will try to develop a model of the decision process in stages, basing it on less demanding assumptions than those of game theory and utilizing some of the decision-criteria developed by Simon and Lindblom.

As to the first point, rather than specifying distinctive pay-offs we use the assumptions underlying chicken and prisoner's dilemma games. As is well known, the decisive difference between these variable sum games is that in chicken games the punishment for noncooperation (DD) is worse than the penalty for exploited cooperation (CD or DC) whereas the reverse is true in prisoner's dilemmata.[46] Practically, however, this means "that both parties prefer the payoff for having their own cooperation exploited by the adversary to the payoff for mutual defection or noncooperation."[47] Let us consider the day to day interactions between states, which, as Fisher[48] and Henkin[49] have amply demonstrated, are rather extensively regulated by legal norms. Although this does not mean that deviance is excluded, it implies that most challenges never escalate: the usual instruments of "judicial interpretation" or "muddling through" are effective. A more serious challenge is reported higher up in the hierarchy of decision-making, where a decision is made to ignore it, protest it mildly by a "note," or call for a new settlement. Only the latter move initiates a bargaining sequence that can lead to the escalation ladder described above.

Ignoring an adversary's move is, however, a widely used device, as shown by the lack of response to Hitler's seizure of the Rhineland or to the initial introduction of Soviet weapons into Cuba. One could then say that the adversary prefers being exploited, and to accept a change in the status quo, rather than to defeat himself and create a more explosive situation. The resulting mild "chicken game" would have the following form:

0	0	-5	5
5	-5	-10	-10

Figure II

The adversary could, however, redefine the situation by engaging new values and thus, countering the challenge, create a "prisoner's dilemma," as Figure III shows:

10	10	-15	15
15	-15	-10	-10

Figure III

This redefinition of the situation, transforming the "mild" chicken game into a prisoner's dilemma, comes about when the threatened party sees the challenge not merely as a particular minor violation of the status quo, but rather as a signal that one party is willing to abrogate cooperation. Whereas in the "mild" chicken game mutual cooperation is taken for granted, and consequently the cooperative strategy CC has no particular payoffs assigned, cooperation becomes a *value in itself* aside from the particular dispute when the challenged party "answers" with a redefinition of the situation.[50] By mutually upping the stakes during the next rounds, the parties escalate the conflict by moving down the main diagonal of Figure I as shown before. Naturally, a party also has the option to try to convince the opponent that its challenge should not be taken as such a signal and that it should be interpreted in terms of a mild chicken game rather than a prisoner's dilemma. Thus, conflict can be avoided if the challenging party can produce excuses or elaborate on its actions by changing the context ("this step was not meant to be a threat," etc.). The importance of this point emerged earlier in connection with Pitkin's treatment of what is accepted as an "explanation" for a "move."[51] The opportunity to persuade and/or deceive results from the conventional character of the signaling systems by means of which we direct social action.

> The freedom to establish the meanings of signals allows actors to influence the relationships that are perceived between some of their actions—i.e., to influence whether others regard things they do as signals and what the meanings of the signals are. They can thus create new signals or destroy linkages previously . . . present.[52]

The reason why we conceptualized the world political process as a "conversation" in Chapter I is now clearer. This means that the shaping of perceptions and expectations, through the manipulation of symbols, is the most encompassing horizon in which certain stages of interactions can be illuminated by "games" like chicken or prisoner's dilemma. But, rather than superimposing upon such strategic-choice models a communication "game," it seems more approprate to use game models *within* the wider framework of symbolic interaction. Although this could be interpreted as merely a matter of preference, it has enormous repercussions for the analysis of decision-making and bargaining, especially in crisis situations, as will be shown below.

4. Rules and Decision-Making

According to game theory, the situations decision-makers face are specified by their respective interest, of which both players are completely informed. Since the alternatives available for each player present a complete set of available strategies, there can be no change in strategy once a course of action is chosen. Consequently, the only way a player can structure the situation is to eliminate some option favorable to the first player's goals. This is done by Schelling's famous "strategy" of commitment, which forecloses all but one option for the adversary. In this view,

interaction among units becomes a race to commit. The first
player to achieve a credible commitment "wins." This two move
paradigm is extended to strategies involving more than one
decision per player through the complex form in which all possible
permutations of multiple decisions form a set of complete
strategies.[53]

But this foreclosure principle provides very little guidance in
actual situations. First of all, only known alternatives can be
foreclosed. But, as information is always fragmentary rather
than complete, the adversary will often have ways to circumvent
the "commitment." Besides, for the player who has to make a
decision it is usually unclear which alternative will bring about
the desired result, because the one-to-one match between
action-alternative and outcome postulated by game theory is in
reality hard to find. Finally, for any decision-maker it will be
difficult to specify the "utilities" of an outcome: the long-range
consequences are usually unknown and outcomes often
encompass several independent dimensions that can hardly be
reduced to homogeneous utilities. Consequently, as decision-
makers usually face ill-defined situations, they prefer to avoid
strategies that commit them to irrevocable course of action:
instead, they develop their strategy sequentially, a procedure
that gives them a cushion for errors.[54] The Cuban quarantine
decision illustrates this point rather nicely.[55] The blockade was
chosen exactly because it allowed the president to retain the
option of initiating hostilities, be it by firing at ships trying to run
the blockade or by marshalling superior air power for destruction
of the enemy's missiles. Because not all future consequences of
an action can be foreseen, as required for the utility calculations
of a perfectly "rational" decision-maker, an actual
decision-maker will only be able to take into account some
consequences of his actions—those he does foresee. In the
Cuban crisis, for example, Soviet pressure against Berlin was
soon discounted by the Kennedy group.

As feedback reveals the consequences of the initial strategy,
and as the discrepancy between goal and actual achievement is
noted, new measures are adopted to "take care" of the things
that went wrong.[56] Attacking the "synoptic ideal"—knowledge
of all alternatives and their consequences—Lindblom points out
the decisive difference between policy problems and "problem
solving" in terms of adopting the "best" available strategy:

If what is to be achieved, then, is not simply (as in the usual concept of a problem) removal or substantial reduction of the frustrations in a goal seeking activity, but also and sometimes instead, reconciliation of interests, then problem solving is a more continuous process than it is ordinarily conceived to be. For whether a possible reconciliation is satisfactory today will depend not solely on the characteristics of today's problem, but also on what yesterday's pattern of reconciliation was and what tomorrow's might be made to be.[57]

This leads us to a stage model of conflict.[58] First, the decision-maker who, through the introduction of a new resource (like new missile systems as in the case of Khrushchev), raises his level of aspiration and sets out to challenge the status quo rarely knows his maximum and minimum points, much less the other party's limits. Experience allows him to judge certain outcomes only as likely or unlikely to occur, as Snyder[59] suggested. Thus, Kennedy's weak performance in Vienna is said to have led Khrushchev to believe that the United States would not hold firm in another confrontation, and this in turn led to the Soviet initiation of the Berlin and Cuba crises.[60] Provisions are made for minor difficulties the challenge might encounter, so that no immediate reconsideration is necessary. Only when the opponent makes a move unexpected by the challenger (second stage), rendering his initial strategy ineffective by either circumventing his challenge or escalating the conflict, must the challenger devise modifications. If neither party can find a "winning strategy"—that is, a move that reduces the opponent to the sole aim of cutting his own costs while leaving the winner with substantial gains (as shown in Figure I)—a deadlock develops and disaster seems unavoidable. At this stage, either a joint solution is attempted or war ensues (stage three). In the first case, both sides engage in the search for an acceptable outcome by revealing their preferences and eliminating goals unacceptable to the opponent, until a compatible goal-set exists. In this view bargaining is a matter of creating a "bargaining space," through disclosing one's preferences in phases two and three, as well as a matter of finally settling on one particular point. (The theory of arbitration—for example, Nash's proposal—assumes too much by presupposing joint knowledge of preferences, an initial move to the boundary of the bargaining space, and a disagreement limited to the question of what position is to be taken on the boundary.)[61]

Classical bargaining theory not only telescopes the three stages into one "game" but strangely ignores the consequences of "bargains," assuming that the deals struck will actually be implemented. This might make sense if bargaining theory is taken as a purely normative enterprise dealing solely with what rational players should do in order to maximize their gain. But in adequate descriptive theory such assumptions create serious distortions. For instance, Coser's remarks suggest that solutions found at the bargaining table will not pass without challenges from competing groups or factions. Such a challenge might arise because a group is outside the decision-making process and therefore lacks information on which to base a concrete assessment of the opponent's bargaining strength, or it might result from opportunism. In any case, outcries against an official bargain, as a "betrayal" or a "sell out," are quite common.

It therefore makes sense to add a fourth stage to the conflict model to deal with opposition, on both sides, to the new definition of the situation and consequently to the bargain itself. The decisive problem here is whether the leadership is challenged in order to sabotage the results of the deal or whether certain groups simply seize upon the situation to press for a change in government without endangering the new agreement. In other words, the decisive point is what has been "learned" by the recent conflict.

In such a perspective, attributing to the opponent a foreign policy plan that extends into the indefinite future is fanciful indeed, even if the adversary claims magical powers of divination by pointing to relentless "laws of history" and the inevitability of the "great world revolution." Assessing the opponent's moves correctly is still further complicated by the fact that force changes, i.e. one of the most important indicators in international relations, are outcomes of decisions usually taken several years earlier and under vastly different circumstances. Furthermore, a government must not only explain and justify its actions to its opponent but also establish a common definition of the external situation for domestic reasons. Under such circumstances, international negotiations not only effect an understanding with the opponent but also define a joint preference-ordering within the domestic arena.

Such considerations have particularly important implications for treaties, which are distinguished from *ad hoc* bargaining deals by their scope and explicitness.

Thus, Abram Chayes, in an illuminating article on the bargaining process of arms control, remarks quite aptly:

> Treaties are often analogized to contracts. But unlike the voluntary exchange of promises between two individuals—itself increasingly misleading as the archetypal contract—the formulation, negotiation and ratification of a treaty is an elaborate bureaucratic and political affair. . . . It is probably fair to say that the principal reason arms control agreements take so long to negotiate and are not more far reaching is not so much the difficulty of one side convincing the other as the need for each side to guarantee a broad base of agreement and acceptance within its own and allied policy making establishment. The argument ... is that this very process of negotiation and ratification tends to generate powerful pressures for compliance if and when the treaty is adopted. At least three interrelated phenomena contribute to these pressures: 1) by the time the treaty is adopted a broad consensus within governmental and political circles will be arrayed in support of the decision; 2) meanwhile principal centers of potential continuing opposition will have been neutralized or assuaged though often by means of concessions; 3) many officials, leaders of the administration or regime and opponents as well, will have been personally and publicly committed to the treaty, creating a kind of political imperative for the success of the policy.[62]

Naturally this does not mean that treaties cannot be broken, or entered into under false pretenses, but it does point out that a decision to abrogate a treaty usually requires a new round of maneuvering and bargaining, which displaces the old consensus. Thus, a treaty fundamentally affects the incentive system within which the policy making bureaucracy works. Research or the development of options in a certain area, which formerly seemed promising for the bureaucrat because it allowed easy advancement, is now frowned upon. Money for such projects will be harder to come by and the intelligence community's "worst case analysis" will be read in the light of newly developed expectations. The threshold for counter-measures against advances permitted to the opponent by the treaty will be higher, and they will probably only be taken when several attempts at consultation fail or when the information provided is not considered reassuring.

> . . . although the treaty will be directed at a reasonably well
> understood range of undesired conduct, it will tend as well to
> inhibit activities in a kind of penumbra surrounding that core. A
> zone of doubtful conduct may arise because the agreement
> establishes what Prof. Roger Fisher calls "a precautionary
> rule"—that is a rule some distance back from the interest we are
> trying to protect, so that a breach of the rules does not necessarily
> offend that interest.[63]

In short, explicit agreements provide the opportunity to develop a signaling system in terms of "roles". Thus a much wider range of situations can be structured in terms of complementary expectations, through the creation of "routines". Role taking no longer depends on *ad hoc* deals defining situations: iterative bargains begin to reveal "structures", and rules emerge as signposts which guide inferences. It will be the task of the next chapter to investigate further the process by which such "rules" impinge upon behavior. Beginning with a discussion of the most prominent set of rules, i.e. laws, I will try to establish a clear demarcation criterion which distinguishes rules of law from other more informal constraints upon decision-making. This in turn will enable us to elucidate more fully what it means "to follow a rule" *in general*. The rest of the chapter is then devoted to the discussion of the more informal rules such as metaphors, myths, doctrines and historical analogies which can thus be understood as subsets of the "grammar of rules".

III The "Grammar" of Rules

1. Introduction

To conceive of political behavior as being regulated by rules is nothing new. Indeed, our whole Western political tradition is based upon a belief in the capacity of law to channel and resolve conflict. The call for a "government of laws and not of men" recurs in political debates from Plato [1] to the American Revolution [2] and the present. At times, this emphasis on law was so overbearing that, for the student of public affairs, politics seemed to be circumscribed by the investigation of constitutional structures. [3] By the same token, international relations were analyzed in terms of international law. But because state practice seemed nearly always somehow at odds with legal prescription, some "filters" of law had to be invoked, i.e. the "prudential rules" of diplomacy. Thus, the failure of international law to provide an adequate mapping of international reality led to several efforts to "close the gaps" and to introduce the rule of law into international life. [4] The Geneva Protocol, the Kellogg-Briand Pact, the advocacy of comprehensive international arbitration agreements, and Sir Hersch Lauterpacht's "proof" that all issues are "justiciable," [5] all resulted from the same underlying conviction that legal procedures are applicable to all areas of public life.

This narrowing of political inquiry, supposedly making public affairs more intelligible, was bought at a heavy intellectual price. First, it hampered critical investigation into the limitations of law by blocking out the importance of the social setting in which

45

law-regulated behavior occurs. Second, preoccupation with legal
logic provoked in reaction the argument that the crucial step in
adjudication was the *application* of legal norms.[6] But this
application could not simply be deduced from the existing norm
structure, as there were acceptable legal arguments "to
vindicate whatever course of action is preferred for nonlegal
reasons." [7] Intellectual dissatisfaction with the conventional
conception of law was enhanced when the rise of totalitarian
ideologies   threatened—domestically   as   well   as
internationally—the concept of a legal order. Law was
"unmasked" as an instrument of the ruling class, or an
unnecessary bridle upon the aspirations of the "stronger race".
Long before law had ceased to be an adequate map of social
reality,[8] the focus on sanctions as the distinguishing
characteristic of a legal order obscured the way in which legal
rules actually impinge upon decisions. The latter problem comes
into sharp focus when we notice that "following a command"
(stop!) is obviously different from "following a rule of law," for
example, applying a stipulation of the penal code to a case at
hand. In both cases a command in the widest sense is being
followed, and both prescriptions can be traced back to the
"sovereign" who enunciated them. But the fact that both rules
have the same source does not prevent them from producing
vastly different mental operations. Furthermore, as "realists"
were quick to point out, individual or class preferences may have
a significant impact upon legal decision-making, yet such factors
are far removed from the supposedly decisive threat of
sanctions. Thus a good many influences may serve as constraints
on behavior and may account for decisions: the primacy of
"sanctions" is at best dubious. Furthermore, it may not be
appropriate to conceive of law mainly in terms of adjudicative
procedures. As Morton Kaplan and Nicholas Katzenbach aptly
remark:

> When we speak of the rule of law or of a "government of laws,"
> we clearly do not mean the rule of judges, or a government of
> judges. We are talking about the larger formal process through
> which members of the society pursue and realize values in an
> orderly way. It scarcely requires argument that "law" viewed as a
> body of authoritative rules pervades all the institutions of modern
> government, and is no monopoly of judges. We have a
> constitutional allocation of functions, supplemented by custom,

experience, and ways of doing business within government, which gives to these processes a "legal" character. [9]

Law then performs a much wider range of functions, than an emphasis on sanctions would at first seem to suggest. Thus, even in systems marked by hierarchial authority patterns, many disputes fail to be resolved by adjudication, despite the law's central role in structuring adversary arguments. For example, the United States Supreme Court recognizes such evasive legal principles as "case and controversy," [10] "no standing to sue," or the flat refusal to grant *certiorari*, as well as elaborate doctrines like the "political questions" doctrine, [11] whose expressed purpose is to avoid adjudication when serious conflicts within the coordinated branches of government are likely to arise. [12] In such "horizontal disputes" accommodation rather than adjudication is usually sought. "The goal is conflict settlement, not the vindication of rights." [13]

These considerations are rather important for a discussion of international law, for "conceptual assumptions about the nature of law operate as a perception-set determining the scope and the subject of investigation." [14] Thus, many characteristics of the domestic legal order, like hierarchical authority structures, have been taken, implicitly or explicitly, as *prerequisites* for any functioning legal order, with the result that international law was declared "deficient," a mere set of rules of comity, or as Rousseau called it, "a chimera." [15] The limitations imposed by inapplicable conceptual tools suggested two main avenues of research that might rescue international law as a special part of "law": either one could construct a legal system pointing to functional international equivalents of domestic structures — "self help" as an equivalent to "sanctions," for example — preserving in this way the status of international law as "true" law; or one could broaden the inquiry by subsuming under the concept of law all kinds of factors that impinge upon legal decision-making. Whereas the first path was followed by Hans Kelsen in his "pure theory of law," [16] the pragmatic tradition of American legal theory directed Myres McDougal [17] toward the latter strategy. Without going into the extensive debate about Kelsen's formalism versus McDougal's move toward "policies" as the proper province of law, one may fairly observe that whereas Kelsen's theory fails to account adequately for the "material side of law," or how norms get translated into behavior, McDougal's encompassing approach blurs the distinctive features of law. [18]

It is the hypothesis of this chapter that both failures spring from an inadequate conceptualization of how rules or norms influence decision-making. Furthermore, an analysis of the language-games that are involved when we speak of "rules" can show why this is so. Thus, we hope not only to find a more adequate conceptualization of international law, but also to learn how to deal more coherently with phenomena often treated as quasi-legal—such as "doctrines" (the Monroe Doctrine, the Truman Doctrine) or foreign policy commitments. Because our aim is to look at the problem of international order in terms of rules of the game as exemplified in analogies, metaphors and strategic doctrines, clarifying their status in decision-making and their respective roles (legal rules, decision rules in the form of commitments, strategic doctrines, and so forth) is of paramount importance. Having devoted much of the previous chapters to a critique of conventional world order thinking, I will now attempt to sketch more clearly the characteristic features of my approach. The plan for this chapter is therefore the following: In the second section various theories of law will be evaluated for their contribution to our understanding of international law and in section three our search continues for satisfactory criteria distinguishing related phenomena, such as informal rules, preferences, and commitments, all of which impinge upon decision-making. Section four will then try to show the importance of "doctrines" based on earlier development of a sufficiently clear demarcation criterion between rules of policy and legal rules. The role of historical analogies, metaphors and myths is investigated in section five and the final section concerned with a more principled treatment of rhetoric and reasoning tries to summarize our discussion of the influence of metaphors, analogies and myths upon inferences in the political discourse. (Section 6).

2. The Problem of Obligation

In the previous section, our argument reached the point where the question of the distinguishing characteristic of the rule of law was transformed into the question of legal obligation. Obligation, indeed, served for a long time as the major focus of otherwise disparate legal theories, before preoccupation with policy itself led to an over-emphasis on the open character of the legal system. Stanley Hoffmann aptly remarked:

> The tendency of some international lawyers is to agree with earlier criticism so much that they throw out the legal baby with the stale bath. It is essential to understand that law in the hands of statesmen is not merely a policy among others, but that it has very special characteristics and roles.
> . . . Law is distinguished from other political instruments by certain formal features: there is a certain solemnity to its establishment, it has to be elaborated in a certain way. More significantly the legal order even in international affairs has a life and logic of its own. . . . Law may be an instrument of policy, but it is one that has an artificial reason.[19]

But although it points out the error in identifying law with the outcome of decision processes, the paragraph quoted above provides no clear statement of the positive distinguishing characteristics of legal rules.

To clarify this problem, I will proceed in two steps: First, I will try to illuminate the nature of custom and, second, I will attempt to show what "following a rule" means in general, and what special operations may be involved in "following a rule of law," thus providing a clearer demarcation criterion.

Above all, we have to remember that international law exists only in the sense that national decision-makers refer to it in their international dealings. In that regard, the conceptualization of international law as a kind of psychological pressure working upon government officials seems to be sound. (The fruitfulness of this approach in analyzing bureaucratic constraints has been shown by the works of Henkin and Coplin,[20] as already mentioned.) Consequently, the normative content of international law depends decisively upon the concerns of these state officials. So far the individual focus and the "psychological pressure" theory of law make good sense. But this approach can lead to serious distortions, in particular when the validity of a norm of law is claimed to derive from the reasons an individual decision-maker advances for his compliance with the law. Obviously, one can follow a rule of law for many different reasons, as exemplified by the great variety of "rationalizations" states and individuals give for their obedience. The requirement of motivational conformity thus seems to involve, logically speaking, a "category" mistake, and should be dropped from any valid theory of law.

In the same vein, one must wonder whether Myres McDougal's idea—to use all "current social science techniques," [21] interviews, surveys and so on, in order to elicit "factual" responses from national decision-makers about their attitudes toward law—would not lead to more social science "busy-work" without providing any bonus for a correct theory of law. This suspicion is enhanced when we remember that international law in particular is used mainly for the validation of claims and *not* for adjudication. The reasons a national official advances for compliance or noncompliance with a particular norm, are therefore seldom the reasons actually determining a certain course of action. Rather, public reasons are an essential part of the bargaining game, which is played by making normative legal statements.

To avoid this flaw in the "internal constraint" theory of law, we must return once more to its origins in the "command" theory of law. As we saw in the first chapter, Hobbes' idea of a sovereign possessing supreme power seemed to be logically necessary in order to structure individual expectations so that contracts would be kept.[22] Hume showed, however, that such coordination is possible without the threat of superior force, and that the threat of force is only a special case among many devices used to resolve the fundamental problem of coordinating choices. In view of this, the binding character of international law seems to result from the "strategic calculations" of decision-makers and not from their private psychological motives.

> What matters to decision makers in state A is not what they believe is the right rule, nor what the counterparts in other states might believe or desire, but rather what rules (they think) . . . are manifested in the conduct . . . of the generality of states. International consensus in conclusion is manifested objectively as a result of the strategic calculations of states that are the creator-subjects of International Law. It is misleading to look for subjectivities or national intentions apart from what the states manifest in their international relations.[23]

It is now clear why a unilateral declaration of policy, even if effectively pursued, is not sufficient to create international custom as long as no further compliance on the part of other states can be observed. Furthermore, it seems that McDougalian social science "theory" may turn out to be highly disruptive for international law, despite its insistence on "upgrading" research and helping law to develop in a realistic fashion. As the validity of a legal norm for a given state depends upon assumptions about how other states assess its validity, the ready availability of such information might seriously weaken legal constraints. Consider a state A no longer agreeing with a particular norm of international law, but obeying it because of the belief that states B, C, D, E, and F accept it as a valid legal principle. As soon as officials of state A learn that their counterparts in states B and C do not feel obliged either but have conformed to the norm because of A's compliance, A, B, and C will be tempted to collude and claim the invalidity of the norm in question. Such an example is not so far-fetched as it first seems: the breakdown of the three mile limit on territorial rights in the oceans at the Geneva Conference of 1958 follows this pattern nicely. Despite widespread dissatisfaction with the three mile limit, states generally presumed its legality; but that presumption very quickly lost its force when it became clear that a great number of states made conflicting claims, in turn encouraging more and more extravagant positions.

Until now our analysis has only refined the idea of internal constraint. But a moment's reflection will show that this is only a necessary, not a sufficient, condition of law, because the binding character of foreign policy commitments and guarantees (who does not remember the famous domino theory!) results from such a strategic calculaton, too. A criterion distinguishing clearly between legal rules and other rules of the game serving as constraints upon the choices of a decision-maker will, consequently, have to be developed. I will try to discuss this issue in terms of the "language game" involved in "following a rule."

3. *"Following a Rule"*

What do we mean by saying that someone is following a rule? Ludwig Wittgenstein makes the following interesting observations:

The use of the word "rule" and of the word "same" are interwoven. 24

> "How am I able to obey (follow) a rule?" If this is not a question about causes, then it is about the justification for my following the rule in the way I do. If I have exhausted the justifications I have reached bedrock and my spade is turned. Then I am inclined to say "This is simply what I do." 25

In this account three ideas are central. Rules first of all define situations and provide guidance by pointing out similarities within what seems at first to be a bewildering variety of circumstances. Secondly, rules serve as inference warrants by providing justifications for possible decisions in choice situations. Thirdly, rules are not subjective preferences or intuitions: they define a social "practice." All this has important implications for the study of law. Let us begin with the idea of a rule defining a social practice and work our way backward. The idea of a social practice was briefly ventilated in the second chapter. Gidon Gottlieb remarks, in a discussion of "learning" how to follow a rule of law:

> Indeed we should not admit that a student has learned a law, if all he were prepared to do were to recite it. Just as a student, to qualify as knowing rules of grammar, multiplication, chess or etiquette, must be able and ready to apply these rules to concrete operations, so to qualify as knowing a law, he must be able and ready to apply it in making concrete inferences from and to particular matters of fact, in explaining them, and perhaps, also in bringing them about, or preventing them. 26

Although "rule" seems, therefore, very closely tied to "training," a rule of law is concerned with a special kind of training or practice i.e. *reasoning*. Thus, in this context, following a rule means to reason and to be guided in this process by devices (rules) that warrant certain inferences. Here, the second problem mentioned above, the problem of "justification," comes into focus. Several important corollaries follow from these observations:

1. There must be room for choice. If physical necessity is present no rule is involved, because, as Wittgenstein remarks, the grammar of "following a rule" contains also that of "making a mistake." 27 Similarly, we speak of a rule of law, but not of a rule of physics.

2. The circumstances in which a given rule is to apply must be

specified, so that it is possible to select certain aspects of a rule as "relevant" to a choice. Indeed, the consideration of the proper "facts" or merits of the case distinguishes a decision made according to a rule of law from one made solely according to a decision criterion like flipping a coin or drawing lots.

The outcome of drawing lots depends on matters unconnected with the total situation in which the decision is required. The outcome of a decision determined by legal or moral rules is on the contrary, heavily dependent upon such a situation. The difference rests, in other words, in the relationship between the prostasis of a rule—that part of the rule which points to the circumstances in which it operates—and the situation which calls for the decision. 28

3. The rule must identify the nature of the inference to be drawn—for example, whether something is permitted, required, prohibited, or what. This element is the "character tag" of the rule, as Gottlieb calls it.

4. From 2 and 3 it follows that the purpose for which the rule was designed becomes an intrinsic part of its application. Thus, a prohibition against swimming in a lake obviously does not apply to a swimmer rescuing a child who has fallen into the water.

The last point deserves further elaboration, for it shows the difference between the logical form and the substance of "reasoning" with rules in practical matters. If law were, as many proponents seem to suggest, a predominantly "logical" discipline, concerned mainly with the proper distribution of facts into pigeonholes and with the resulting syllogistic conclusions, the life-saver in the above case would be convicted. Under that kind of law, the only relevant question that could arise would be whether the facts as ascertained by the general statement were actually given. This would seem to nearly all of us bad "judicial" reasoning, because we assume a mainly implicit statement of purpose contained in the enumeration of "relevant facts" within the scope of the rule. But because such statements are often eliptic, the purpose of a law is usually expressed by the invocation of "higher" legal principles (equality, civil rights, liberty, and so on) in the courts.

Now the similarity and difference between legal rules and political "rules of the game" can be elaborated further. First, it is clear from the discussion above that rules in general provide

guidance for decision-making; Wittgenstein's comparison of a
rule to a sign-post fits this interpretation very well.[29] Thus, all
rules limit the space in which choices have to be made. But the
following difference between a rule of law and a policy rule or
commitment is worth noting:

> Policies are designed to guide inferences toward fixed results or
> to use Dewey's term toward ends in view. Rules of law
> contemplate specific contexts or settings of application and fixed
> decisions designed to promote specific objects. They provide
> relatively firm guidance, not only with respect to ends, but also as
> to the means to be adopted; they elaborate what has to be done
> when, and to what end. The reasoning appropriate to decisions in
> terms of policies . . . Policies contemplate the delegation of a
> considerable degree of authority to their executants and
> presuppose a correspondingly significant area of indeterminacy
> for the measures to be adopted. Rule guidance on the other hand,
> typically requires the performance of specific acts in
> predetermined circumstances for stated ends.[30]

Several corollaries follow from these thoughts.

First, law requires a consistent and evenhanded application
transcending the contingencies of the single case, i.e., law must
be self-consistent and constant. For if no intelligible pattern of
judicial law-making resulted from the activity of judges, people
would not be able to steer their lives in a reasonable manner.

Second, law requires the acceptance of guiding principles that
cannot be altered unilaterally at a decision-maker's discretion.
The difference from policy is perhaps clearest here. Thus, people
can "violate" legal rules, but not policies.

Third, as this approach to rules in general and to law does not
focus on authority structures or institutions, but on *modes of
reasoning*, a further difference can be found: legal reasoning
must at least in principle accept certain procedures that establish
what is to constitute a legally relevant proof, whereas in politics
this question is usually a decisive part of the argument itself. In
legal proceedings, that is, reference must be made to "texts"
(contracts, treaties, codes, and so on) that structure the
argument by authoritatively prescribing what is allowed to be
introduced as "evidence."

Having mapped out the distinctive features of legal rules, as
compared to mere preferences and commitments, we can now

turn our attention to the latter category of rules and their importance for the strategic interaction between nations. In this context, the way in which two adversaries translate aspirations and power potential into strategy is of particular interest. A clearer understanding of the role strategic considerations play in policy formation is the objective of the next section.

4. *The Meaning of Strategy*

Strategy has conventionally been defined as the science of art practiced by the commander-in-chief. But if it is true, as a French statesman said about war, that strategy is too important to be left to the generals, then one would do well to examine the above definition critically instead of whole-heartedly embracing it. Now, it is obvious that battles in war can have no other rational function than overcoming the resistance of the opponent, and as we saw in the last chapter, they can serve this purpose only until the enemy has capitulated. It is therefore quite possible, at least in theory, to maneuver an opponent into such a hopeless position that surrender without a direct clash of arms is the only reasonable way out. [31] In such a "war of nerves" the role of force is clearly minor as compared to psychological and political instruments. Seeing the capitulation point in psychological rather than purely military terms, Lenin once quite aptly remarked, "the soundest strategy in war is to postpone operations until moral disintegration of the enemy renders a mortal blow both possible and easy." [32] Although Lenin was speaking particularly of revolutionary activity within the armed forces, aimed at crippling their combat readiness, it is fair to say that in most cases battles are a very costly way to disorient the enemy and thus destroy his will and capability to resist.

The above remarks suggest that a wider and more appropriate definition of strategy is necessary. In the words of André Beaufre:

> Strategy is the art of the dialectic of force or more precisely the art of the dialectic of two opposing wills using force to resolve their dispute. [33]

This definition neither limits strategy to an aspect of combat operations nor loses its proper focus on force, which distinguishes strategy from mere bargaining. This interconnection between political goals and force, as well as the willingness to pay for those goals, raises the problem of strategic doctrine, as it is the task of the strategic debate to come to terms with such difficult matters. Noting that the penalty for miscalculation in the field of strategic doctrine—though not immediately obvious like failures in technical fields—is finally "catastrophic," Henry Kissinger wrote in *Nuclear Weapons and Foreign Policy* more than a decade ago:

> It is the task of strategic doctrine to translate power into policy whether the goals of a state are offensive or defensive, whether it seeks to achieve or to prevent a transformation, its strategic doctrine must define what objectives are worth contending for and determine the degrees of force appropriate for achieving them
>
> . . .
> Whatever the problem, then, whether it concerns questions of military strategy or of coalition policy or of relations with the Soviet Bloc, the nuclear age demands above all a clarification of doctrine. At a time when technology has put in our grasp a command over nature never before imagined, power must be related to the purpose for which it is to be used. . . . Strategic doctrine transcends the problem of selecting weapons systems. It is the mode of survival of a society, relating seemingly disparate experiences into a meaningful pattern. By explaining the significance of events in advance of their occurrence, it enables society to deal with most problems as a matter or routine and reserves creative thought for unusual or unexpected situations.[34]

The role of doctrines serving as rules, as guidance devices for inferences in the formulation of foreign policy, becomes visible. But the influence of strategic doctrines upon policy is even more subtle today than the preceding paragraph might suggest. The shift from defense to deterrence brought about a more thoroughgoing alteration of foreign policy, which can be described as a change of emphasis from possession to milieu goals.[35] As the struggle for a congenial international milieu involves the shaping of international legitimacy, the "symbolic dimension" of foreign policy has become increasingly salient.[36]

This has important repercussions for the continuous strategic debate between the two superpowers. Whereas the actual employment of force has decreased in utility, the importance of doctrine has been heightened, because the strategic debate about "sufficiency," "superiority," "limited war," and so on becomes the major means of influencing peacetime bargaining with the opponent. The strategist of today who can convince both sides that the limitation of war is feasible and that superiority in terms of weaponry is not a useful political goal, is not merely describing political reality "but changing it," as Robert Jervis has pointed out.[37] An empirical investigation into the strategic debate in East and West is, therefore, not merely of peripheral interest, but comes to terms with the "stuff" international politics is made of in the nuclear era.

5. *Historical Analogies and Metaphors as Inference Warrants*

Up to now we have dealt with two types of rules: legal and doctrinal or policy rules. Both types shared the characteristics of "inference warrants" but were distinguished by different degrees of explicitness in the guidance they provided for reasoning in choice situations. Legal rules allow only for "principled choices," or decisions that refer to guidance in regard to goals as well as means, whereas policy rules, as exemplified by "doctrines," implicitly confer a great deal of discretion upon the decision-maker as to the time, place and means of their implementation. These two types of rules display, as was pointed out, rather complex and elaborate structures for guiding inferences. But in a way, even individual *components* of such structures seem to have some of the features of rules. It would seem, writes Gidon Gottlieb,

> that the very words and concepts of a language are themselves rule-like. That is, they embody instructions as to the circumstances and purposes for which they may be used in much the same way technical directives and recipes do. . . . If words are rule-particles, so to speak, then every form of human communication may well be a type of normative activity which displays some of the characteristics of reasoning with rules.[38]

This idea has important repercussions upon political discourse, especially if we consider the symbols by which goals are made explicit. Consider, for example, a decision-maker who advocates a certain course of action because it aims at restoring the "balance of power." Obviously he is not describing reality, as all our previous remarks about words as "signals" rather than "labels" imply.[39] He uses a metaphor that allows unknown and bewildering events to be apprehended by a large audience through the "perception of identities with the familiar." [40] Conversely, his opponent will respond in terms of a different set of images—"empire building," "aggression," and so on. Metaphors are, in short, "instruments for shaping political support and opposition, and the premises upon which decisions are made." [41]

In our effort to explicate the "grammar" rules, we thus move further away from the *cognitive explicitness* that characterizes "laws" and "doctrines" and try to investigate the process by which *goal conceptions* themselves are formed and choice situations are defined. It is the hypothesis of this section that, in addition to metaphors, which serve as a rudimentary means of defining situations, historical analogies and myths are of particular importance because they provide guidance for the individual as well as the collectivity in their search for identity. First of all, historical analogies make bewildering situations comprehensible and establish criteria for the choice of appropriate responses by pointing to similar cases in the past. Second, aside from helping to draw such parallels, historical analogies are usually part of a larger context which is seldom fully articulated but which is significant for the definition of the "self" and the "mission" of a collectivity.

In order to investigate these phenomena a bit closer and to uncover the links between historical experiences and "identity" we will have to utilize a *Gedankenexperiment*.

Let us once more start with the imaginary example of two actors interacting with each other. As we have seen, the crucial problem in such a case is how one makes "sense" out of the other's actions. Assuming that actor A and B do not share the same assumed knowledge, which provides ready-made interpretations of all sorts of social acts, A will watch B perform and attribute to him motives and intentions that, in light of A's knowledge, made sense in such a situation. A will therefore see B's action "in terms" of the ready-made stereotypes A's assumed knowledge has provided. Whether or not A's imputations are congruent with B's intentions, A will be able to predict B's typical behavior. Thus, two foreign cultures may interpret each other's typical actions in terms of their own traditions: as long as B's reactions to A's cues, and vice versa, do not lead to major unforeseen events both actors develop "roles" vis-a-vis each other. Note that a match between the role images of A and B is unnecessary, as long as the mutually imputed stereotypes are good indicators of future performance. Interaction thus becomes routinized and

> . . . relieves both individuals of a considerable amount of tension. They save time and effort not only in whatever external tasks they might be engaged in separately or jointly but in terms of the respective psychological economies. Their life together is now defined by a widening sphere of taken for granted routines. . . . This means that the two individuals are constructing a background . . . which will serve to stabilize both their separate actions and their interactions The construction of this background of routine in turn makes possible a division of labor between them opening the way for innovations . . . which will lead to further habitualizations . . . in other words, a social world will be in process of construction containing within it the roots of an expanding institutional order. 42

Again, the introduction of a third party changes the game profoundly, as the institutional world created by the interactions between A and B congeals and attains the status of an objective datum that "confronts the individual as an external and coercive fact."43 Only as such an objective datum can the institutional order created in the course of A's and B's relationship be transmitted; thus it becomes the objective world for the new generation, which enters the game as a new third party through socialization. Under such circumstances, it is not astonishing that many practices institutionalized by A and B will lack functional as well as logical coherence, and consequently the new generation encounters strong incentives to deviate from established practices. To reinforce social control, as well as to satisfy the psychological preference for consistency, legitimizing formulas will be developed that link the various social practices in a meaningful whole.

> The logic does not reside in the institutions and their external functionalities, but in the way these are treated in reflection about them. Put differently, reflective consciousness superimposes the quality of logic on the institutional order . . . 44

> The primary knowledge about the institutional order is knowledge on the pre-theoretical level. It is sum total of "what

everybody knows about a social world," an assemblage of maxims, morals, proverbial nuggets of wisdom, values and beliefs, myths and so forth, the theoretical integration of which requires considerable intellectual fortitude in itself as the long line of heroic integrators from Homer to the latest sociological system builders testifies. On the pre-theoretical level however, every institution has a body of transmitted recipe knowledge that is knowledge that supplies the institutionally appropriate rules of conduct.[45]

It is this "recipe knowledge" that is particularly important for the interpretation of an opponent's actions. His moves are understood in terms of precepts about what one should do in such a situation. But since the lessons derived from experience are never unambiguous, rival schools of interpretation arise and compete for adoption as socially relevant assumed knowledge. This naturally creates stress in a society, which can be resolved by selecting the "correct" practical lesson in light of the commonly accepted theoretical superstructure. A special problem arises, however, if dissent on the practical or theoretical level persists after such an authoritative decision. As the complex theoretical symbolizations are rather far removed from day-to-day practice, and are maintained by social rather than empirical support, "tests" that would determine the correct frame of reference are unavailable. Persuasion and socialization procedures, including the use of force, are brought to bear in order to convince recalcitrant members of the group to accept the authoritative interpretation of reality. Oddly enough, at this stage a pragmatic test for the accuracy of a comprehensive theory become available. A particular theory can now be shown to be correct if it "works," in the sense that it has actually become the standard assumed knowledge of the society. In other words, behavior becomes predictable and institutionalization sets limits on choices.

This observation has important implications for the management of deviance. Someone who systematically misinterprets the actions of his fellow men, who interprets these actions as meaning something quite different from what the socially accepted assumed knowledge proposes, will need the help of a socially accepted professional—psychiatrist, shaman,[46] priest—as does the individual who, though able to interact, comprehends his life as a meaningless sequence of events. Similarly, social groups understand themselves in terms of such social "theories," whether in the form of mythical accounts of a given institutional order, or in the form of a particular *historical* understanding of triumph and defeat, mission and subjection.

This last point is especially important because historical knowledge is virtually the only symbolic universe that provides political actors with an image of the whole of the intersocietal interaction process. This function of history is explicitly acknowledged by many early historiographers. Herodotus [47] for example intends, in his words, "to save the memory of the great deeds"; his second purpose is to show that nothing in human history occurs without a cause. Thus, he becomes a "searcher" [48] of stories that provide clues as to why particular events occurred in a certain way, and his history becomes an attempt to construct a meaningful universe in which various political events can be placed. Thucydides, [49] assuming the constancy of human nature, writes—as Machiavelli does later—to provide lessons an intelligent statesman can use in his dealings with other states. Polybios, [50] finally thinks that historical developments point to the universal dominion of Rome and that history also teaches best how luck and disaster can be borne with dignity by the responsible statesman. History in this sense of an encompassing horizon, therefore, fulfills the same function for inter-societal interaction as various "theories" do for society, or as a "biography" does for the individual.

Here the link between historical reconstruction and identity becomes visible. Erik Erikson pointed out that "by accepting some definition as to who he is . . . the adult is able to selectively reconstruct his past"; [51] but it is also true that by coming to terms with the past, by accepting certain past events the identity of an individual as well as that of a collectivity is redefined, as our discussion above showed. Furthermore, it becomes clear that the encompassing horizons which unite discrete historical experiences are of particular importance. In this context the structure of "myths," which are a particular kind of such encompassing frames of reference, will have to be investigated further.

Political Myths

What then is a political myth? in line with the above argument about the decisive importance of expectations for practical choices, George Sorel's definition of political myth[52] seems at first to be the most appropriate one for our purpose. He sees it as a vision that allows the workers, despite great sacrifices and setbacks, to sustain belief in the revolution and to "picture their coming action as a battle in which their cause is certain to triumph."[53] The treatment of political myths as "gnostic," or more generally as secularized forms of eschatological expectation, figures prominently in the work of Cohn[54] and Voegelin.[55] But there seems to be no reason to deny the status of a political myth to Socrates' vision of Earth in the *Republic*[56] or to Cicero's[57] and Livy's[58] accounts of the Roman foundation. Finally, the American Revolution and the Founding Fathers are for all intents and purposes proper political myths, despite the fact that they concern *past* occurances. Rather than looking for specific symbols, we will have to look for certain functions that all political myths fulfill, regardless of their direction in time.

Myths, we said, are above all accounts of either past glory or future events that render the experience of the present more coherent. Thus what distinguishes the mythical discourse from other "inference guidance devices" is not its content but rather the mode by which a *link between selfhood and action is postulated*. Myths depict the present as an episode in an ongoing drama in which the individual and, in the case of the political myth, the community has to play a specific role.

> What marks its account as being a myth is not its content, but its dramatic form and the fact that it serves as a practical argument. Its success as a practical argument depends upon its being accepted as true, and it is generally accepted as true if it explains the experience of those to whom it is addressed, and justifies the practical purposes they have in mind.[59]

But besides explaining coherently what happened and providing a practical understanding of the potentialities of the future, myths serve as a justification of action. Here the problem of identity and responsibility emerges:

> It is evident that the question of responsibility cannot be separated from the problem of identity. In practical activity, a man must consider among other things whether the action he proposes to take is appropriate to the kind of person he conceives

himself to be. If he is to perform his role, he must know what character he is supposed to play, and it is by defining his character, by establishing his identity, that he delimits the area of his responsibility . . .

If the revolutionary myth maker is like John of Salisbury's prince to shed blood blamelessly, then he must sink his individuality into the identity of a greater whole. He must regard himself as the representative of the group movement whose cause he has espoused.[60]

The limitation of personal responsibility for political acts, through the creation of a "representative" type who acts for his public, shows that to characterize myths merely as cognitively deficient is more than misleading. Besides, myths need not always resort to explanation by miracles, for example the foundation of a community by "gods," as the myth of the American Founding Fathers shows; and very often rational and irrational explanations are intertwined in political myths. Thus, on the one hand Cicero attributes Roman greatness to the structural arrangement established by its constitution,[61] but on the other hand, he views the rise of Rome as a result of its divine origin[62] and of the institutionalization of its charisma in custom (*mos maiorum*], which served as a standard for behavior. Obviously, these two "explanations" are logically incompatible, but the inclusion of "rational elements" (like Cicero's structural argument) is rather the rule than the excetion in political myths.

This characterization of myths allows us to distinguish them from similar concepts, like fables and ideologies, and to see much more clearly their particular inference guidance in the decision-making process. Like fables or parables, myths *do not* provide *instrumental knowledge* suitable for technological application: they are "object lessons" that guide the formation of *attitudes* rather than confer specific advantages in a given situation by teaching a special manipulative skill. Within this frame of reference, myths in particular are characterized by a certain concreteness in the ways they give coherence to the experience of the individual in a group. They differ from a fable, parable, or fairy tale, where the miraculous predominates and where, in order to illustrate a moral precept, appeal to a particular "history" is unnecessary because the lesson can perfectly well be illustrated by a fictitious story. By contrast, the historical messages of myths would suffer if the practical point they convey is "unmasked" as merely fictitious.

On the other end of the spectrum, myths shade into full-fledged ideologies when the rational component dominates the mythical account and promises to provide not only the insights of an object lesson but *usable technical* knowledge. Ideological argumentation avails itself, therefore, of the conventional canon of scientific discourse save the principle of refutability. No one saw this more clearly than Sorel, who stressed the attitudinal impact of ideologies, an impact he called "myth." In the idea of the "revolution" the suppressed workers find, despite all the disproven predictions of socialist ideology, a mythical account that explains their past and present and throws light on an anxiously awaited future.

Our discussion of myths and metaphors brought to the fore a link between reasoning, emotions, and the definition of identity which is no longer reflected upon in our prevalent analytical division between the cognitive, evaluative and cathectic elements of social action. But since the connection between emotional arousal and reasoning in practical matters was part of "rhetoric" from Aristotle[63] to Vico[64], a short discussion of this tradition could be a useful contribution to the understanding of the link between emotions and "perceptual shifts," as discussed above in connection with the mild chicken and the prisoner's dilemma games.

6. *Rhetoric and Reasoning*

In a time when we are accustomed to equate rhetoric with "propaganda," it seems quite strange to point to a connection between practical reasoning and rhetoric. The modern view that rhetorical imagery suffers from a "cognitive deficiency" might nevertheless be an unwarranted simplification. There is, naturally, a sense in which such suspicions are appropriate; but to dismiss political rhetoric as cognitively deficient might not do justice to political discourse and debate in general. In situations in which political choices have to be made, it is seldom possible to determine, by means of "objective referents," how to advance the "security" or "freedom" of a country or the "happiness" of its citizenry. (The widely accepted rule of liberal utilitarianism, to secure the greatest happiness of the greatest number, turns out to be one of the more successful rhetorical slogans, despite its appeal to "scientific" numbers.) [65] Furthermore, because the situations in which rhetoric plays a part—Aristotle's "things one has to deliberate about" [66]—are defined for practical and not analytical purposes, an appeal to moral sentiments and an ornate and suggestive rather than analytically rigorous style is not so much due to the trickiness of politicians (although they usually exploit such situations) as it is the result of the way in which we create our social and political universe.

> Whatever appears important for our wishing and willing, our hope and anxiety, for acting and doing: that and only that receives the stamp of verbal meaning. . . . Only what is related somehow to the focus-point of willing and doing, only what proves to be essential to the whole scheme of life and activity, is selected . . . and . . . receives a special linguistic accent, a name. [67]

This process of "naming" has already been dealt with above in discussing "defining situations." But it was modern role theory that provided further theoretical underpinning for Ernest Cassirer's speculation about the importance of emotions and their arousal for practical reasoning. First of all, there is mounting evidence that, contrary to Freud's conception of motivation, it is not so much sustained oppression and deprivation as fear of being frustrated in one's expectations that stimulates the escalation of conflict. [68] As we tried to show in the previous chapter, such fear leads to a redefinition of the situation through the engagement of new values, transforming a "defection" in a "mild chicken" game into a "prisoner's dilemma." [69] As we have seen, a mediator understands how to motivate the two antagonists to mutual role taking: in this process, taking the perspective of the "other" leads to a sharing of aspirations, of weaknesses and fears, and thus reassures the opponents. A mutual limitation of demands or a compromise then becomes possible.

> As a concomitant of mutual role taking and the exchange of significant symbols, feeling is part of understanding: an adjunct and a necessary condition of the very process of sharing perspectives that makes it possible for politicians and leaders of clientele groups to enter into a symbolic pattern of action . . . the visible, publicized process of role taking in politics becomes a

ritual which chiefly functions to shape a myth of a symbolic social order in which the weak are protected. In this case, the myth contributes to political quiescence for masses and to political craftsmanship for leaders.[70]

It is now obvious why "metaphors" used by the government become such pervasive cues for group action. As Mead [71] has pointed out, the shared beliefs of a group and the development of an individual's identity are the result of the same process of role taking. And because—despite various group memberships—"nationality" becomes a very important part of one's identity, it is part of self-respect to be loyal and obedient to one's "representatives."

> Insofar as people's hopes and anxieties are salient to politics, they turn on status in society and on security from perceived threat. For the great mass of political spectators cues as to group status and security, and especially as to their future status and security can come chiefly or only from governmental acts. This is one of the few forms of activity perceived as involving all groups and individuals in society and as reflecting the range of public interests, wants, and capabilities. In an ambiguous but salient area of public affairs, therefore, political cues serve in Lasswell's terms as "symbols of the whole" in a way acts or promises of individuals or private groups rarely can.[72]

All these considerations set the stage for the second part of this work, which investigates the interaction of the superpowers in the postwar era in terms of policy and strategic doctrines. Chapter IV will deal with historical analogies and their respective roles in the policy formulation process of the United States and the Soviet Union. Chapter V will take up the role of myths and metaphors and Chapter VI traces the development of strategic doctrines and the part played in international politics by the strategic debate.

IV Historical Analogies

1. Introduction

The Cold War, its origins and demise, can serve as a case study for the approach to international order problems developed in the previous chapters.

Circumscribing our case study in time, few people would object, I think, to the view that President Nixon's 1972 visits to Peking and Moscow are a convenient historical landmark signalling the end of the era of Cold War hostility. Certainly, major changes in Soviet-American relations had already occurred—a test ban treaty was signed, the Soviet incursion into Czechoslovakia had evoked little protest on the part of the United States, as had the mining of Haiphong and the bombing of North Vietnam on the Soviet side. But it was on the occasion of the two visits that the significant changes that had taken place in the configuration of power since World War II received their fullest official expression. Stepping from the plane on May 22, 1972, exactly twenty-five years after President Truman's signing of the bill providing economic and military aid to Greece and Turkey, President Nixon declared that "we meet at a moment when we can make peaceful cooperation a reality..."[1]

Yet if a fair consensus exists on the date of the demise of the Cold War, there is little corresponding agreement as to its origins.[2] Behind the endless argument about whether the Cold War actually began with the Peace of Versailles in 1918,[3] or resulted from particular actions on the Soviet or American side in the aftermath of World War II,[4] lies deep disagreement as to the

67

causes of this era of hostility. Delving into the discussion
concerning the inception of the Cold War is therefore not merely
of interest to our study but is directly related to a most crucial
question: what characteristics define this particular period, and
who or what actions were responsible for its emergence?

Let us begin with the question of responsibility, because its
elucidation will provide us in turn with some answers about the
proper delimitation of the Cold War as a historical
phenomenon. During the fifties and early sixties "conventional
wisdom" saw Soviet intransigence,[5] lack of cooperation, and
sometimes even brutality (as in the Berlin Blockade or earlier in
Soviet strong-arming of satellite regimes) as the main causes of
East-West conflict. But a significant shift in the evaluation of
particular interactions took place in the mid-sixties. The
revisionist school of historians [6] put the blame for the
exacerbation of conflict more or less squarely on the side of the
United States and its allies. She, the revisionists said,
misunderstood the "purely defensive measures of the Kremlin"
in Eastern Europe, and their aggressive behavior forced the
Soviets to alter what were initially limited aims in this area.[7] A
third group of historians rejects both interpretations, and sees in
the protracted East-West struggle an "irreducible dilemma," a
"tragic predicament" that should properly evoke an attitude of
"compassion" for both parties.[8]

We are confronted with such a wide variety of interpretations
of "what happened" that reality seems to dissolve into
"perspectives": while not necessarily mutually exclusive, they
have indeed very little in common. This dilemma cannot be
solved simply by resort to the "facts," of which all accounts are
full, because not facts themselves but their meaning is in
question. This is not to say that all criticism has to cease, nor that
choosing one perspective is as reasonable as choosing another.
There is, first of all, a good deal of self-deception in the
traditional accounts of the Cold War, a flaw the revisionists
rightly attacked.[9] Unfortunately the "New Left's" argument
considered in toto, does not rest on a much better foundation.
Many of these works violate elementary rules of scholarship in
their treatment of sources and in drawing inferences from
them.[10] Do we therefore have to resign ourselves to the rather
trite third position of "aurea mediocritas," which holds that both
actors were to blame and that consequently such questions as

who is responsible have to be answered in terms of the ominous circumstances under which Soviet-American antagonism began? Although this answer might in the end contain a good deal of truth, it is hardly acceptable when stated in such a summary fashion, because it presents the progression of events as historically inevitable and consequently excuses everything and explains nothing. But how then can the paradox of escalating conflict due to defensive moves on both sides be resolved, or at least given more theoretical precision? Furthermore, what does "responsible" mean in such a context? Could the Cold War perhaps, as some revisionists maintain, have been avoided? Obviously, this question cannot be answered in a straighforward fashion, as the historical process cannot be rerun with changed parameters. But it is here that our approach, which is heavily indebted to language analysis and symbolic interaction, can contribute considerably to a clarification of the problem.

Let us consider the term "responsible" more carefully. Obviously, it is used in two different language games, in that of casual inference ("the blow-out of the tire was responsible for the car swerving around") and in that of moral concern ("he is responsible for this accident"). In the latter case a particular occurrence could have been avoided by choosing an alternative course of action.[11] What is important in this context is that any assessment of culpability resulting from a particular choice clearly presupposes a "stock of knowledge" that is taken for granted or assumed.

In the above example, this knowledge would include considerations such as "he should have known better than to drive so fast, as everybody knows that going 50 miles per hour on this road must lead to an accident." If we impart responsibility we can do so only within the boundaries of the second language game, because pointing out casual sequences is insufficient to come to terms with the problems of culpability. The question of responsibility for the Cold War consequently boils down to the problem of what was the knowledge about interstate affairs when the crucial decisions were made on both sides (before the announcement of the Truman Doctrine and the full Sovietization of Eastern Europe).

Here the argument becomes rather complex, much more so than either "traditionalists" or "revisionists" admit. Practically, in order to answer the question of culpability, it is not

Practically, in order to answer the question of culpability, it is not sufficient to explain moves in terms of the actors' intentions alone, without any reference either to their opponents' ambitions or to the assumed knowledge on the basis of which the protagonists assessed each other's moves.

What is striking in this context is the assumption, common to both traditionalist and revisionist historians, that Cold War actions can be explained or evaluated solely in terms of the goals and intentions of the two major antagonists. Revisionism far from being a new and more reflective approach to the problems of international order in the postwar period, is simply a mirror image of traditionalist historiography, substituting deviousness for the high-sounding official reasons usually given. In such a universe the intentions and goals of the European actors simply do not exist. It is true that, debilitated as they were, the Europeans did not count for much, but nevertheless they participated in the international political process. A further shortcoming of revisionism is that it attempts an assessment of culpability without reference to the common conventions that serve as aids in interpreting policy moves. In this respect Stalin seems to have been much more clear-sighted than today's defenders of his European policies realize. Milovan Djilas reports that Stalin was convinced the Cold War was a radically new era, because now "whoever occupies a territory also imposes on it his social system...it cannot be otherwise."[12] If the characterization of Stalin's views is correct, then the question of the mere sequence of events is of lesser importance, because the source of East-West conflict is clearly the lack of a common conception of a legitimate international order. But, given the preferences of the two antagonistic powers to extend their respective social systems, every defection from the cooperative status quo must immediately be interpreted in the much more ominous terms of a prisoner's dilemma instead of in terms of the mild chicken game, as elaborated in Chapter II. Thus, the paradox of conflict escalation due to mutually defensive moves can be resolved without recourse to explanations based on either "misunderstandings" or on ulterior motives that work themselves out in mysterious ways in the foreign policy decisions of the United States. In the latter view, as an illustration, the Marshall Plan can become, despite the intentions of its creators or the reactions of the recipients, an example of Dollar

Diplomacy and the Open Door Principle; thus, responsibility for the Cold War can be assigned solely to the United States.

Even within the frame of such an interpretation of history, to condemn morally or politically the unilateral transfer of billions of dollars from the United States to the European countries seems, to me, senseless. Even if the Soviet Union, because of its poverty or because it attributed aggressive intentions to the capitalist states, could only respond by isolating itself, this does not mean that Truman and Marshall were at fault in provoking the Kremlin to furious response. The Soviet response was in that case simply the price that had to be paid for aiding Europe. Unless they regret that Stalinism was prevented from advancing to the Atlantic coast, Europeans still obstinately refuse to consider the price excessive.[13]

Having dealt with some popular arguments concerning the *origins* of the Cold War, we can return to the question of what characteristics defined this era. According to Hans Morgenthau, the Cold War can be defined in the following way:

The Cold War between the Soviet Union and the West owes its existence to the unique coincidence of two historic factors in the aftermath of World War II: First, the impossibility of peace, because of conflicting incompatible conceptions of the post war world which rendered both sides more intractable by dint of their identification with incompatible ideological positions and aspirations; and second the improbability of war because of the possibility of nuclear war.[14]

In short, it was the collapse of the European state system together with its conventions that transformed the conflict of interest between the United States and the Soviet Union into a hostile struggle between two mutually exclusive ways of life. The conventions of the European state system had provided decision-makers with a common stock of assumed knowledge in light of which the policy moves of their opponents could be assessed. But neither of the powers that emerged in a dominant position after the Second World War had participated wholeheartedly in the European game before, although they had both cast ominous shadows over the political landscape after Versailles. In fact, Bolshevism as well as "American liberal democracy" had originally defined their interests and goals in opposition to

European diplomatic practice. Without the rudimentary
understanding of what a policy move meant, the new competing
powers had no assumed knowledge to guide them. They had to
depend on their own historical experiences, which offered
convenient analogies and made complex and bewildering events
understandable. Thus, considering only the "lessons" of the
immediate past, both powers had reason to be unyielding and
suspicious. While "no more Munichs" was the guiding principle
for a good many American actions from Truman to Johnson, fear
of being double-crossed again and awareness of the great
damages inflicted by the war must have figured prominently in
the calculus of Soviet leaders. The dangers the superpowers
believed they faced were heightened by the fact that the collapse
of Germany and Japan opened vast opportunities to the most
determined survivor. The latter point deserves particular
attention, because much has been made of the psychological
epiphenomena of the Cold War, which like tensions, have often
been considered the cause rather than the accompaniment of
conflict. Placing psychological variables like "tensions"
and "detente" in the wider setting of international interactions,
Morton Kaplan aptly remarks:

> Just as the popular images of the Cold War were in part a
> response to the frustrated hopes of international cooperation that
> were held during the war period, the psychology of the detente is
> in part a reaction to the exaggerated fears of the Cold War period.
> . . .
> The period 1945-50 was . . . the period in which the wartime
> images of the world and in particular of the Soviet Union had to be
> readjusted. The main wartime image was an image in which
> the victorious and "democratic" allies would reconstruct a new
> world while holding down the vicious fascist states. The
> simple-minded picture could not survive the end of the war for
> . . . the United States and the Soviet Union discovered a fact that
> could no longer be ignored. Each was the greatest potential threat
> to the other, to its image of the world and its own stability. And
> each faced a highly unstructured world which was susceptible to
> rapid change if either nation did not quickly counter the moves of
> the other.[15]

Thus, it is important to remember that American policy, even
though it resulted in a rather open display of hostility against the
Soviet Union, was hardly as disastrous as many observers claim.

After all, Tito's break with Stalin as well as the Sino-Soviet rift occurred when the West treated Tito and Mao as "stooges" of Moscow; a case can even be made that the West's undifferentiated approach to communism helped bring the dormant conflict between Moscow and its satellites out in the open. Moreover, a relatively amenable Eastern and Western rhetoric, during the "thaw" after Stalin's death, contributed to the spirit of Geneva or that of Camp David but failed to produce solidly beneficial results. It was the affable Khrushchev, not the tyrant Stalin, who intervened in Hungary and recklessly tried to expand his influence in the Congo and the Western Hemisphere. Similarly, high levels of tension during the Cuban missile crisis did not hinder subsequent measures for avoiding deadly clashes. Rather, they laid the groundwork for a common perception of mutual vulnerability and of shared fate in the face of the nuclear threat, a perception crucial for the development of roles, as pointed out in Chapter I.[16]

Policies cannot, therefore, be evaluated by observing the epiphenomenal psychological states which are their corollaries. They can be judged much more soundly according to whether or not they promote the growth of conventions promising a significant reduction of international violence. This is what Henry Kissinger calls the establishment of a legitimate international order, an order that safeguards the three essential elements of social coexistence developed in Chapter I.

> An international order in which the basic arrangements are accepted by all the major powers may be called "legitimate." A system which contains a power or a group of powers which rejects either the arrangements of the settlement or the domestic structure of the other states is "revolutionary." A legitimate order does not make conflicts impossible; it limits their scope . . . A legitimate order is distinguished by its willingness not to press the quest for security to its limits. Instead, safety is sought in a combination of physical safeguards and mutual trust. It is legitimate not because each power is perfectly satisfied but because no power is so dissatisfied that it will seek its remedy in overthrowing the existing system.[17]

These considerations suggest the plan of the present chapter. The second section will expand on the idea of conceptualizing international systems in terms of rules of the game or conventions, and will describe how the rise of the two peripheral powers to dominant positions changed the nature of the international game. Section three will be devoted to the discussion of assumed knowledge, studying in particular the role historical analogies play in the construction of such background knowledge. It is followed by empirical investigation into the "lessons" of history, with a special emphasis upon the early postwar era, which will set the stage for the treatment of myths and metaphors in the next chapter.

2. The Problem of the International System

Our preliminary sketch attributed the rise of the Cold War to the breakdown of the rudimentary rules according to which states in the European state system customarily pursued their political goals. This conceptualization of the international system in terms of perceptions and strategic calculations is crucial for the present argument and thus deserves closer examination.

In Chapter I, the discussion showed the shortcomings of the predominant mode of world order thinking, which posits what was called the "one-power world." The argument there was cast mainly in epistemological terms, demonstrating the inadequacy of a model of international politics that does not allow for interdependent decision-making. Now I will try to point out the bearing of these considerations upon the emergence and persistence of conventions or rules of the game, as we have called them. For this purpose I will avail myself of a short *Gedankenexperiment.* [18] Let us for the moment assume a "one-power world." An instance of this system would be an empire that has subordinated virtually all political decision-making centers under its rule. Needless to say, such states of affairs have endured only for brief spans of time, but despite their historical rarity and fragility they are enormously useful in helping us organize our perceptions of political reality. In a "one-power world" outsiders do not exist. There are always some who disturb the imperial peace, but imperial authorities treat them as "barbarians" on the frontiers and as "non-subjects *within* the ecumenic territory but not *of* the ecumenic society." [19] The implications for formal relations between these two entities are obvious: in such a world, resistance to imperial authority on the part of the barbarians is considered criminal, and treaties or other sorts of agreements, though tactically necessary, seldom attain much legitimacy or any formal status. In case of obstinate challenges from a powerful neighbor on the periphery of the empire, it can make necessary adjustments without granting equal status to the disturber: agreements may become legitimate instruments of inter-unit relations as long as the neighbor's subordination to the center is clearly maintained in principle. This could be called the "one-and-a-half-power" system, as no equality between the decision-making centers is acknowledged.

The ideal type of a two-power world differs from the "empire plus challenger" or the one-and-a-half-power-world to the extent that both parties accept each other as at least potential equals. Inter-unit relations are now clearly regulated by strategic calculations for which game theory provides major insights. Treaties and compacts achieve greater legitimacy in the "theory" that evolves to justify such a state of affairs, but conflicts are at least potentially total as long as both powers harbor imperial aspirations and accept the two-power world only as a respite in the struggle to impose an imperial peace. If, however, equality is accepted, the theory of "law without sanction", alluded to in the first chapter, showed that under certain conditions conflicts can be resolved in terms other than the minimax theorem of strict game theory. It is through the transformation of such a dyadic relationship into a triad that two parties are able to move from the DD cell of the game matrix to more cooperative solutions. Such a triad might well be implicit—the "Gods" may be invoked as a third party or "precedents" or common practices may be adduced. The presence of an actual third power is more revolutionizing because its mere existence profoundly changes the strategic calculations of the other players. ("Implicit third parties" do not have the same impact, because both powers are free to ignore them or deny their relevance to a specific conflict.) With the appearance of a third player new strategic options emerge and "reputation" becomes an important part of the game. Thus, "pacta sunt servanda . . . is in a three power anarchy a counsel of prudence as well as a moral imperative." [20] Naturally, as more players engage in our imaginary example, "systemic" considerations become more important for each player in choosing his strategy.

The above examples, concerned with the logic of interactions

rather than with historical occurrences, should have made one
thing clear: a sequence of "systemic" models does not by itself
provide an adequate image of international relations, because
the crucial "step-level" effects of systemic transformations, for
example, from a one-and-a-half-power world to a two-power
world, depend on the protagonists' perceptual changes, with
which systems theory does not deal. Certainly, roughly equal
power may produce an awareness of equality, but it need not. It
is entirely conceivable that two roughly equal powers retain their
universalist aspirations despite the gap between te actual state
of affairs and the theoretical constructs by which they interpret
their relations. The gap may persist even if a third and fourth
player emerge, because each power could theoretically claim
new parties as vassals rather than allies, the important
distinction being that a vassal is a subordinate whereas an ally is
on equal footing.

These considerations have important repercussions upon the
development of rules and conventions. If the observance of
treaties is the counsel of prudence in a multi-power world, it is
also the precondition for the functioning of rules in a horizontal
authority environment. [21] Safeguarding national independence,
then, is not so much a Machiavellian ambition of statesmen as it
is the result of the particular game in which all players are
involved. Viewed from this angle, the deficiencies of the command theory of law become obvious, as does the untenability of
proposals to expand international law and conventions through
the centralization of authority. [22] Thus, the European state
system emerged after the peace of Westphalia not only because
neither the Holy Roman Empire nor any other power could
enforce its will *de facto*, but also because the deep cleavages that
had surfaced in Europe demonstrated that conceiving
international reality in terms of an empire no longer served any
ordering function. Preventing any universal hegemony became a
paramount concern for continental European statesmen:
Voltaire, reflecting upon this conception of international order,
writes in his "Le Siecle de Louis XIV":

> Christian Europe except Russia could be regarded as a sort of
> Grand Republic divided into a number of states, some
> monarchical others of a mixed complexion; . . . but all of them
> thinking alike all with a similar fundament of religion, even
> though it was divided into a number of sects, all of them with

similar principles of public law and politics unknown to other parts of the world. It is owing to these principles that the European nations do not enslave their prisoners, respect their enemies' ambassadors, all subscribe to the preeminence and to certain rights of certain princes such as the Emperor, the King, and other lesser potentates and above all that they concur in the wise policy of maintaining among themselves to the best of their ability an equal balance of power, constantly employing negotiations even in the midst of war, while maintaining in each others countries ambassadors or less honorable spies who are able to warn all Courts of the designs of any one court and at once sound the alarm for Europe and safeguard the weakest against the invasions which the strongest power is always prepared to undertake.[23]

Nothing can be more foreign to this train of thought than the idea of an international "police force" for the enforcement of peace, such as figures so prominently in President Roosevelt's postwar plans for the reorganization of international relations.

The Council of the United Nations must have the power to act quickly and decisively to keep the peace by force, if necessary. A policeman would not be an effective policeman if, when he saw a felon break into a house, he had to go to the Town-Hall and call a town meeting before the felon could be arrested. . . . If we do not catch the international felon when we have our hands on him, if we let him get away with his loot because the Town Council has not passed an ordinance authorizing his arrest, then we are not doing our share to prevent another World War.[24]

Clearly, an image of a different "game" is here superimposed upon international reality. This domestic image, already inadequate to deal with the problem of large-scale disregard of law in the domestic arena itself—one cannot simply arrest 25,000 demonstrators for "trespassing"—is all the more inadequate for comprehending international reality. The interpretation of international politics in legalistic terms is therefore due not so much to the inherent idealism for which American foreign policy is often blamed as to an inadequate conceptualization of group conflict.[25] A possible explanation for this intellectual trait might be the strongly ingrained individualism in American social thought, as well as the lack of historical experience with an environment characterized by bargaining relationships. "The

free states of North America," wrote Hegel, "have no
neighboring state with respect to which they are situated as
European states are situated to each other that is to say a state
which they must regard with distrust and against which they
must maintain a standing army." He noted: "Canada and
Mexico do not inspire them with fear and England has learned
from fifty years of experience that America is more useful to it
free than subjected.[26]

Significantly, the Indians, the only "disturbers of the peace"
the U.S. had to deal with, were treated as "nationals" but not
"citizens" thus fitting well the imperial model in still another
respect! Even the clashes with European powers at the turn of
the century required no reassessment of the American
conception, because quick and decisive action assured the
implementation of all war goals. As a result, the theoretical
elaboration of international politics in the New World viewed
peace not only as the normal state of affairs—a reflection of
geographical isolation as well as the protection provided by the
British fleet—but as a state that does not rest upon complicated
mutual power calculations.[27] Thus, American foreign policy
oscillated between isolation from the balance of power game
played by "wicked" Europeans and activism in which
comprehensive and rather implausible security claims were
made.[28] Military policy, intended to assure victory, was thus
divorced from diplomacy, concerned with the self-evident state
of peace—a confusion that produced not only self-deception and
self-contradiction but a good deal of self-congratulatory
moralism. Thus, President Roosevelt "opposed British
imperialism yet counted upon the power of Great Britain . . . as
an equal democratic partner in the postwar world."[29] Secretary
of State Cordell Hull's comment on the 1943 Moscow
conference—which supposedly had done away once and for all
with "spheres of influence"[30]—not only overlooked the ample
warning the Soviets had served for their nonadherence to the
universalistic norms of the Atlantic Charter[31], but also totally
ignored the American claim to predominance in its own
hemisphere, a claim that finally surfaced at the San Francisco
conference.

The inadequacy of the universalist American approach to
postwar planning soon became painfully obvious, as discussion
between Secretary of War Stimson and United States delegate

John McCloy reveals: McCloy, worried about Russian aspirations for a similar sphere of influence in Eastern Europe, had in his words "been taking the position that we ought to have our cake and eat it too; that we ought to be free to operate under this regional arrangement in South America and at the same time intervene promptly in Europe; that we oughtn't to give away either asset."[32] Stimson's response to McCloy's position reveals that power political considerations clearly played a part in American policy formulation, and thus casts considerable doubt on the traditionalist interpretation of American goals as pure "universalism." But Stimson also shows the central dilemma of American policy in the wake of the collapse of the European state system and before the establishment of a new world system with its proper conventions. He asserts rather naively, or cynically, that it "is not asking too much to have our little region over here which never had bothered anybody" and consequently the Soviet Union "has no legitimate right to object to our hemispherical situation over here. That ought to stand by itself."[33] The alleged similarity between the two spheres of interest is dismissed with the following argument:

> I think you ought to be able to prevent Russia from using that thing in her parallel, alleged parallel position. It isn't parallel to it. She is not such an overwhelmingly gigantic power from the ones which she's probably going to make a row about as we are here, and, on the other hand, our fussing around among those little fellows here doesn't upset any balance in Europe at all. That's the main answer. It doesn't upset a balance there where she may upset a balance that affects us. That's the difference. I think you ought to maintain that although it seems to be a little thing, it's been a pretty well developed thing and I think you can say that it isn't parallel to what she threatens to do.[34]

Here Stimson clearly recognizes that international order cannot be based on a naively assumed adherence to "universal norms" but has to be founded upon bargaining relationships that allow each power to assess its interests in terms of the costs and expectations their pursuit creates for the members of the system. Stimson was one of the few members of the administration who advocated a general political settlement before the inauguration of the United Nations as a peace keeping organization.[35] Official American policy mostly ignored such suggestions, however, and was busy devising a whole set of institutions intended, as it was later claimed, "to transform foreign policy into an aspect of domestic policy, to bring about a situation abroad in which the will of the other nations or at least that of the enemy is no longer a significant factor."[36]

As late as January 1946, Secretary of the Navy James Forrestal complained in a letter to Walter Lippmann that insufficient planning had been done for an international order that had to rely on bargaining relationships among actors with widely different outlooks. "There is no place in government," he writes, "where a study has been made which addresses itself to the 'nature of Soviet foreign policy,' 'its relationship to Marxism, Leninism' and the 'possibility of accommodation between the democratic and communist systems' despite the fact that 'the fundamental question in respect to our relations with Russia is whether we are dealing with a nation or a religion.' "[37]

Basically, the question addressed here by Forrestal is whether both sides posess an "assumed knowledge" concerning legitimate aims and methods of foreign policy that would allow for the adjustment of differences. As Forrestal had put it after Harry Hopkins' return from Moscow in June 1945:

> I expressed it as my view that it would not be difficult to work with Russia, provided we were dealing with her only as a national entity; that the real problem was whether or not Russian policy called for a continuation of the Third International's objective, namely world revolution and the application of the political principles of the dialectic materialists to the entire world. Hopkins said he doubted if anyone could answer this question and I added that I doubted if even the Russians themselves could answer it.[38]

The American conception of what constituted legitimate interference in the opponent's sphere of influence, especially in Europe, rested upon some crucial practical assumptions. First of all, the belief was widespread that a Europe united under any single power would decisively shift the world's balance of power to the disadvantage of the United States.[39] It was this fact above all that caused America twice to intervene in European affairs. In that sense, Stimson's claim that American and Soviet aspirations in their respective spheres were not comparable expresses, though clumsily and in a logically questionable form, a rather important consideration. Second, as a revisionist correctly points out, "Eastern Europe had been critical to the entire European economy and this was not less true in 1945!"[40] Thus, American officials believed that even if an exclusive Soviet sphere of influence were limited to Eastern Europe, it would have enormous repercussions upon Europe as a whole and would thus be "generally important to America's well-being and security."[41] But this view undermines the revisionist argument that America's opposition to Soviet predominance was due to a direct American interest in investment opportunities in this area rather than to traditional security considerations focusing on Europe's well-being. As American position papers drawn up for the Yalta and Berlin conferences show, the United states did *not* want to challenge Soviet influence in Eastern Europe but only to prevent the total exclusion of American influence there.

> Politically, while this government probably would not oppose predominant Soviet influence in the area (Poland and the Balkans), neither would it wish American influence to be completely nullified. . . .[42]

> While the Government may not want to oppose a political configuration in Eastern Europe which gives the Soviet Union a predominant influence in Poland, neither would it desire to see Poland becoming in fact a Soviet satellite and have American influence there completely eliminated. . .

> Mikolajcyk does not expect the full freedom which he would like for Poland and the Polish people...he freely accepts that Poland's security and foreign policy must follow the lead of Moscow...[43]

It was thus the Soviets' rather peculiar interpretation of their own security that led Americans to realize that such demands could not be accomodated within the assumed knowledge of the defunct European state system. Some historians obscure this most important point simply by making "social forces" (especially a mythical European "left") rather than states the actors in their historical account. Even more astonishing than such writers' claim that the "left" somehow miraculously has the power to represent the "true" wishes of European societies, is the fact that they apparently introduce subservience to Soviet security claims as a criterion of genuine "leftism." Social Democrats, like Reuter or Bevin, who strongly objected to the Soviet embrace, are treated as more or less reactionary "stooges" of American imperialism. Discussing American policy without the slightest consideration of European interests as voiced by governmental leaders considerably distorts history, especially in regard to the question of responsibility. First it makes every historical occurrence appear to result from an American action intended to be inimical to Soviet interests, against which, quite naturally, the Kremlin had to take "defensive" steps. Secondly, it creates the illusion of parallelism between Soviet and American actions, which in the language game of moral responsiblity is rather questionable. Despite the fact that each antagonist brought its power to bear within its sphere of influence in order to insure friendly regimes, there still seems to me a difference worth mentioning between the methods of Stalin as exemplified in the Slansky processes (significantly never mentioned in Kolko's supposedly exhaustive study of the Cold War) and the American pressures on France and Italy in the wake of the Truman Doctrine. Thus, although in a sense one is justified to point to a certain parallelism between American and Soviet views on international order—especially as both powers had formulated their goals in opposition to the conventions and rules of the European state system—the extension of this parallelism to the language game of moral responsibility seems to me rather capricious.

In short, the extensive security claims of the Kremlin, although misperceived by the West as an all-out bid for world domination, were surely not like traditional great power interests, as the tensions between Tito and Stalin soon showed. Furthermore, a rather cynical if perhaps useful arrangement between the United States and the Soviet Union of respective spheres of influence—such as George Kennan proposed to Charles Bohlen in a letter on the eve of the Yalta conference [44]—would have presupposed American willingness and capacity to "deliver" Western Europe's agreement. But the rapid demise of England, whose vital interests were threatened by nearly all Soviet postwar goals from the bases in the Dardanelles to an African trusteeship, was not at all obvious in 1945. It was after all Bevin, not an American official, who refused to see in Soviet probes only limited aspirations. Given

British security interests, Bevin's assessment that "a great power was cutting across the throat of the British Empire"[45] was not overly alarmist. The very fact that Soviet aspirations violated deeply cherished English interests—a fact Stalin must have known all too well—made it quite impossible to interpret such demands as "legitimate" within the conventions of a multi-power world, for they would have led to a systemic transformation eliminating England as a viable power. Significantly again, it was an English statesman, Winston Churchill, who sounded one of the first alarms against Soviet intransigence in his Fulton address.[46]

The same single-mindedness with which Moscow pursued its interests against Britain was evident in Germany, convincing French negotiators at the 1947 Moscow conference that the Kremlin did not want to play by the rules of a multi-power game.[47] Thus, after he realized that no give and take was possible, Bidault accommodated his policy to the American position and pooled his vote with the United States, instead of pursuing a policy of shifting coalitions. The time for ambiguity had ended, and with the announcement of the Truman Doctrine and the foundation of the Cominform, the world was put on notice that a new international system had emerged in which the rules of the game corresponded closely to a bipolar configuration. If, as is reasonable to assume, Stalin would have preferred to avoid such a clear-cut confrontation and to preserve instead some measure of ambiguity in the political situation as shown by his stalling on the problem of German administration—and his remarks to Secretary of State Marshall could be interpreted in such a fashion[48]—then his tenacity at the Moscow conference backfired (as had his intransigence during Molotov's visit to Berlin in 1940). The West, confronted with economic problems that required decisive action in Germany, was no longer willing to leave matters in a state of uncertainty.

3. *Assumed Knowledge, Historical Analogies and the Origins of the Cold War*

Our discussion has revealed the importance of assumed knowledge in assessing an opponent's moves. It is only against the background of these half-consciously understood conventions which make up the international game that certain actions can be characterized as specifically "aggressive." If a game is distinguished from mere "play" (where roles can be taken freely and rules can be made as one goes along)[49] by the structure that interrelates all the players' moves, then an aggressive move in a game is one that threatens to upset the accepted rules. The reasons why a player may take such a step are then of minor importance. Endless discussion of whether Soviet moves were dictated by national security considerations rather than by ideological aspirations, for instance, is not very helpful for two reasons. First, it mistakes private reasons for the rules of behavior in which the historian or political scientist should be interested. Second, as Watergate has amply demonstrated, in order to avoid stretching terms like national security or national interest, one has to refer to a particular set of conventions and practices, to a "game" that can give more precision to such claims. Thus, a break-in violating another person's civil rights might be permissible under specified circumstances in cases of dire national emergencies, but is hardly legitimate in an election campaign or in a planned attempt of political slander. The one who has broken the "rules" (in this case legal rules) may cite considerations of national security as his "reasons" but such a rationale has no validity under the set of rules governing political interactions. If we apply these insights to our problem, we can see that the justification of Stalin's actions in terms of the classical "national interest" language game is hardly convincing, because, despite the formulation of his policy goals in territorial rather than ideological terms, his aspirations had a *system transforming* character. On the other hand, the United States' assumed knowledge was no more conducive to building up a reliable mutual assumed knowledge that could have helped de-escalate conflict. Prone to mistake particular American goals for universal moral aspirations—repeatedly likening the Four Freedoms to the Decalogue[50]—President Roosevelt only courted disaster by delaying political decisions that would confront the emerging power realities [51] and by blurring differences through high-sounding formulas or "personal diplomacy." But the reasons for enmity went far beyond personal foibles or occasional mistakes and our discussion showed why this is so: it described how decision makers' perceptions are shaped and influenced by certain experiences when statesmen face rather unstructured situations and contradictory pieces of evidence about the opponent's preferences and intentions. The adversary's moves are then interpreted in terms of an historical framework.

It is therefore not surprising that plans for the future are deeply influenced by what one thinks the lessons of history are, and that practical action is geared toward avoiding the "errors" of the past. Viewed from this angle, American postwar planning is a classic example of this pervasive human inclination. "Nothing," writes John Gaddis, a perceptive historian of this era, "shaped American plans to prevent future wars more than a determination to avoid the mistakes of the past." [52] The moral of American involvement in World War I and of America's subsequent withdrawal seemed to be clear: lenience toward Germany at Versailles paved the way for Hitler's later aggression, and American isolationism abandoned control of political events until it was too late. Translated into practical political terms this meant not only the "unconditional surrender" of Germany but her demilitarization and economic weakness, according to the Morgenthau Plan and other similar plans for the postwar era.

Beyond this immediate goal, which grew out of the common effort to defeat the Axis and keep it disarmed, American postwar planners aimed at the creation of a congenial environment for "peace-loving nations" through two devices thought to reinforce peace and deter aggression: free trade, and a world organization with "teeth" to "enforce the peace."

4. Economic Planning

Looking back on American efforts to come to terms with the problem of international order after the surrender of the Axis powers, Secretary of Defense James Forrestal remarked "that American diplomatic planning was far below the quality of the planning that went into the conduct of the war." [53] Plans for a restructured world economy were perhaps the exception. Indeed, revisionist and traditionalist historians alike argue that reconstructing world trade was one of the most important goals of the American government. But whereas the revisionists maintain that America's political expansion was dictated by the need to find foreign markets for its goods and capital, traditional historians see economic interests playing an important but not decisive role in the formulation of postwar policy. "If one accepts the revisionist argument," writes Robert Gilpin, "then the Cold

War should have been between the United States and Western Europe, particularly the United Kingdom rather than between the U.S.S.R. and the U.S."[54] After all, the British imperial preference tariff was a major stumbling block to a multi-lateral economic order. Although considerable tensions arose between London and Washington over this issue,[55] "in the end the United States, facing what it felt to be a Soviet challenge, drastically reversed its international economic policies. In contrast to its earlier emphasis on multi-lateralism and non-discrimination, the United States accepted trade discrimination in the interest of rebuilding the shattered West European economy."[56] Even such free trade ideologues as Will Clayton advocated a European customs union, surely in the hope that "in the long run" it would serve as a stepping stone toward multilateralism,[57] but nevertheless in opposition to the tenets of strict liberal trade philosophy.

But, if the economic orientation of American foreign policy cannot be explained as a single-minded pursuit of profit maximization, then the roots of the predilection for multilateralism have to be sought in a particular belief-system and in the historical experiences that seem to bear out those ideological premises. Indeed, behind all the rhetoric about the blessings of free trade lies the conventional liberal wisdom about the causes of war. The events of the inter-war period seemed to confirm this theory. The enormous dislocations created by the Great Depression were attributed to economic nationalism, the hoarding of currencies, trade barriers, and investment restrictions. And it was the depression, in turn, that had led to Japanese expansionism as well as to the unpalatable phenomenon of Fascism. From these lessons of history Secretary of State Cordell Hull concluded:

> To me unhampered trade dovetailed with peace: high tariffs, trade barriers and unfair economic competition with war. Though realizing that many other factors were involved, I reasoned that if we could get a freer flow of trade—freer in the sense of fewer discriminations and obstructions—so that one country would not be deadly jealous of another and the living standards of all countries might rise, thereby eliminating the economic dissatisfaction that breeds war, we might have a reasonable chance for lasting peace.[58]

It was this reasoning that led to American plans for an

International Trade Organization and to American insistence on revision of some of the trade agreements between the Soviet Union and Eastern European countries. Soviet Foreign Minister Molotov was quick to point out that "the unlimited application of the principle of equality, is . . . convenient for those who have the power and wealth" and are therefore "trying to use their capital to subjugate those who are weaker";[59] he forgot, however, to mention that exploitation was and is by no means limited to capitalist economic systems, as the scandalously unequal trade treaties and joint stock companies of the Soviet Union and her satellites later showed.[60] Recalling Hitler's use of economic ties before the war, American officials were, in the words of Herbert Feis, "not merely striving to obtain a few extra million dollars of trade or profit" but trying also to preserve at least a minimal "openness" in these countries.[61] Besides, Soviet monopolization of Yugoslav trade was one of the decisive factors in Yugoslavia's decision to resist the Russian embrace.

Needless to say, the prescriptions of the multilateralists "proved on the whole inadequate, leading directly to major initial weaknesses in postwar international ecnomic policy"[62] and aggravating the developing tensions between the two leading powers, for whose economic as well as political coexistence inadequate provisions had been made. The fixation upon past "mistakes" prevented American decision-makers from coming to terms with the problems resulting from two radically different political and economic systems. Instead of investigating the preconditions for the coexistence of these differing conceptions of order, responsible statesmen in Washington merely assumed "that a way could be found whereby nations with capitalistic, socialistic and mixed economies could live together in harmony."[63] Russia's participation at the Bretton Woods conference was, therefore, taken as a significant sign of cooperation although the negotiations soon revealed that Soviet interests were rather different.

When the Soviets finally refused to join either the World Bank or the International Monetary Fund, "the dream seemed to be shattered and the Department of State passed on to the [American] embassy [in Moscow] in tones of bland innocence the anguished cry of bewilderment that had floated over the roof of the White House from the Treasury Department on the other side."[64] George Kennan, then counselor at the embassy, availed himself of the opportunity to send a long telegram to the State Department in which he tried to put the recent Soviet refusal and all the other irritating disagreements encountered in the immediate postwar era in a wider perspective.[65]

The "sensational effect" this telegram had in Washington was mainly due to Kennan's attempt to provide an alternative interpretive framework for Soviet actions. What seemed to show the superiority of Kennan's view over the conventional interpretation of Soviet conduct was the thesis that these misunderstandings were of a *systemic* nature and could be explained in terms of the particular historical experiences that informed the Soviet outlook on international affairs.

> At the bottom of the Kremlin's neurotic view of world affairs is the traditional and instinctive Russian sense of insecurity . . . Russian rulers have invariably sensed that their rule was relatively archaic in form, fragile and artificial in its psychological foundations, unable to stand comparison . . . For this reason they have always feared foreign penetration, feared direct contact between Western world and their own, feared what would happen if Russians learned truth about world without or if foreigners learned truth about world within. And they have learned to seek security only in patient but deadly struggle for total destruction of rival power, never in compacts and compromises with it. . . . Thus, Soviet leaders are driven by necessities of their own past and present position to put forward a dogma, which pictures the outside world as evil, hostile and menacing, but as bearing within itself germs of creeping disease and destined to be wracked with growing internal convulsions until it is given final coup de grace. . . . This thesis provides justification for that increase of military and police power in Russian state . . .[66]

For American audiences, even these admittedly rather sweeping sketches of historical developments were still too subtle. American officials were disappointed by Soviet actions; more seriously, they had to persuade the American public that enormous sums were needed for the economic reconstruction of Western Europe and that continued American involvement in world politics was essential. They therefore found it necessary to dramatize Soviet noncooperation and to present Stalin's moves as ominous portents of unlimited expansion. Thus, East-West political differences attained the character of a world-wide

Manichean struggle between the forces of "light" and those of "darkness," or, as President Truman said in his message to Congress: "At the present moment in world history nearly every nation must choose between alternative ways of life."[67]

Before we treat this mythical struggle in greater detail and see how the Munich analogy contributed to the mythical image of conflict, we have to focus on another aspect of American decision-makers' assumed knowledge, which seemed to indicate that international peace and cooperation were not only desirable but realistically attainable. The American vision of a harmony of interests between the great powers, which could serve as the foundation for peace keeping machinery, found its most perfect expression in plans for a world organization.

The United Nations Organization

The first section of this chapter cast some doubt on the proposition that universalism was the sole or decisive guiding principle in American postwar planning. What emerges from a closer study of the historical record is rather an unacknowledged ambiguity between the half-hearted toleration of "power politics" and the pursuit of universal aspirations. Already at the time of Pearl Harbor, President Roosevelt envisaged the future international order as a "Big power trusteeship or guardianship" and later the metaphor of the Four Policemen was used for such an arrangement.[68]

This pragmatic side of policy, acknowledging the oligopolistic position of the big powers in the global political arena, was largely hidden from public view by the rather autocratic and secretive way in which Roosevelt conducted foreign relations. The deception led later to aggravation and disappointment, when "these efforts brought Roosevelt to a nearly impossible position from which death delivered him."[69] These unresolved tensions between realism and morality, between global aspirations and the desire to avoid political entanglements, were displayed clearly at Yalta when Roosevelt told Stalin that the United States would probably not maintain military forces in Europe for more than two years after the end of hostilities.[70] The sources of these tensions have to be found largely in the "lessons" American decision makers learned from Wilson's failure to gain support for the League of Nations.

The most promising strategy, therefore, seemed to be to delay

the most important political decisions until after the defeat of the
Axis, to involve Republic party leaders peripherally in postwar
planning, and to maintain tight Presidential control of foreign
affairs. Critical voices like Stimson, who wanted a general
settlement of outstanding political issues before the inauguration
of a new world organization, were brushed aside, although
everyone from Hull to Stalin agreed that the United Nations
would work only if the big powers were acting jointly. Despite
this agreement, discussions about the effective functioning of
the United Nations always pointed to the indefinite future, as if
"the establishment of an international organization were some
sort of talisman which would possess a powerful virtue to heal
disputes among the nations."[71] Thus, the preconditions of a
world organization were in such speculation easily transformed
into consequences. Naturally, political reality was less pleasant.

When the San Francisco conference was under way and as
Soviet territorial ambitions in Eastern Europe became more
obvious, it was Vandenberg who perceived new opportunities for
using the United Nations. On March 7, 1945, he wrote to his
friend, the Polish-American leader, Frank Januszewski:

> I have not altered my view respecting Poland—both for her own
> precious sake and as a "symbol." I could get no greater personal
> satisfaction out of anything more than from joining—aye in
> leading—a public denunciation [sic] of Yalta . . . It would be a
> relatively simple matter to dynamite the new League. What
> would *that* do for Poland? It would simply leave Russia in com-
> plete possession of everything she wants . . . Would it not be bet-
> ter to go along with the new League . . . and to seek to give it
> specific authority to examine at any time whatever injustice may
> have been inherited from the war era and to recommend correc-
> tion?[72]

One need not be unusually perceptive to realize that in this
letter Vandenberg's conception of the United Nations had
undergone a fundamental change. The world organization is no
longer seen as an expression of big power unity but as a powerful
instrument of American foreign policy, which could change the
international environment in the interest of the United States,
even against the will of one of the "four policemen."

Nevertheless, such views were still far from being
well-crystallized policy. They were only the first inklings of
things to come. Vandenberg himself, as well as the official

American position, seemed to have vacillated between two conceptions. For a while at least, it still seemed that the most urgent task of the United Nations would be to maintain the peace brought about through the subjection and permanent demilitarization of the notorious disturbers of the peace, Germany and Japan. The Charter (Art. 107) exempted enforcement actions against these powers from the requirement of Security Council approval; thus even the preparations for the organization, which should have looked far beyond the war, were characterized by a silently accepted analogy between the postwar era and the interwar years.

> What is surprising is how completely their (Roosevelt and his associates') post-war planning was controlled by a handful of analogies and parallels, all from their own lifetime.
>
> . . . What seems unaccountable is that they appear never to have imagined that the pattern of events after World War II could differ significantly from that after World War I. The administration's vision of the post-war world seems to have been dominated by a single image. 73

It is here that our approach can lead us a bit further and show why this was so. As already mentioned, for most American decision-makers peace was an unambiguous symbol, because their particular interpretation of it was easily enforced in America's few early encounters with opposing powers. The United States could carry out a foreign policy without the uneasy compromises and political bargains so characteristic of continental politics. Thus, in the American "theory," the pursuit of enlightened self-interest and the preservation of peace never seemed fundamentally at odds. As a corollary of this "theory," peace was easily identified with its social epiphenomena, like personal friendliness between statesmen, "good neighborliness" and "personal diplomacy."

In this context it is important to mention that Roosevelt's predilection for "personal diplomacy," which led to considerable problems in dealing with Stalin, dates back to Roosevelt's "good Neighbor policy" in Latin America. Forgetting the particular setting that promoted the success of this policy, Roosevelt generalized from his experience and wrote to Churchill, even before his first meeting with Stalin:

> I think I can personally handle Stalin better than either your

Foreign Office or my State Department. Stalin hates the guts of all
your top people. He thinks he likes me better and I hope he will
continue to do so. [74]

Roosevelt's remarks to Ambassador Bullit concerning Stalin
have to be understood in the same light. Warned about Stalin's
intentions, the President tried to downplay the danger of Soviet
noncooperation:

> If I give him everything I possess and ask from him nothing in
> return *noblesse oblige* he won't try to annex anything and will
> work with me for a world of democracy and peace. [75]

"It is not far-fetched," writes Willard Range, a student of
Roosevelt's conception of international order, to say "that
Roosevelt looked upon the basic problem of transforming
international relations as something of a psychiatric
problem." [76] His conviction that what had worked in Latin
America would also be beneficial for the world at large led him to
try to win Stalin's friendship, by sometimes taking sides with
him against Churchill, by refraining from criticism of the Soviet
Union, and by showing understanding for the Soviet's often rude
or provocative behavior.

Roosevelt's belief also led to particular prescriptions for
Germany and Japan. When the "madmen" in power had
rejected his therapy, forcible confinement and treatment became
necessary. The fact that a genuine madman like Hitler, whose
psychic maladjustment became increasingly obvious, was ruling
Germany reinforced the American assumption that international
reality could be adequately interpreted in such simplistic terms.
From these premises followed the idea of personal responsibility
not only for properly established war crimes but for "conspiracy
against peace," a charge included in the Nuremberg indictment.
What is interesting in this context is the phrasing of the rather
complex problem of international order in terms of purely
personal intentions, to the exclusion of contextual considerations
like the Molotov-Ribbentrop pact, which had covered Germany's
flank and thus made the attack on Poland possible.

Even a few years later, when all the great hopes of personal
friendship among the leaders of the four powers were shattered
and had given way to undisguised hostility, the extreme
individualistic bias in American theory persisted. It underlay the

rhetoric of "liberation" and "roll back." Instead of viewing the new power relationships in Eastern Europe as the basis of a possible future diplomatic adjustment,[77] the West rather naively assumed that political pressure would somehow enable the suppressed peoples of Eastern Europe to rid themselves of the "criminals" ruling them.

Within such a frame of reference, the other critical assumption for a functioning United Nations—an effective collective security arrangement—could be neatly accommodated. Again America's particular historical experiences were of decisive importance, at least to Roosevelt, who viewed collective security as part of his "good neighbor policy" on a global scale. For him it was "one of the basic principles of good neighborliness," for it required "cooperative action to keep the peace and to give stability to the international neighborhood."[78] The painful difference between collective and individual rationality, brought out in the collective goods debate,[79] was obscured by two important symbolic devices that immunized this theory from criticism. These devices were, first of all, the idea of the "extended self," by means of which each nation was to realize that its own welfare depended upon that of every other nation, and second, the metaphor of a peace-keeping "machinery." Although the advocacy of such a machinery seems to be only the logical outgrowth of the realization that a state of anarchy exists in international relations, the idea of a mechanism or machinery reveals, at closer scrutiny, a whole host of unstated assumptions. It seems to suggest a device that, once set in motion, provides for the almost automatic resolution of conflict. Thus, the settlement such a device produces seems essentially *independent* of the wills and preferences of the parties in conflict, because it is determined by the operations of the peace-keeping gadget.

It is not surprising that special Soviet historical experiences—alluded to in Kennan's long telegram—led to an assumed knowledge and a "theory" of international politics rather different from the conceptions that prevailed in the United States. Peace, for Soviet leaders, is not a self-evident state of affairs, regulated or brought about in a half-automatic fashion by a machinery, but is rather the result of a particular distribution of power or, to use the notorious Soviet term, of a particular "correlation of forces." Trained to see the world historical process as a battleground of forces, Stalin had little difficulty sacrificing good will for concrete gains, even if it meant the affront of an ally.

Viewing conflict rather than harmony as the norm sharpened the Soviet perception of concrete advantages as opposed to mere desiderata. The consequences of the division of Poland in the aftermath of the German-Soviet Nonaggression Pact can serve to illustrate this point. Even if one accepts the official Soviet version, that this arrangement with Germany resulted from "defensive considerations," Stalin never lost track of the immediate gains that might accrue to him. Thus, the Soviet Union *annexed* the sphere of influence assigned to her in the secret protocol of August 23, 1939, although this was against the understanding arrived at, as Hitler pointed out to Molotov during his visit to Berlin in November 1940. Furthermore, Stalin's seizure of a corner of Lithuania assigned to Germany, as well as his unilateral revision of the status of the Bukowina, (although afterwards accepted by Germany) had annoyed Hitler. These differences showed that German and Soviet interests were bound to clash: war, which Stalin supposedly wanted to avoid at all costs, would surely break out if Moscow did not use extreme caution.[80] Nevertheless, Stalin decided to take full advantage of the opportunities opening up in the Balkans when Hitler proposed Russia's accession to the Tripartite Pact. More important, Stalin pursued his goals even at the risk of a war for which he was, after the Finnish disaster, evidently unprepared. Moscow renewed pressure on Bulgaria in November 1940 and January 1941, and immediately recognized the anti-German government in Yugoslavia, which had taken over after the Yugoslav Crown Council decided in March to accede to Hitler's Tripartite Pact. When Germany crushed the resistance in the Balkans, Stalin recognized that he had overplayed his hand. He retreated and tried to appease Hitler by withdrawing recognition from the Yugoslav government with which Molotov had signed a treaty of amity only a few weeks earlier.[81]

In all these moves, Stalin adhered rather closely to the position Molotov outlined to German Ambassador von der Schulenburg on November 6, 1940, despite the fact that Russia's weakness, together with the risk of a Soviet-German clash, made the pursuit of such extensive foreign policy goals dangerous and unrealistic. Stalin was ready and willing to accede to the proposed Four Power pact provided Germany would withdraw all

German troops from Finland, allow a Soviet mutual assistance pact with Bulgaria, and force Turkey to grant base facilities for Russian land and naval forces within the range of the Bosporus and the Dardanelles.[82] Furthermore, Germany was to acknowledge that "the area south of Batum and Baku" in the general direction of the Persian Gulf was the "center of the aspirations of the Soviet Union," and she was to back the Russian plan for Japan's renunciation of oil and coal concessions in northern Sakhalin.

This "shopping list" displays rather obvious parallels to Stalin's postwar policy. Though eager to divide with Germany the "real estate of the British Empire,"[83] Stalin was not easily deflected from Eastern Europe by Hitler's promises of greater and more secure gains in the direction of the Indian Ocean. Stalin's regrets and gestures of appeasement towards Berlin came too late. On the night of June 21/22, 1941, Germany invaded the Soviet Union. The life and death struggle that ensued made the pursuit of the extensive foreign policy goals outlined above quite fanciful, at least in the short run. Nevertheless, Stalin's ambitions were well known (although not to their full extent), and Churchill came close to recognizing some Soviet territorial gains in Eastern Europe in the wake of the infamous Molotov-Ribbentrop pact.

The reversal of the military situation after the battle of Stalingrad in January 1943 brought the question of the future political order into sharp focus. It became clear that the Soviet Union would survive and most probably win the war together with its allies. But such a peace was still far away and likely to be extremely costly, especially because neither the United States nor Great Britain showed much eagerness (at least in Stalin's opinion) to open the promised second front. Besides, American refusal and British reluctance to agree to Soviet demands must have raised the question in Stalin's mind whether an imperfect peace with Germany might not be preferable to an elusive victory, which would surely lead to severe quarrels over Eastern Europe and over some other areas, held by Great Britain but considered vital for an improved Soviet power position after the war. Although this part of the politics of the Great Alliance has not been dealt with extensively in the literature, there are several indirect indications that Stalin at times considered a wartime rapprochement with Germany.[84] Indeed, there seems to have been a secret meeting between German and Soviet envoys during April and May of 1943 in Stockholm. [85] If Voitech Mastny's information is correct, Germany was at that point ready to "make peace in return for a satellite Ukraine and for economic concessions in other parts of the Soviet Union whereas the Russians insisted upon the frontiers of 1941." [86] By May 1, the negotiations seem to have been broken off by the Kremlin. A marked improvement in relations between Moscow and the Western powers ensued, only to be impaired by Roosevelt's and Churchill's message to Stalin announcing the delay of the second front until May 1944. [87] The pro-Western diplomats Maisky and Litvinov were recalled, and a new series of contacts with German representatives seems to have followed in Stockholm. An article in the ideological journal *Voina i rabotchii klass* objected to the Allied theory of collective German guilt and "hinted at the possibilities that Germany might be allowed to keep some of her conquests". [88] The German offensive of June 5th, however, buried all hopes for such settlement. Yet even after the battle of Kursk in July 1943, which was probably the most decisive one on the Eastern front, Stalin seems once more to have weighed his options carefully, although he was now clearly in a superior position.

But from September on, the Soviet Union knew that Germany would be beaten decisively. Therefore, it concentrated on coming to terms with its Western allies, for they were now the ones who could frustrate Soviet attempts to acquire a favorable position in the "correlation of forces" of the postwar era. [89]

A few months later at Teheran, President Roosevelt assured Stalin that he would not challenge a dominant Soviet influence in Eastern Europe and that he "personally agreed with the views of Marshall Stalin" on this matter although he could not participate in any formal decision because of the Polish-American vote in the upcoming elections. [90] Thus, ironically, the Western powers, uneasy about their long delay of the promised second front and worried about rumors and intelligence reports of a possible deal between Moscow and Berlin, decided to accommodate Stalin when he no longer had any feasible alternative, and, on the contrary, concessions of the Western powers stimulated Soviet aspirations.

> . . . (At Teheran) Stalin hinted that his goals would expand with expanding opportunities: "there is no need to speak at the

present time about any Soviet desires but when the time comes
we will speak."91

The time soon came. Soviet pressure began to appear in those
areas mentioned in the shopping list Stalin had submitted to
Hitler. In addition, the Soviet search for a favorable "correlation
of forces" required first a massive program of economic recovery
and expansion in order "to be insured against every
eventuality," as Stalin significantly observed. In the "election"
speech that set forth these goals, he also justified the brutal
collectivization of the 1920's as a necessary precondition for the
recent victory of the Red Army: the parallel seemed grim indeed.
Second, Soviet aims required retaining freedom of action in
foreign policy. This meant a certain isolation from the West,
allowing the Soviet Union to conceal its weaknesses. It also
counseled a firm resistance to any global organization with
"functional responsibilities"—with the authority to replace
bilateral bargaining relationships by compulsory measures—or
with an autonomous "peace-keeping machinery."92

When the United Nations assembled in San Francisco to
debate their future organizational structure, it soon became
evident that the U.S.S.R. approached this issue—as she had the
negotiations at Dumbarton Oaks—in terms of continuing the
wartime alliance rather than inaugurating a peace-keeping
machinery.

It was, however, already clear that future practice rather than
the Charter—with its contradictions between universal concerns
and regional organizations, self-help and collective security,
domestic jurisdiction and supranational authority—would shape
the future role of the United Nations. Thus, whereas Western
powers stressed the "constitutional character" of the Charter,
pointing to its hidden functional logic and its "implied powers"
in the hope that the international system could be transformed,
just as "necessity" and clever lawyers had transformed the
character of the United States' Constitution, the Soviets
emphasized the coalition character of the United Nations. From
the first General Assembly in 1946 these differences in
perspective were pronounced, as the following passage from
Molotov's speech on that occasion proves:

> Of late an extensive campaign has been launched against the
> recognition of this (veto) principle. . . . The debate on the veto

. . . makes it necessary to speak openly of the contradiction and
the chief political tendencies existing in international life in our
day. Two main tendencies are struggling within the United
Nations organization to influence the fundamental trend of its
work. . . . Imagine for a moment that the campaign for the
abolition of the so called "veto" is successful. What would be the
political consequences? It is perfectly obvious that the rejection of
the principle of unanimity of the great powers—and that
essentially, is what lies behind the proposal to abolish the
veto—would actually mean the liquidation of the United Naitons
organization; for this principle is the foundation of the
Organization. 93

For the Soviets, the bitter experience of the Korean War, in
which the politics of the "empty chair" failed to block United
Nations action, led to a certain re-evaluation of this approach.
Participation seemed to be required even if only to bar action
detrimental to Soviet interest. The special character of this
coalition, called the United Nations, intruded so forcefully that
active membership in it even seemed to outweigh considerations
of "socialist solidarity," for Peking's membership was no longer
vigorously pursued. Unlike classical coalitions, where
nonparticipation insures that action will be blocked, the United
Nations seemed to constitute a forum in which one could not
simply abstain without losing. The importance of sanctions also
subtly changed under such circumstances, because "nonparticipation" rather than "enforcement" now posed the critical
problem. 94

The need to "keep the game going" had superceded attempts
to use the world organization for particular political purposes,
and this had far-reaching repercussions on the policies of the
superpowers as well as on the United Nations itself. Indeed this
was the underlying reason for the success of "preventive
diplomacy," invented by Secretary General Dag Hammarskjold,
which sought to prevent the great powers from engaging their
vital interests in critical areas through interposition of UN forces.
It was exactly at the moment when "preventive diplomacy" in
the Congo engaged in the pursuit of particular political goals of
its own, instead of merely facilitating communications between
the superpowers, that the Soviet Union and then the United
States tried once more to transform the character of the global
institution according to their respective preferences. The troika

plan advanced by Krushchev would have dissolved the rudiments of institutionalization and returned the United Nations to the form of a coalition with the lowest possible denominator.*94* The American plan, on the other hand, would have used the procedures outlined in Article 19 of the Charter to emphasize the organizational character of the United Nations. It is important to notice that neither side could mobilize sufficient support for its position among the uncommitted nations, as this third bloc wanted to use the international organization for purposes which required the continued functioning of the organization in the traditional manner.[95] Practically, this meant that the security issues that both superpowers had been pushing for a long time within the United Nations increasingly had to be taken outside this forum.

> The interesting thing in the present context is that, starting with radically different a priori philosophical and tactical premises, the United States seems now to have ended up with something very close to the Soviet Union's special position vis-a-vis the United Nations.
> First, both the Soviet Union and the United States seem now agreed that the United Nations is not a suitable arena for the negotiation or settlement of the really serious conflicts in contemporary international relations.
> Second, even where the Soviet Union and the United States accept to negotiate within the framework of the United Nations, — as with Disarmament; or in the context of a multilateral treaty, — as with Space problems, — the operational methodology for achievement of the final settlement will be direct bilateral Soviet-United States negotiations. . . .[96]

Having recognized this state of affairs, both powers increasingly use the United Nations as a legitimizing agency for deals arrived at outside the organizational framework, as the Cuban crisis, the Vietnam settlement, and the Mideast settlements show. Oddly enough, detente between the superpowers, envisaged by the Charter as the foundation and guarantee of the proper functioning of the organization, might thus turn out to be as detrimental to its development as was the unabated hostility of the Cold War, which was blamed for the world organization's failure to create a stable and just world order.

The Ghost of "Munich" and the "capitalist encirclement"
Two historical events had a profound impact upon the

assumed knowledge decision-makers used for interpreting political moves. The first was the outbreak of World War I, a nearly unlimited conflict that seemed to unfold uncontrollably; the second was the traumatic experience of Munich, which made appeasement a much despised policy. Ironically appeasement was justified at the time of Munich in terms of the lessons drawn from the collapse of the European state system after 1914. [97]

The result of all these efforts to prevent precipitous action was that the "defections" of Hitler and Mussolini—both widely acclaimed as "nationalist" leaders [98]—were interpreted in terms of a mild chicken game rather than a prisoner's dilemma. The young John Kennedy, travelling at that time in Europe, wrote in his diary the following remark, not untypical of "educated" opinion of the day: ". . .(I) have come to the decision that Fascism is the thing for Germany and Italy, Communism for Russia and Democracy for America and England." [99] However, events of the late 1930's showed that concessions had only whetted the appetite of the defectors. The policy of appeasement engendered in the Western democracies a sense of guilt and self-hatred for having been "gutless," and a sense of inferiority because of what seemed an inherent shortcoming of democracy. [100]

Exactly how traumatic Munich was for the generation whose formative political experience it constituted can be seen from Anthony Eden's remarks some twenty years later on the Suez crisis of 1956:

> Success in a number of adventures involving the breaking of agreements in Abyssinia, in the Rhineland, in Austria, in Czechslovakia, in Albania had persuaded Hitler and Mussolini that the democracies had not the will to resist, that they could now march with the certitude of success from sign post to sign post along the road which led to world dominion. . . . As my colleagues and I surveyed the scene in these autumn months of 1956, we were determined that the like should not come again. [101]

The Soviets themselves had apparently drawn similar conclusions from the events of the 1930's, or at least they found it profitable to exploit the inferiority complex of the Western democracies in this respect. It was, after all, Chairman Khrushchev who told the American poet Robert Frost, shortly before the Cuban missile crisis, that "democracies were too liberal to fight." [102] Thus, Dean Acheson's policy of "building strength," [103] as well as Kennedy's later efforts to avoid "miscalculation" and establish a credible military posture, were not the products of merely imaginary fears, as some historians want to have it. If there were errors in judging the opponent, they arose not from groundless phobias but because each side, instead of correcting errors as they appeared, willingly or unwillingly reinforced them.

The creation of an "honest" communications system, as well as the accretion of a common assumed knowledge in terms of common conventions, gained paramount importance particularly with the advent of total mutual vulnerability to nuclear attack. All the lessons of both wars seemed then to point in one direction: the avoidance of miscalculation.

> "A favorite Kennedy word from my earliest association with him," writes Ted Sorensen, "was a 'miscalculation.' "
>
> "Hitler," said Kennedy, "thought that he could seize Poland, that the British might not fight or . . . after the defeat of Poland might not continue to fight." And, then in Korea . . . the North Koreans "obviously did not think we were going to come in and . . . we did not think the Chinese were going to come in . . ."
>
> Thus, "three times in my lifetime" he told the nation at the time of the Berlin crisis "our country and Europe have been involved in a major war. In each case serious misjudgments were made on both sides of the intentions of others which brought about great devastation. . . ." [104]

But if at the time of Kennedy's presidency such a common stock of knowledge had not yet been built up, making an accurate evaluation of the opponent's move possible, the situation was naturally worse when Harry Truman took office. Deprived of such an interpretive framework it is not surprising that historical analogies and the lessons derived from precedents, had a powerful hold on the minds of decision-makers confronted with a bewildering array of problems. How important the lessons of history were for Harry Truman, for example, is shown by his deliberations preceding the decision to intervene forcefully in Korea.

> I had time to think aboard the plane. In my generation this was not the first occasion when the strong had attacked the weak. I recalled some earlier instances: Manchuria, Ethiopia, Austria.

. . . Communism was attacking in Korea just as Hitler, Mussolini
and the Japanese had acted ten, fifteen years earlier . . . if this
is/was allowed to go unchallenged it would mean a third world
war, just as similar incidents had brought on a second world
war. 105

Truman was not alone in placing Korean events in such an
historical frame of reference. Averell Harriman, returning from
Europe, reported that "people there had been gravely concerned
lest we fail to meet the challenge in Korea" 106 and, when
Charles Bohlen informed French Foreign Minister Robert
Schuman about the American decision to intervene, Schuman's
"eyes filled with tears. 'Thank God,' he said, 'this will not be a
repetition of the past.' "107

It is this concern with the nature of the international game,
rather than with tangible gains in territory or economic
opportunities, that distinguishes postwar conflicts from earlier
crises. Yet revisionists are strangely insensitive to this
distinction, despite the fact that from the beginning, the
Truman Administration explicitly focused its concern on how
Soviet actions would affect the structure of expectations about
the basic nature of postwar politics. Hopkins made this point
rather emphatically on his last mission, when he told Stalin
that:

> He wished to state this position as clearly and as forcefully as
> he knew how. He said that the question of Poland per se was not
> so important as the fact that it had become a symbol of our ability
> to work out problems with the Soviet Union. He said that we had
> no special interests in Poland and no special desire to see any
> particular kind of government. That we would accept any
> government in Poland which was desired by the Polish people and
> was at the same time friendly to the Soviet government.
> . . . Poland had become a symbol in the sense that it bore a
> direct relation to the willingness of the United States to
> participate in international affairs on a world wide basis and that
> our people must believe that they are joining their power with the
> Soviet Union and Great Britain in the promotion of international
> peace and well-being of humanity. 108

And it was in the context of a discussion on the prospects for
Soviet-American cooperation within the United Nations
framework that Senator Vandenberg made the first and rather

tentative interpretation of the postwar era in terms of the Munich analogy. Disturbed by Soviet insistence on three voting representatives not only in the future General Assembly but also at the San Francisco conference, he wrote in his diary:

> The Conference opens today—with Russian clouds in every sky. I don't know whether this is Frisco or Munich. . . . The decision is one of judgment—At what point is it wisest to stop appeasing Stalin? Otherwise, a new Munich will be followed by comparable tragedies. 109

The historical analogy slowly gained ground in the administration throughout 1946. [110] When, in the spring of 1946, Russian troops refused to withdraw from Iran and backed a separatist government in Azerbeidjan province, Iran's ambassador to Washington did not fail to point out that this "was only the first move in a series which would include Turkey and other countries in the Near East." Failing vigorous American action, the "history of Manchuria, Abyssinia and Munich would be repeated and Azerbeidjan would prove to have been the first shot fired in (a) third world war." [111]

It was the Iranian crisis that convinced virtually all Washington policy-makers that Byrnes' policy of "patience with firmness" offered the only sure means of countering the Soviet challenge. [112] After strong demonstrations and perhaps a threat of actual intervention, [113] the Soviet Union backed down and thus seemed to confirm the conclusion that the medicine that should have been prescribed for Hitler at Munich had worked this time. In the words of the Clifford report of September 1946, "the language of military power is the only language which disciples of power politics understand." [114]

Finally, after prolonged uncertainty, the last pieces in the puzzle of "what were the Soviets up to" seemed to fall into place when Stalin, on August 7, 1946, asked for a revision of the Dardanelles regime. The implications were ominous, for he had prepared his way in 1945 by denouncing the twenty-year pact of friendship and neutrality with Turkey, thus letting everybody know that the revision of the Montreux convention was not merely a modest proposal. [115] The "timetable" of which the Iranian ambassador had warned the United States seemed to be a correct metaphor for Russia's expanding aspirations.

When American decision-makers in the joint War-Navy

Committee assessed renewed Soviet pressure they made the following recommendations to the President:

> We believe that if the Soviet Union succeeds in introducing into Turkey armed forces with the ostensible purpose of enforcing the joint control of the Straits the Soviet Union will use these forces in order to obtain control over Turkey . . .

> If the Soviet Union succeeds in its objective obtaining control over Turkey it will be extremely difficult if not impossible to prevent the Soviet Union from obtaining control over Greece and over the whole Near and Middle East. . . .

> When we refer to the Near and Middle East we have in mind the territory lying between the Mediterranean and India. When the Soviet Union has once obtained full mastery of this territory . . . it will be in a much stronger position to obtain its objectives in Asia and China. [116]

It was through this identification of the various Soviet "defections" from cooperation with the idea of a "timetable"—and that idea was thought all the more applicable as the communist side boasted of its superior skill in using "salami tactics"—that the "Ghost of Munich" became such an overpowering influence. Thus every conflict of interest was transformed into a "test case" that showed the correctness of the initial assessment.

Similarly, years later when a new "row of dominoes" in Southeast Asia suggested a preconceived timetable, President Lyndon Johnson advanced the following interpretation of the events in Vietnam:

> Everything that happens in this world affects us because pretty soon it gets on our doorstep. We thought we could sit out World War I, but we could not. The Kaiser misunderstood us and didn't think we could fight . . .

> We thought we could sit out World War II and said "let's let them take care of these problems themselves." What happened? . . . Hitler went through Poland. . . .

> There are three billion people in the world and we have only 200 million of them. We are outnumbered 15:1. If might did make

right they would sweep over the United States and take what we have. We have what they want.[117]

One might be tempted to pass off these extemporaneous remarks as pure presidential "salesmanship," which need not accurately reflect the true thinking of decision-makers at the time, were it not well corroborated that decision-makers indeed thought along these lines. Johnson, who took pride in never having been "any Chamberlain umbrella man"[118] and who had categorically declared that "no more Munichs"[119] were acceptable, was joined by Secretary of State Dean Rusk. Rusk had called Mao's regime a "colonial Russian government — a slavic Manchukuo,"[120] and he saw in recent "wars of liberation" the kind of "laboratory experiments in the anatomy and physiology of aggression" that the "seizure of Manchuria, Ethiopia, the Rhineland, Austria and Czechoslovakia" had been 30 years ago.[121] The decisive difference between a classical seizure of territory and revolutionary warfare was obscured by such a frame of reference.[122] In a 1962 memorandum of the Joint Chiefs of Staff, the connection between the Vietnam conflict and the communist world conspiracy, advancing according to a fixed *timetable*, was once more emphasized.

> The Joint Chiefs of Staff wish to reaffirm their position that the United States must prevent the loss of South Vietnam to either communist insurgency or aggression. . . . It is recognized that the military and political effort of Communist China in South Vietnam and the political and psychological thrust by the U.S.S.R. into the Indonesian archipelago are not brushfire tactics nor merely a campaign for control of the mainland area. More important it is part of a major campaign to extend communist control beyond the periphery of the Sino-Soviet Block and overseas to both island and continental areas in the free world, through a most natural and comparatively soft outlet, the South East Asian Peninsula. It is, in fact, a planned phase in the communist timetable for world domination.[123]

This advice, based upon the then current interpretation of history, not only ignored the widening Sino-Soviet rift but viewed the Vietnam war as the last link in a chain of events set in motion a long time ago. Alexis Johnson, American Ambassador to Thailand, believed that "communist designs for taking South East Asia dated back before World War II,"[124] and Walt

Rostow reconstructed the "communist strategy" in the following manner:

> In a manner resonant of Russian history, Stalin's effort to exploit the postwar disarray of Eurasia had two phases. He pressed first in the west and then when frustrated turned to apparent opportunities in the east. 125

Thus, guerrilla activity in Asia is seen not as an effect of the breakdown of colonial rule and the end of Japanes occupation, but as the product of a new communist policy introduced by the Cominform's announcement of "ambitious new objectives." The climax of this development, according to this particular view, was Mao's victory in China and the two communist powers' joint venture against South Korea. 126

But such an interpretation is open to question on several grounds. First of all, it assumes a measure of control over foreign communist parties and revolutionary activities that Moscow rarely enjoyed, with the exception of those parties that had taken refuge in Moscow during the war. Second, the successful pursuit of a long-range "master plan" requires capabilities and knowledge of circumstances and events that no statesman can possess. Thus, the Korean conflict was not so much a planned shift of revolutionary activity to the East as it was an apparently safe and convenient mop-up operation, to which Stalin acceded when the North Korean leader Kim Il Sung promised that "the first poke would touch off an internal explosion in South Korea and the power of the people would prevail." 127 After all, the United States had acquiesced in the "fall" of China, and official statements had excluded Korea from the American "defense perimeter." 128 A quick *fait accompli* promised to evoke little resistance from the West, while gaining the advantage of a foot in China's door by obliging one of her oldest clients.

All of this naturally does not prove that Stalin's moves were purely defensive. But they were obviously more cautious and more dependent upon circumstances than the image of a relentless timetable suggests. What then were the criteria by which Stalin evaluated situations, and what were the lessons of history *he* had learned?

On the most general level, Stalin had seen that war, with all its dislocation and turmoil, provided a good opportunity for a

"socialist" takeover. He did not forget that it had been the First
World War, *not* the predicted world revolution, that had brought
the Bolsheviks to power. Thus, a coup d'etat in the face of total
disorientation had provided the opportunity for a subsequent
transformation of society; the revolution properly speaking
followed during the civil war and Stalin's collectivization.

Furthermore, the failure of the Polish campaign (on that
occasion the Polish proletariat sided against the invading Red
Army instead of welcoming their socialist "brothers")[129], and
the only ephemeral success of communists uprisings in the wake
of World War I, reinforced Stalin's contempt for the foreign
proletariat. Having operationalized the term "good communist"
in terms of personal loyalty—enforced by purges—Stalin took no
chances with future "national crises" that might develop after
another "imperialist war." [130] Western communist party
leaders in exile in Moscow had to measure up to the same
standards and had to endure the same purges.[131] Even then,
Stalin was very careful to restrain "revolutionary romanticism"
among these loyalists, recognizing the constraints imposed by
the international situation.[132] In this respect, Stalin followed
quite closely Lenin's theory of the "general crisis of
capitalism," which transferred the center of revolution from the
industrialized West to the underdeveloped East. Contrary to
Marx's original assumptions,

> . . . the world revolutionary process came to be conceived of not
> as an all European proletarian Revolution on Marx's model but as
> a long drawn out revolt of the colonial East against European
> hegemony on the model of the revolution in semi-Asiatic peasant
> Russia.[133]

The paramount importance Stalin assigned to international
factors in bringing about world revolution is revealed in his
attempts to formulate a coherent theory generalizing the lessons
he learned during World War I and its aftermath. In viewing
imperialism as the last stage of capitalism, Stalin not only
followed Lenin but elaborated a theory of imperialism that
envisions the revolution as a result of *international* rather than
national or societal factors. Revolution, in this view, occurs in
particular countries not as a consequence of local or societal
developments, as earlier Marxists had predicted, but because

the whole world capitalist system has become ripe for such an upheaval. [134]

> Formerly it was usual to speak of the presence or absence of objective conditions for proletarian revolution . . . in one or another well developed country. . . . Now we must speak of the presence of objective conditions of revolution in the entire system of the world imperialist economy as an integral whole; the existence within this system of some countries that are not sufficiently developed industrially cannot serve as an insurmountable obstacle to revolution . . . because the system as a whole is already ripe for revolution.[135]

With this formulation the classical dilemma of Marxism as a pure "second image" theory seems to be solved. It not only explains why the revolution takes place in the underdeveloped East rather than in the industrial West, but also shows the paramount importance of the Soviet state for the final success of the world revolution. It thus lays the groundwork for the identification of the world revolutionary process with Soviet interests. This is a rather ingenious solution, for it reconciles the universalist aspirations of socialism with the systemic constraints imposed by the international system. Stalin incorporated this concept of Russia as the nucleus for the world revolutionary process in the famous "Two Camp Theory" he first expounded in an interview with American workers in 1927.

> In the further progress of development of the international revolution . . . two centers will be formed: the socialist center attracting to itself all the countries gravitating towards socialism and the capitalist center attracting to itself all the countries gravitating towards capitalism. The struggle between these two centers (for the conquest of the world economy) will decide the fate of capitalism and communism throughout the whole world, (for the final defeat of world capitalism means a victory of socialism in the arena of the world economy).[136]

Bukharin, in contrast, envisioned only peaceful economic competition and a final socialist victory through economic superiority—a theory revitalized by Khrushchev after the Twentieth Party Congress.[137] But Stalin's historical experience, as well as his desire for control, led him to emphasize war, thus elevating the Red Army to the status of a surrogate proletariat. The image of the two camps then also explains why Stalin himself could not understand "national liberation struggles"—neither that of Tito nor that of Mao—despite the fact that in those struggles, the decisive pre-condition for communist accession to power was *war* rather than social revolt.

The importance accorded to the Red Army later fostered the conception of a "people's democracy," which was basically a theoretical formulation of the fact that communist regimes in Eastern Europe had come to power through the help of the occupying Red Army. The Polish communist Bierut defined a "people's democracy" as "a special form of revolutionary authority which came into being under new relations among classes in the international arena."[138]

What were the implications of these experiences and ideas for Soviet policy?

First of all, it seems that the emphasis placed upon international power considerations led to cautious but tenacious and often contradictory policy moves. For instance, Wolfgang Leonhard's instructions for political agitation in the eastern zone of Germany were already changed by the summer of 1945, as the political picture there began to resemble more and more that of the other Eastern European countries. Western accommodation apparently encouraged bolder actions. Land reform, favoritism to communist organizations, and the dissolution of the various antifascist groups that had spontaneously sprung up after the end of the war were now vigorously pursued.[139] In the spring of 1946 Stalin seemed to have been rather confident of his ability to control the rest of Germany as well, as he told Yugoslav and Bulgarian leaders that "all of Germany must be ours, that is, Soviet Communist.'[140] But a year later, when the West drew a line through Germany, Stalin settled for a division.

When the U.S. tried to consolidate Western Europe, Stalin was convinced that the Marshall Plan was designed mainly to create the industrial base for political and military pressure against his sphere of influence. Polish and Czech interest in the plan showed that controlling these countries would be much more difficult if they could free themselves from nearly total dependence on the Soviet Union. So Stalin set out to organize his bloc systematically. The foundation of the Cominform, with its emphasis on ideological uniformity, "left no doubt as to the close links between domestic Soviet developments and the reassessment of the East European scene." [141] Fearful that western influence seeping through Eastern Europe might endanger his regime, Stalin took no chances. He dealt with the problem of control in the only way he knew: repression and purges.

Oddly enough, his preoccupation with total control within his own sphere of influence—taken in the West as confirmation of ruthless aggressiveness—left little room for large-scale military probes across the now clearly established dividing line in Europe. Being in total control of his satellites ensured Stalin that no "national crisis" could develop, and Soviet demobilization continued throughout 1947 and 1948. At the end of that year Soviet armed forces were down to about 2.9 million men, "hardly an excessive figure in view of the Soviet garrisons from Port Arthur to Berlin.' [142]

Ironically, the Berlin blockade, which finally convinced nearly everyone in the West of Stalin's aggressive intentions, was most probably a rear guard action intended to force the issue of Germany once more and to reintroduce some fluidity into a rapidly congealing situation. When it became obvious that the Western powers did not want to reopen the whole question but were ready to give in on the currency question in Berlin—the alleged "cause" for the Soviet blockade—Stalin departed Moscow, leaving behind the Western ambassadors with their carefully drafted proposals, which Molotov and Stalin had already informally approved. [143] Having overplayed his hand once more, Stalin at last recognized that the division of the world would become final.

V Myths and Metaphors

Myths

1. The Rise and Demise of Myths

The above discussion of historical sequences that serve as constructs for interpreting political action led us to the point where the connection between these comprehensive symbolic typifications and "myths" became visible. As pointed out at length in Chapter III, myths are—on the most general level—dramatic stories that establish a socially supported identity and suggest a collective course of action to allay the anxiety created by bewildering events. As we have seen from the historical account of the last chapter several factors contributed to the interpretation of the great power antagonism as a mythical contest. There was first of all the lack of an assumed knowledge which endowed historical experience of the recent past with paramount importance. Second, there was the anxiety created by the perceived threats against one's "way of life," and, last but not least, there was the notion of a "timetable" or an "encirclement" which reinforced the mythical conceptualization of world politics. Political myths, writes Murray Edelman,

> fall into a small number of archetypical patterns though they vary widely in detail. Either they define an enemy who is plotting against the national interest and may need to be exterminated; or they define a savior hero leader of a popularly or divinely sanctioned social order who is to be followed and obeyed and for

whom deprivation, suffering or sacrifice are gratifying. All sorts
of political concerns are translated into these forms. 1

An instructive example in this respect was the world reaction
to President Kennedy's murder. As Presidents are "symbols of
the whole" *par excellence*, their unexpected death induces anxieties totally out of proportion to the likely disruption of the
political process. A panic at the stock market may follow, and
free-floating anxieties may be focused on a mythical conspiracy
of which the death of the president is only the first manifest example. Geyelin reports:

> When Kennedy was killed everybody was looking for a wider plot.
> The Communists were calling it a rightist conspiracy and tied it to
> the Ku Klux Klan and the John Birch Society. The Arabs saw it as
> a Zionist plot and Africans and Asians as a racist affair. Nigeria's
> president hurried off a message to President Johnson saying that
> the killing of Kennedy shows clearly that among some Americans
> there is a deep seated hatred of the black man as a human being. 2

Similarly, when an opponent's foreign policy moves create
anxiety but defy analysis, they become highly susceptible to
mythical interpretation. Thus when Japanese and American
interests clashed in the Far East at the turn of the century,
Franklin D. Roosevelt, then a student at Harvard, had been
profoundly impressed as

> (at that time in 1902) a Japanese friend had unfolded to him a
> hundred year plan made in 1889 whereby Japan would conquer
> Asia and the Pacific. This plan of conquest was revealed to the
> whole world, he told Congress shortly after Pearl Harbour, by
> Japan's 1894 attack on China, by her subsequent occupation of
> Korea, by her attack on Russia in 1904, by her illegal fortification
> of mandated Pacific islands after 1920, by her seizure of Man-
> churia in 1931 and finally by her invasion of China in 1937. 3

Such shared beliefs in a plotting enemy and in a competent
hero-leader not only "explain" a state of affairs experienced
with anxiety, but also reassure an aroused public and strengthen
cooperation and even sacrifice for the sake of national welfare.

The connection we noted earlier between emotion and
cognition allows us to carry our analysis a step further. Freud
observed that we seem to have a tendency to convert inner

stimuli in to a sequence of outer events, e.g., as in a dream when an inner struggle is translated into a dramatic story. Through externalization, the containment of "terror and impulse is made possible by the decorum of art and symbolism."[4] But what is objectified can be communicated to and shared by others. Private experience loses its particularity and becomes "common," creating a social and political phenomenon. As Robert Tucker has shown, the individual experience of alienation Marx focused on in his early writings is later transformed into the external social and political struggle between the capitalist and the proletarian[5]

Lenin and Stalin then extended Marx's theory to the even wider setting of international relations. The former believed that success at home could only be sustained by revolution abroad; the latter maintained that a capitalist war against the Soviet Union would give rise to "nation-wide crises," which would give the Soviet Union new opportunities to expand its influence through the revolutionary transformation of a significant part of the international system.[6] But violence—whether in war or in revolution (especially in a revolution believed to be inspired by foreign subversives)—is one of the most anxiety-producing experiences an individual or a society has to endure. As the threat of violence grows, it is all the more likely that international conflict will be described in terms of dramatization rather than as a negotiable disagreement. The perception of such a threat is heightened particularly when an opponent's behavioral and rhetorical signals deviate from what the assumed knowledge would predict. Language styles are thus of particular importance because they signal conformity with or rejection of the prevailing outlook.[7] Revolutionary rhetoric, even if not followed by revolutionary practice, serves as an indicator for the maintenance or rupture of the common symbolic universe which is decisively important for the appraisal of each player's moves.

This has important implications for our discussion of the Cold War, since the discrepancy between rhetoric and reality has often led contemporary American commentators to conclude that leaders like Mao and Tito had been "nationalists" above all, and that the international communist movement has always been a myth—myth in the sense of a pure phantasm that ought to be dispelled.

But such sweeping statements are historically false. After all,

Tito was for a time the most loyal and militant anti-Western leader, and at one time he probably even hopd to succeed Stalin as helmsman of the communist movement. [8] Furthermore, such a view of communism hardly does justice to the complexities of the symbolic structures that serve as inference guidance devices for political action. There is little doubt that both Tito and Mao thought they were acting strictly in accordance with the precepts of communism, with the ironic result that some of their policies were more Stalinist than Stalin's. How strong, for example, Tito's adherence to the CPSU and to Stalin actually was, is shown by his remarks at the party congress when he made the final break with the Soviet leader. He concluded his five hour speech with: "long live Comrade Stalin."[9] Mao's attitude was similar. In 1956, when several East European leaders insisted on the right to take their own "way to socialism," thus challenging Moscow's claim to ideological supremacy, Mao insisted:

> The socialist camp must have a head and this head is the USSR . . . the Communist workers' parties must have a head and this head is the CPSU.[10]

Only when the Kremlin refused to back China's fight against "American imperialism" with a nuclear guarantee, thereby departing from the accepted communist dramatic script, did Sino-Soviet differences become pronounced. If the "nationalist" theory were correct, it would indeed be hard to explain why foreign communist parties consistently subordinated their welfare to that of the Soviet state, or why they endured purges of their exiled leaders and obediently fell in line when Moscow rejected different roads to socialism by ostracizing the Yugoslav communists from the Cominform.

Thus, if Western policies of this period were indeed based on delusions, these delusions prevailed in the East as well as the West. And because such myths directly or indirectly informed the decision premises of decision-makers on both sides, and both sides' self-images, they cannot fairly be seen as simple errors that could have been corrected by looking harder at the facts. Interpretive frames of reference die hard in spite of contradictory evidence, and the new CPSU party program still sees all disturbances of the status quo as a "single revolutionary process undermining and destroying capitalism."[11]

Can we conclude from this that nothing has changed and

that, then as now, the "myth" was only a verbal smokescreen? This raises in general the question of how political myths relate to behavior and how the functions of myths change over time, for example, from an operational imperative to a sanctified principle that has lost its importance for day-to-day decision-making. Our theoretical discussion in Chapters II and III is directly relevant to this point.

We said political myths are archetypal in character and rather few in number. Furthermore, societies whose aspirations are "plotting enemies," endowed with incredible foresight and cunning which the myths objectify and transform into "dramatic stories," reassuring the people and inducing political action. As we have shown, the sense of frustration itself results from interpreting defections in a mild chicken game as ominous signs of non-cooperation in future rounds. As already mentioned, it is this step that transforms the game into a typical prisoner's dilemma, where cutting one's own losses leads to the choice of the noncooperative solution as exemplified in the DD cell of the game matrix.

The perceptual shift implied in the redefinition of the game can in turn be broken down into a three-stage process. First, an opponent's initial defection need not have such dramatic consequences, if it is interpreted as a deviation not exceeding customary limits, as understood in light of the prevailing assumed knowledge. Such principles as "reasonableness" and "adequacy" of excuses are of decisive importance here. Thus, nonconformity with a rule supposed to guide behavior in a particular case need not result in mutual hostility or in the breakdown of orderly intercourse, because the grammar of "following a rule" contains the possibility of "making a mistake" or "violating a rule."[12] Nevertheless, defections *do* introduce uncertainty into the game, and the wronged party will naturally try to ascertain what the defector was up to and what his defection means for future interactions. Reassurance will be sought that an accepted rule exists for a class of events of which the dispute was a case. If such reassurance is not forthcoming or is not satisfactory, the wronged party will try to construe a test case that will avoid some of the ambiguities of the previous case. The opponent will be put on notice that issue X will have far-reaching consequences. The second stage has been reached.

The opponent now has three basic strategies available for

countering such a challenge. He can flatly reject the
interpretation tendered by the wronged party, asserting that the
rules or their interpretation in terms of a common assumed
knowledge are merely a sham. In this case communication
breaks down and the parties move to strategy DD (stage three).
A second possibility is that the opponent will choose the
cooperative solution (CC), trading off short-term loss for
long-term gain and reaffirming the existence of a common
assumed knowledge, essential to maintain trust in case of future
defections. Thirdly, the defector might argue that, in spite of the
existence of a common assumed knowledge, the rule in question
was irrelevant in the case at issue. Depending on his persuasive
skills and conciliatory gestures, the defector might thus buy time
and delay the redefinition of the game. But such tactics will
surely heighten suspicion and anxiety. The wronged player will
now search his memory for relevant precedents in order to
assess correctly the motives of the opponent. Historical
analogies, especially those taking the form of lessons derived
from recent traumatic experiences, seem to play a decisive part
in the search for an interpretive frame of reference and in
gauging one's strategy accordingly. Needless to say, the
escalating charges and countercharges might also have
convinced the defector (who incidently might have constructed
his own test cases) that little common ground is left. Against this
escalating sequence, which heightens anxiety, the events that
have occurred are translated into the dramatic form
characteristic of myths. Since no common assumed knowledge
remains to provide the basis for trust, cutting one's losses
becomes imperative and both parties become locked into a
classical prisoner's dilemma.

As experiments with repeated rounds of these games show,
the best way of building up a common assumed knowledge
seems to be the "tit for tat" strategy. 13 This strategy relies on
the emergence of common norms for the transformation of the
game—norms that incidently serve as implicit "third parties."
But the appearance of an actual third player changes the game
fundamentally, as has been shown extensively.

Let us consider for a moment the strategy of changing the
game through the mutual recognition of norms. Obviously,
changing the character of the game in this way requires that one
player takes the initiative by announcing his choice of the

cooperative strategy. He not only risks being exploited in this particular round but may also encourage the opponent to make further demands in future rounds, as the opponent may view choosing the cooperative strategy as a sign of weakness. But if instead the first player's initiative is rewarded by a cooperative response from the opponent, these experiences can be ordered into a new set of historical recollections. The new lessons of history, however, are likely to contradict central tenets of both players' original myths. For example, resolving a crisis situation successfully, and thus escaping the mythically predicted catastrophe will have important repercussions upon each side's image of the opponent. Empathetic mutual role-taking during a crisis may reveal that the opponent is neither so cunning nor so reckless as the myth makes him. Beyond that, the experience of regaining control over a chain of events that had seemed "out of hand" might enlarge both players' understanding of the range of viable solutions. But the reassertion of control in a situation that should have unfolded "logically" and inevitably, according to the myth's plot, drastically restructures the situation. The dramatic story of the myth ceases to provide a script for future developments.

Throughout these experiences, the players' goals may undergo very little change, but postponing their attainment to the indefinite future fundamentally transforms the meaning of the myth by revising its implications for social action. Exactly because myths are dramatic stories, changing their time-frame affects their character profoundly. Those who see only the permanence of professed goals, but who neglect structural changes—the incorporation of common experiences into the myths of both sides, shifts in the image of the opponent ("there are reasonable people also in the other 'camp'"), and modifications in the myths' periodization—overlook the great effects that may result from such contextual changes.

As metaphors are structurally less complex than myths and can therefore more easily be used in an *ad hoc* fashion, they indicate actual decision premises more clearly than do the more elaborate structures of mythical symbols, which might obfuscate rather than reveal the changed meaning of a myth for quite some time. For example, Protestant reformers' stress on "innerwordly ascesis" in terms of "doing God's work here and now," rather than on the contemplative expectation of the "kingdom of God,"

changed ways of life fundamentally despite the fact that
Protestant sectarianism shared with Catholic orthodoxy the
common myth of the church as *civitas dei*, on a pilgrimage to its
predestined goal.[14] An inventory of the metaphors used in
describing social reality therefore gives important clues as to the
changing meaning of myths for social action. In fact, we are
justified in saying that another way in which the structure of
myths can change is by the degree of *elaboration* with which
inconsistencies between mythical prediction and actual behavior
are explained. The mythically dogmatic will maintain that an
opponent's unexpected behavior does not indicate a change in
plans, that on the contrary it only proves a central tenet of the
myth: the deviousness of the opponent, who, by slightly
modifying his tactics, makes one's own camp relax in order to
attack more effectively later. Interpreting inconsistent behavior
as the result of disagreements within the opposing leadership,
rather than as merely a tactical shift, influences decisively what
strategy one is willing to employ. As myths are responses to
unsettling emotional experiences, a leader who had cued his
society and himself in certain mythical terms might derive
considerable comfort from the dogmatic maintenance of the
original myth. This is the reason why structural changes in
myths—by explanatory elaboration or by time frame
changes—usually result from a change in leadership, as our
theoretical discussion shows. The new "generation"[15] has
constructed different historical frames of reference, consequently this generation is less limited by the dominant myth. The
"new beginnings" so often invoked on the occasion of
inaugurals or other significant power transfers symbolically express this commonsense notion.

Let us now return to the second factor that can transform a
game locked into a classical prisoner's dilemma: the appearance
of a third party. The implications for transformation have been
spelled out in Chapter IV, 2, so no repetition seems necessary
here. There is however a way in which emerging third parties
play a role long before they are admitted as full players to the
game. As I tried to show, it is important to realize that, for example, the emergence of a "tribe on the periphery of a one-power
world does not alter the character of the game as long as this
party is not recognized as an autonomous decision-making
center. Relations between the two entities in such a one-and-a-

half power world will not resemble the interdependent decision-making of a full-fledged two-power world. The example of the Chinese empire shows that strong resistance to a perceptual shift may inhibit the adjustment to the horizontal authority structure characteristic of an n-power world for a long time. Similarly, we will see that decision-makers in a two-power world can treat changes on the periphery as nuisances rather than changes in the character of the game for quite a considerable time, reinforcing the mythical belief that whatever happens must have been caused by one of the two protagonists. But the mere existence of an incipient third player creates new opportunities, especially if, alongside the mythical structure, an in stitutional framework exists that is not organized according to the two-power model and that therefore allows for divergent expressions of political reality. Competition for the favors of the third force in this arena will therefore not depend upon strategic calculations in terms of the usual indices of power-potential; and parties with vastly inferior strength can exert a disproportionate influence, thereby showing the irrelevance of the polarized mythical world view for a whole variety of political issues. Thus, peripheral third parties will encourage leaders who perceive new opportunities to advance competing interpretations of reality and to restructure the original myth. It has, for example, been the merit of Zbigniew Brzezinski's work on the Soviet bloc to show how the change in leadership after Stalin's death, and the formation of the non-aligned bloc, encouraged Eastern European leaders to look for their own path to socialism.[16] *Mutatis mutandis,* this was naturally also true of the Western communist parties. Having paid the heavy price of subjection under Stalin's absolute rule in accordance with the originally expounded myth, the mere existence of forces outside the rigid two camps—forces that displayed not only independence from the "West," but often considerable sympathy for the Socialist side—lessened the anxiety of the Western communists that deviations from the prescribed scenario had to be bought at the price of political disaster.

To trace these developments more extensively on both sides, the next two sections will deal with changes in the mythical structure brought about both by changes in time frames and by metaphorical elaboration.

2. The Myths of the Cold War

When the German surrender took effect on May 8, 1945, the problem of postwar cooperation between the victorious powers arose ominously, as a whole gamut of virulent issues had been postponed until after the German defeat. With Britain's Balkan interests in jeopardy, it was only logical that Winston Churchill should sound one of the first official alarms. On May 12, only four days after the German surrender, he dispatched a telegram to President Truman clearly reflecting his anxiety about Russian intentions. In this message one of the most dramatic metaphors of the Cold War made its first appearance.

> I am profoundly concerned about the European situation. I learn that half the American Air Force has already begun to move to the Pacific theatre. . . . Meanwhile what is to happen about Russia? I have always worked for friendship with Russia, but, like you, I feel deep anxiety because of her misinterpretation of the Yalta decisions, their attitude towards Poland, their overwhelming influence in the Balkans, excepting Greece, the difficulties they make about Vienna, the combination of Russian power and the territories under their control or occupied coupled with the Communist technique in so many other countries and above all their power to maintain very large armies in the field for a long time. . . . An iron curtain is drawn upon their front. We do not know what is going on behind. There seems little doubt that the whole of the regions east of the line Lübeck-Trieste-Corfu will be completely in their hands. . . . Meanwhile the attention of our peoples will be occupied in inflicting severities upon Germany which is ruined and prostrate and it would be open to the Russians in a very short time to advance, if they chose, to the waters of the North Sea and the Atlantic. . . . 17

Churchill presents a nearly classical inventory of the themes that foster a mythical interpretation of conflicts of interest. There is first of all an objective threat to one's position within the international system; this threat is heightened by uncertainty about the intentions of the opponent, and by his employment of unconventional means of attaining his goal (subversion). The resulting anxiety is reinforced by the secrecy with which the adversary surrounds himself and his actions (iron curtain) and their potentially ominous implications.

Truman's response to these remonstrances is also quite typical. America's position did not seem to be in danger, and

American attention was focused on "finishing the job" in Japan. [18]

Thus, despite Truman's tough talk to Molotov in April 1945, there is precious little evidence that the new President was pursuing form the outset a well-planned strategy of confrontation.[19]

By early summer 1945 and for the rest of the year, American decision makers were constructing the first test cases, in order to find out what "the Russians were up to," rather than embarking upon a new policy. The Hopkins mission in May and Secretary Byrnes' moves at the London and Moscow conferences reinforce this view.[20] In fact, despite all the irritations produced by the confusing London and Moscow conferences, they also produced agreement on a wide variety of issues. Secretary of State Byrnes' confidence and satisfaction, reflected in the radio address he delivered after his return, contrasted sharply with British Foreign Minister Bevin's gloom and disappointment.[21]

Nevertheless, it was the series of events during 1946 that led to a critical reappraisal of American foreign policy. Apparent internal and external threats heightened the American sense of vulnerability, and led to the first dichotomization of the historical process, which seemed to display the features two conflicting ways of life. In order to understand the construction of this symbolic universe, let us briefly recount the most important historical incidents. On February 9, Stalin made his famous "election" speech reviving the two-camp theory;[22] and on February 16 the Canadian spy case broke, creating a good deal of anxiety in the United States and undermining hopes for the future great-power harmony. Kennan's "long telegram" reached the State Department on February 22, and five days later Robert Murphy, political adviser to General Clay in Germany, warned about Soviet "sabotage" of the Potsdam agreement.[23] Republican foreign policy spokesman Senator Vandenberg, himself under growing criticism for working together with the "appeaser" Byrnes, tried to focus the free-floating anxiety by asking "what is Russia up to now?"

> We ask it in Manchuria. We ask it in Eastern Europe and the Dardanelles. We ask it in Italy. We ask it in Iran. We ask it in Tripolitania. We ask it in the Baltic and the Balkans. We ask it in Poland. We ask it in the capital of Canada. We ask it in Japan. We

ask it sometimes even in connection with events in our own United States.

. . . It would be entirely futile to blink away the fact that two great rival ideologies—democracy in the West and communism in the East—here find themselves face to face with the desperate need for mutual understanding in finding common ground upon which to strive for peace for both. In the final analysis this means that the two greatest spokesmen for these rival ideologies—Soviet Russia and the United States—find themselves face to face with the same need for mutual understanding both in and out of the United Nations. . . .

If this is so Mr. President I assert my own belief that we can live together in reasonable harmony if the US speaks as plainly upon all occasions as Russia does; if we abandon the miserable fiction . . . that we somehow jeopardize the peace if our candor is as firm as Russia's always is; and if we assume a moral leadership which we have too frequently allowed to lapse. . . . We can speak with the extraordinary power inherent in . . . unselfishness. We need but one rule: What is right? Where is justice? There let America take her stand. [24]

Although this speech does not yet exhibit hostility or anger—which became standard features of later Cold War rhetoric—and although it even manages to sound a hopeful note on the possibility of mutual understanding within the framework of the United Nations, the political process is already cast in the dramatic language of a medieval morality play. America's role and mission, its claim to moral leadership, are now seen to be world wide. The character of conflict seems to have changed so fundamentally that speaking of other players and their actions, or interpreting the difficulties at hand as conflicts of interest, seem inadequate descriptions of reality. Under such circumstances the plea for a mutual endeavor to find some common ground is dwarfed by moral aspirations and by the stakes at issue.

It is not surprising that such first expressions of concern, signalling a change in attitude, came from the opposition because it had no particular stake in the policy-line advanced by the administration. As a matter of fact, expounding new frames of reference is one of the main functions of the opposition in the policy process and its chief technique for gaining support in the electoral competition. The administration, on the other hand, though already slowly shifting gears, remained cautious in its official announcements and overt acts.

Again it was a member of the "opposition" who, freer to express the growing apprehension, underlined the deterioration of the political climate. On March 5 Winston Churchill delivered his famous "Iron Curtain" speech in Fulton, Missouri. In Truman's words, it "was admirable and would do nothing but good though it would cause a stir." [25] Aside from painting a dark picture of the situation in Eastern Europe, Churchill spelled out the implications for Western policy in a way that a large segment of American public opinion was not yet ready to endorse. Churchill maintained that although the Soviets did not want war they "wanted the fruits of war and the indefinite expansion of their power and doctrine." To this purpose, "in a great number of countries...Communist fifth columns are established and work in complete unity and absolute obedience to the directions they receive from the Communist center." [26] The prescriptions that flowed from this dramatic plot were clear. They not only entailed a particular application of the lessons of recent history but specified new roles for Great Britain and the United States to play. Neither hopes for a functioning United Nations nor a return to the conventional balance of power game could serve as a substitute.

> From what I have seen of our Russian friends and allies during the War I am convinced that there is nothing they admire so much as strength and there is nothing for which they have less respect than for military weakness. For that reason the old doctrine of a balance of power is unsound. We cannot afford . . . to work on narrow margins offering temptations to a trial of strength. . . .
>
> Last time I saw it all coming and cried aloud to my own fellow countrymen and to the world, but no one paid attention. We surely must not let that happen again.
>
> The United States stands at this time at the pinnacle of world power. . . . With primacy in power is also joined an awe-inspiring accountability to the future. It is necessary that constancy of mind, persistency of purpose and the grand simplicity of decision shall guide and rule the conduct of the English speaking peoples in peace as they did in war. . . .
>
> There is however an important question we must ask ourselves. Would a special relationship between the United States and the British Commonwealth be inconsistent with our overriding loyalties to the world organization? I reply that on the contrary it is probably the only means by which this organization will achieve

its full strength . . . "in my father's house are many mansions."
Special associations . . . which have no aggressive point against
any other country . . . far from being harmful are beneficial and
as I believe indispensable. [27]

In retrospect it is hard to deny that this speech was an accurate
inventory of things to come. First of all, the leading role of the
United States is acknowledged and the transformation of the
international system into a two-power world is implicitly
recognized. With France prostrate and England struggling to
revive her economy, the alliance of the "English-speaking
peoples" is introduced as a new actor, replacing the notion of
Great Britain as a third party that may shift alliances in
accordance with the requirements of an n-power   game.
Two other reasons, in Churchill's view, make a return to the
balance of power as a means of conflict resolution impossible:
first, the unlimited ambitions of the Kremlin and its use of
subversive methods, which are contrary to the systemic
requirements of the old European state system; and, second, the
enormous stakes in the new conflict, which might encourage
armed probes formerly deterred by the narrow margins of
superiority states or alliances could attain. Finally, there was the
leitmotiv of later years that the "building of strength" has to
precede diplomatic accommodation and that the United Nations,
although providing a framework for such accommodation, can be
nothing more than a coalition.

Although the administration tried to disassociate itself from
such sweeping statements, its own reassessment of policy was
well under way. First, Kennan's telegram had stirred a good
deal of interest within the government and Forrestal had made it
required reading for hundreds of higher officers. Second, the
Soviet refusal to withdraw its troops from Iran at the agreed upon
time seemed to recommend a "get tough policy." Last but
not least, there was the famous "test case" of a four power
guarantee against German rearmament which was supposed to
take care of Russian objections to Allied policy in Western
Europe. When Molotov objected to a twenty-five year term of
such a treaty and Byrnes declared his willingness to consider a
forty-year term, Vandenberg noted in his diary: "If Molotov
finally refuses this offer, he will confess that he wants expansion
not security." [28]

With Eastern Europe practically written off by the peace

treaties of February 1947, the containment of Soviet influence within Eastern Europe became imperative especially in view of the West's steadily deteriorating economic and political situation. Thus, there might be a good deal of truth in Richard Powers' observation that the Truman Doctrine was a policy "in search of an occasion which the British withdrawal (from Greece and the Eastern Mediterranean) provided." 29

Perhaps the clearest expression of what would be required for such a policy shift is Will Clayton's March 5 memorandum, sent to the Secretary of State:

> I am deeply disturbed by the present world picture and its implication for our country. The reins of world leadership are fast slipping from Britain's competent but now very weak hands. These reins will be picked up either by the United States or Russia. If by Russia there will almost certainly be war in the next decade or so with the odds against us. If by the United States war can almost certainly be prevented. The U.S. must take world leadership and quickly . . . But the United States will not take world leadership effectively unless the people of the United States are shocked into doing so. To shock them it is only necessary for the President and the Secretary of State to tell them the truth and the whole truth. . . . Meantime we have discussed with the Congressional leaders a program to help Greece. . . . This goes only part of the way; it tells only part of the truth. We must go all out in the world game or we'd better stay at home and devote our brains and energies to preparations for the Third World War. 30

A fundamental reorientation of the government's information policy had also figured prominently among Kennan's recommendations. But he had advocated it in order to dispel the hysterical American response to Soviet action;31 in his view this was a precondition of realistic diplomatic adjustment. Kennan underestimated, however, the crucial symbolic dimension of politics, the problems of quiescence and arousal that set decisive parameters for political action.

Clayton's analysis, on the other hand, emphasized the importance of a thoroughly unsettling emotional experience in producing widespread acceptance of the reordered political priorities. Indeed, Secretary of State Marshall's speech to congressional leaders, laying out the facts on the situation in Greece and Turkey, failed to persuade them—but Acheson's mythical dramatization turned the tide at the crucial February 27 meeting. The Secretary of State rejected the allegations of some congressional leaders who, eager to reduce taxes, metaphorically described new American commitments abroad as "pulling British chestnuts out of the fire."

"Only two great powers remained in the world," Acheson continued, "the United States and the Soviet Union. We had arrived at a situation unparalleled since ancient times. Not since Rome and Carthage had there been such a polarization of power on this earth. Moreover the two powers were divided by an unbridgeable ideological chasm. For us, democracy and individual liberty are basic; for them dictatorship and absolute conformity. And it was clear that the Soviet Union was aggressive and expanding. For the United States to take steps to strengthen countries threatened with Soviet aggression or Communist subversion was not to pull British chestnuts out of the fire; it was to protect the security of the United States.' [32]

When Acheson was done the mood had changed. Vandenberg declared that he had been "greatly impressed, even shaken" [33] and that aid to Greece and Turkey were only part of a much wider picture. Acheson's metaphor had hit home.

Like apples in a barrel infected by one rotten one, the corruption of Greece would infect Iran and all to the east. It also would carry infection to Africa through Asia minor and Egypt and to Europe through Italy and France . . . [34]

Vandenberg was not only persuaded by Acheson's presentation but also felt that any request for funds "should be accompanied by a message to Congress and an explanation to the American people in which the grim facts of the larger situation should be laid publicly on the line as they had been at their meeting there that day."[35] When President Truman addressed Congress on March 12 in order to request support for the "Truman Doctrine," the national security rationale—mentioned as early as the second sentence of the message—provided the background for the mythical phrasing of conflict.

At the present moment in world history nearly every nation must choose between alternative ways of life. . . . I believe that it must be the policy of the United States to support free peoples who are resisting attempted subjugation by armed minorities or by outside pressures. I believe that we must assist free peoples to work out their own destinies. . . . It is necessary only to glance at a map to realize that the survival and integrity of the Greek nation are of great importance in a much wider situation. If Greece should fall under the control of an armed minority, the effect upon its neighbor Turkey would be immediate and serious. Confusion and disorder might well spread throughout the entire Middle East. Moreover, the disappearance of Greece as an independent state would have a profound effect upon those countries in Europe whose peoples are struggling against great difficulties to maintain their freedoms and their independence while they repair the damages of war.[36]

Although the administration was eager in subsequent hearings to dispel the impression that the Truman Doctrine was a "pattern out of a tailor's shop to fit everybody,"[37] a rather significant expansion in the concept of United States security interests had found official recognition. "By interpreting security as a function not only of a balance of power between states but of the internal order maintained by states and not only by some states but by all states, the Truman Doctrine equated America's security with interests that evidently went well beyond conventional security requirements."[38]

Oddly enough, it might have been the Marshall Plan rather than the more sweeping Truman Doctrine that fueled Stalin's suspicions and led him to translate his mythical vision of the "two camps" into repressive measures at home.[39] This interpretation is borne out by the lack of Soviet reaction to the announcement of the Truman Doctrine. True, Izvestia took issue with Truman's interpretation of events in Greece,[40] but Stalin did not mention the President's message to Congress in any of the discussions he had with Americans in early 1947. He complained neither to Elliot Roosevelt nor to Harold Stassen nor to Secretary of State Marshall about the sweeping redefinition of American security interests. Although the replacement of British influence by United States influence in the Eastern Mediterranean was surely not to his liking, Stalin was realistic enough to recognize that very little had changed in the actual distribution of power. This was especially true in view of the fact that the Greek insurrection had not been approved by Moscow, a fact Stalin took care to conceal from the West as it would have disproved the carefully cultivated myth that all communist parties paid obedience to Moscow.

The effect of the Marshall Plan seemed to be quite different. After a period of vacillation, Stalin apparently decided that this plan posed an actual threat to his exclusive domain in Eastern Europe, as Polish and Czech interests seemed to indicate.[41] Economic aid, especially if administered in a supranational fashion as envisaged by the Marshall Plan, would have undone the rather crudely spun ties of Eastern Europe's economic dependence upon Moscow. Besides, the procedures outlined for arriving at an estimate of the consolidated deficit of all recipients would have revealed Soviet economic vulnerability.[42] Faced with a threat—or what he believed to be a threat—to his domain, Stalin reacted in the very same fashion as he had directly after the war, when widespread hopes for Soviet liberalization had endangered his power position.

At that time, the steps Stalin had taken to preserve "the political system were swift and decisive. Soviet prisoners of war who had been exposed to close contact with Westerners were sent to labor camps.[43] The military was put in its place by the discovery that victory in the Great Patriotic War had not been the work of the Red Army or of the superior leadership of such Marshals as Zhukov or Vasilevski,[44] but of Stalin's genius. And finally, by 1947/1948 the arts and sciences were brought to "reason" by Zhdanov's vicious attacks. How much the Soviets feared contamination by Western ideas can be seen in the following passage from Zhdanov's essay on philosophy, which was originally a speech delivered at a conference on philosophy called by the Central Committee in June 1947.

> Contemporary bourgeois science supplies clericalism, supplies fideism with new arguments which must be mercilessly exposed. . . . Many followers of Einstein, in their failure to understand the dialectical process of knowledge, transpose the results of the study of the laws of motion of the finite limited sphere of the universe and arrive at the idea of the finite nature of the world, its limitedness in time and space. Today the center of the struggle against Marxism has shifted to America and England. All the forces of obscurantism and reaction have now been placed at the service of the struggle against Marxism. Brought anew and placed at the service of bourgeois philosophy are the instruments of the atom and dollar democracy—the outworn armor of obscurantism and clericalism: the Vatican and racist theory, rabid nationalism and decayed idealist philosophy, the mercenary

yellow press and depraved bourgeois art. Today under the banner of ideological struggle against Marxism large reserves are being mobilized. Gangsters, pimps, spies and criminal elements are recruited. [45]

It was clearly the internal threats he perceived rather than specific foreign policy measures in Western Europe that confirmed Stalin's suspicions and promoted a mythical conception of politics. In contrast to the West, which hoped for an international order founded on the universal recognition of liberal democratic constitutionalism, Stalin seems to have been ready for a postwar settlement only if it guaranteed his absolute security from dangerous Western influences. Kennan's analysis was probably correct, that Soviet expansion proceeded from a feeling of insecurity and backwardness, necessitating absolute rather than indirect control.

For example the West argued that the Polish government was well aware of political constraints imposed on it by Russia's dominant position, and that Poland was most unlikely to take up an anti-Soviet stance. But Stalin justified his controls by remarking at Potsdam that "a freely elected government in any of the (Eastern European) countries would be anti-Soviet—and that we cannot allow." [46]

In short, as shown by the purges he made before the Molotov-Ribbentrop pact, Stalin might have been amenable to diplomatic deals but only when he had established absolute control and secured the elimination of rivals who might challenge his position by interpreting international reality in a different fashion. What Stalin especially feared was that an economically strong Western Europe might eventually create a magnetic attraction for the Eastern European countries, thus endangering the Soviet Union's position in the long run. This is reflected in Andrei Vishinsky's denunciation of the Marshall Plan before the United Nations General Assembly on September 18, 1947.

> Moreover this plan is an attempt to split Europe into two camps and, with the help of the United Kingdom and France, to complete the formulation of a bloc of several European countries hostile to the interests of the democratic countries of Eastern Europe and most particularly to the interests of the Soviet Union. [47]

Such an indictment of the formation of blocs must have

sounded hypocritical even to a Soviet spokesman, for it was
exactly the polarization of world politics that had been the official
Soviet line since 1946 when Stalin and Zhdanov had revived the
"two camp" theory of international relations. At the foundation
of the Cominform, too, Zhdanov expounded the importance of
the emerging bipolar configuration.

> The more the war recedes into the past, the more distinct
> become two major trends in postwar international policy,
> corresponding to the division of the political forces of the
> international arena into two major camps; the imperialist and
> anti-democratic camp on the one hand and the anti-imperialist
> and democratic camp on the other. The principal driving force of
> the imperialist camp is the U.S.A. Allied with it are Great Britain
> and France. . . . The anti-fascist forces comprise the second camp.
> The camp is based on the U.S.S.R. and the new democracies.[48]

Confronted with the challenge of revitalized West European
economies and faced with the apparent interest of some of the
"people's democracies" in the West's economic program, the
Kremlin required an immediate effective centralization of
authority. Under such circumstances the "domesticism"[49]
prevalent among the East European communist parties was no
longer tolerable. Secret police control, familiar in Stalin's
Russia, was now extended to the Eastern bloc. During the next
year, the last reminders of a free and democratic political life
were erased there. Independent political initiatives of East
European communists were no longer accepted by Stalin, as Tito
and Dimitrov were soon to find out. Eastern European
enthusiasm for a Balkan federation, an old dream dating back to
the time of the Comintern,[50] obviously irked Stalin, especially
when even Poland and Rumania showed interest. Sensing a
challenge to his supremacy, Stalin promptly withdrew his
imprimatur from this design. Dimitrov and the Yugoslavs were
ordered to appear in Moscow, where Stalin accused Dimitrov of
acting like a "young Komsomol member" or as if he were still
the "Secretary of the Comintern."[51] Dumbfounded but
remorseful, Dimitrov and his Yugoslav companions admitted
mistakes; but as Stalin brutally pointed out, "mistakes are not
the issue: the issue is conceptions which are different from our
own."[52]

In view of the mounting tension with Yugoslavia during the

summer of 1948, the Soviet example was more and more emphasized and the former stress on an "independent road to Socialism" was discredited. Consequently, one of the most serious charges brought against the Yugoslavs during the controversy leading to their expulsion from the Cominform was their "inadequate understanding" of the role of the CPSU and U.S.S.R. [53]

As the heightened international tensions that resulted from the vigorous suppression of a viable opposition in Eastern Europe seemed to confirm the mythical prediction of a plotting enemy trying to subvert "socialism," the identification of the interests of those countries with that of the "fatherland of socialism" seemed once more compelling. Even the French Communist Party, not under Stalin's immediate and coercive control, fell duly in line. In 1948 Maurice Thorez, the French Communist leader, stated that French Communists would not fight against the Soviet Union and would even actively support the Red Army if it occupied French territory in a future war. [54] Such assertions, together with the French and Italian communist parties' invitations to full participation in the Cominform, were taken by the West—and quite correctly so—as ominous signs of Communist militancy. That such fears and suspicions were not entirely unwarranted was shown by an account of the discussions of the Cominform published by the Italian Communist Eugenio Reale, who, along with Luigi Longo, had participated in the founding of the Cominform in Szklarska Poreba in September 1947. [55] This account revealed that the Italian and French communist parties were indicted for their "loss of revolutionary character" and their failure to try to "seize power"; it also revealed that the Cominform meeting was called not only to consolidate communist power in Eastern Europe but also to organize "propaganda and struggle by all means available against American assistance in Europe." [56]

If this analysis is correct, then some apparent contradictions in Soviet behavior can be explained. First of all, harsh domestic measures and a "thaw" in foreign relations need not exclude each other, as foreign observers often assume. On the contrary, the above considerations indicate that suppression of internal opposition is to a certain extent the precondition for an external adjustment. Second, this analysis helps to explain why a diplomatic adjustment to postwar realities took so long. Only

after the East as well as the West accepted the effective division
of Europe and the unchallenged right of each superpower to an
exclusive sphere of influence, could fears subside and a tacit
arrangement evolve. As long as each side saw in the bargaining
offer of the other only a sign of weakness, which had to be
exploited in order to reverse the political facts of life, no serious
settlement was possible. Thus, whereas the East saw the
Marshall Plan as a plot against its own existence, the West
refused to discuss Moscow's interest in a settlement of the
German questions on terms that would have meant the loss of
Germany from the Western alliance.[57]

These considerations suggest that a dynamic Western policy
intended to penetrate the Iron Curtain—whether by a "rollback"
or more recently by "little steps" leading to a "change through
rapprochement"—would have very little chance of advancing
beyond the official legitimization of the *de facto* political
situation. The invasion of Czechoslovakia, where internal
dynamism followed a thaw in external relations—especially with
West Germany—demonstrated that Moscow is unlikely to allow
the pursuit of both internal liberalization and external
rapprochement for any length of time.[58] Similarly, West
German hopes for a normalization of relations with East
Germany, including wider opportunities for East-West contact,
have been disappointed in spite of the *Grundvertrag*; and
Soviet-American detente[59] has produced a considerable
hardening of the Soviet stance on internal liberalization.

Because of their second image conceptualization of
international politics, the Western powers did not perceive the
incompatibility of internal liberalization and external diplomatic
adjustment in the "theory" that informs Soviet decision-making.
As a matter of fact, the selection of containment as the major
decision-premise of Western policy was, in my view, due to an
ingenious blending of these two eagerly pursued goals. When
experience eventually showed the contradictory implications of
the containment nexus, the two goals could be pursued
separately without necessarily violating the well-established
containment policy. Thus, on the one hand it became possible to
advocate a general European settlement, as Kennan himself did
in his Reith[60] lectures (external adjustment); on the other hand,
those decision-makers mainly concerned with the "building of
strength" in order to ferment internal changes in the Soviet

Union could also invoke the containment metaphor. Thus, a more detailed discussion of this important decision premise seems to be in order.

3. Metaphors

a. Containment

In our discussion of myths and metaphors as inference guidance devices, we saw that myths are "dramatic stories" that provide a meaningful frame of reference for the interpretation of events, while the structurally less complicated metaphors more clearly reflect the actual decision-premise (or at least the decision-premise which the actor wants to communicate to his opponent). This nexus between myth and metaphor and metaphor and actual decisions is clarified in the following discussion of a policy that was essentially based upon a particularly instructive metaphor and fitted well into the authoritatively selected myth. Here, naturally, we are talking about the policy of containment, which promised to bridge the gap between the universal aspirations of the Truman Doctrine and day-to-day policy actions, for which abstract principles provided little guidance. Actual political practice somehow had to be shown to be in accordance with the socially accepted interpretation of reality so that political actions could be understood as attempts to change reality's most undesirable aspects. Thus, the containment thesis of Kennan's *Foreign Affairs* article added little either to the Long Telegram's analysis or to actual decision-making, as Acheson ironically remarked.[61] But by molding the perceptions first of decision-makers and then of the attentive public, and by suggesting a clearer means-end relationship for policy actions, it gave containment nearly doctrinal standing. The key phrase in this exposition was

. . It is clear that the main element of any United States policy toward the Soviet Union must be that of a long term patient but firm and vigilant containment of Russian expansive tendencies. . . .

Soviet pressure against the free institutions of the Western world is something that can be contained by the adroit and vigilant application of counterforce at a series of constantly shifting geographical and political points corresponding to the shifts and maneuvers of Soviet policy. . . . In the light of these circumstances the thoughtful observer of Russian-American

relations will find no cause for complaint in the Kremlin's
challenge to American society. He will rather experience a certain
gratitude to a Providence which by providing the American people
with this implacable challenge has made their entire security as a
nation dependent on their pulling themselves together and
accepting the responsibilities of moral and political leadership
that history plainly intended them to bear.[62]

Here the decision-premise of the "vigilant application of
counterforce" is clearly tied to the "mission" that history has
conferred upon the American nation. Many of the
"misunderstandings" that Kennan tries to correct in his
Memoirs spring from his rather sweeping characterization of
American interests. The aspiration underlying this policy is
clearly global in scope, and the lack of territorial
specificity—Kennan lamented later that he forgot to mention
that containment referred only to Europe—is perhaps not so
accidental.[63] There seems, after all, to be an intrinsic link
between the decision-metaphor of containment and the
mythically conceived historical process, as can be gathered from
the following passages:

> . . . the possibilities for American policy are by no means limited
> to holding the line and hoping for the best. It is entirely possible
> for the United States to influence by its actions the internal
> developments both within Russia and throughout the
> international Communist movement by which Russian policy is
> largely determined. . . . the United States has in its power to
> increase enormously the strains under which Soviet policy must
> operate to force upon the Kremlin a far greater degree of
> moderation and circumspection . . . and in this way to promote
> tendencies which must eventually find their outlet in either the
> break up or the gradual mellowing of Soviet power.[64]

As important as Kennan's prescription for American foreign
policy was, his use of metaphors to describe a Soviet
decision-making process that could be influenced by American
actions was perhaps his most influential contribution.[65]

Soviet political action, wrote Kennan, "is a fluid stream which
moves constantly wherever it is permitted to move toward a
given goal. Its main concern is to make sure that it has filled
every nook and cranny available to it in the basin of world
power."[66] He described the "whole Soviet governmental

machine" as "moving along the prescribed path" once a policy line has been laid down, and likened this process to "a persistent toy automobile wound up and headed in a given direction, stopping only when it meets some unanswerable force."[67]

Without reviving the debate on the meaning of the containment policy, it still is clear that all the major themes running through the discussion of American foreign policy during subsequent years can already be found in Kennan's "X" article. There is first of all the idea that the Soviet threat consists in a challenge to the vitality and viability of the American political and social system. The appropriate answer to this challenge is therefore the demonstration that America, the "beacon of freedom," can set an example of a just political order at home and thus claim moral leadership in the world. Although this tradition never became official policy, it is a recurrent theme among "dissenters" from Henry Wallace to George McGovern.

The second strand of thought, which became dominant after the Korean War and was in its heyday under Secretary of State John Foster Dulles, was that "world communism" might be contained not only by building alliances as dams against the communist flood all over the world, but also by taking the domestic-change thesis of Soviet foreign policy literally. Pressuring the communist movement in various geographical areas would crack the monolithic structure of the Soviet regime, and Soviet influence could then be not only contained but "rolled back." The link Kennan had established between Soviet policy and the world communist movement made Dulles' policy—despite its new and inflammatory "liberation" rhetoric—part of the established containment syndrome.

Finally, containment could be interpreted as a prescription to prevent further Soviet political or military encroachments by building up "positions of strength" that could maintain the status quo and preserve the option of a diplomatic adjustment at some future date. This seemed to be the main rationale of Acheson's policy. To that extent Kennan's and Acheson's views were not so far apart as it might have seemed at first. Where they differed was on how to build the strength necessary for containment: Acheson, after the Korean experience,[68] increasingly emphasized military power as the key ingredient of strength, whereas Kennan objected to this "militarization" of foreign policy. They also offered different assessments of the chances for fruitful negotiations: Similarly, Kennan insisted on a European settlement along the lines of a "disengagement" in the late 1950's;[69] Acheson believed that time was on the side of the West and that delaying negotiations would be beneficial.[70]

Consequently, at that time American foreign policy was mainly concerned with tying Germany and Japan to the Western Bloc. The link between this rather sudden impetus to "rehabilitate" the former enemies and global power considerations is clearly reflected in Acheson's account.

> To me one conclusion seemed plain beyond doubt. Western Europe and the United States could not contain the Soviet Union and suppress Germany and Japan at the same time. Our best hope was to make these former enemies willing and strong supporters of a free world structure. Germany should be welcomed into Western Europe not kept in limbo outside as had been the case after the war of 1914-18, relegated to maneuvering between the Soviet Union and the allies. If the former was to be done Western Europe must become more than a phrase.[71]

The German Social Democratic leader Kurt Schumacher, who strongly opposed such integration because he felt that only a Germany neutralized between the power blocs had a chance of reuniting with the Eastern zone, was told quite bluntly by Acheson that

> . . . an attempt by the Social Democratic Party to curry favor with the voters or the Russians by baiting the occupation would be given short shrift. . . . If he believed that the occupation would tolerate an attempt to play the Western allies and the Russians off against one another he would find himself mistaken.[72]

But because Adenauer[73] as well as Robert Schuman[74] shared Acheson's view—although probably for different reasons—there was little official opposition to the integration of Western European coal and steel production.[75]

Similarly, under the impact of Korea, President Truman decided to initiate negotiations on a Japanese peace treaty. John Foster Dulles, the U.S. Chief negotiator, was charged with the task "to secure the adherence of the Japanese nation to the free nations of the world and to assure that it will play its full part in resisting the further expansion of communist imperialism."[76]

What finally emerged from Philippine fears of a revitalized Japan, Australian preferences for bilateral United States defense ties against a rearmed Japan, and British requests for guarantees of its possessions in Malaya and Hongkong, was a United States-Japanese security arrangement and a tripartite defense agreement among the United States, Australia and New Zealand aimed at external aggression. The building of positions of "strength" had been expanded to the Pacific.

The next round in the European theater was the Western announcement in September 1951 that Germany would be invited to provide troops for a European defense plan. [77] The Soviet response was swift and rather effectively presented. Drafted with the help of the Soviet envoy to Eastern Germany, a plan making vague promises of Soviet concessions on German reunification in return for the acceptance of neutrality and the Oder Neisse border was submitted by East German leader Otto Grothewohl. [78] Subsequent West German sounding concerning the prospects of free elections were however rebuffed and Adenauer[79] as well as Acheson sensed a trap: the Western European integration was to be undone.

Exaggerated as these fears might seem to an observer[80] with the advantage of hindsight, it is nevertheless true that the West's "loss" of Germany would have entailed far-reaching changes in the newly emerging international system. In particular, neutralization of Germany would have brought out the conflicting interests of the other European countries with regard to Germany, a conflict that was muted by American predominance in the Western bloc.[81]

When in 1957/1958 some plans for a neutralization of Germany were circulated in the context of the "disengagement" debate, Secretary of State Dulles dismissed such speculations in the following words:

> We do not think well of the concept of a so-called disengagement because of the fact that the practical application of it would be to neutralize or demilitarize Germany and we do not think that it is either a desirable or practical thing to do. . . . I do not think that it has any intrinsic merit as a safeguard against war. . . . I think that an attempt to neutralize a great nation like Germany would be almost certain to come to trouble. . . . My own feeling about Germany is that Germany is not safe for the world unless

Germany is tied to other countries in some way that there cannot
be a disengagement. But to say that Germany is going to be a safe
country neutralized I think is a most dangerous concept. If I had to
choose between a neutralized Germany and Germany in the
Soviet bloc, it might be almost better to have it in the bloc. That
clearly is not acceptable but disengagement is absolutely not
acceptable either.[82]

Thus the continuity of American foreign policy was not
interrrupted during the Eisenhower years.[83] "Containment"
focused increasingly on Washington's overriding concern to
reinforce the solidity of the Western bloc, and moved away from
the domestic change thesis or the diplomatic adjustment thesis,
despite public assurances that a "roll back" of Soviet influence
and the "liberation" of Eastern Europe were strategic goals of
American foreign policy. The next section will show why this was
so.

b. *Liberation and "Capitalist Encirclement"*
In 1953, when the Eisenhower administration took office,
domestic as well as international circumstances were rather
inauspicious for an accommodation with the Soviet Union, even
though United States strength vis-a-vis the Soviet Union was at
its height and should have worked to the advantage of the West
in any negotiation.[84] The American homeland was still
invulnerable, as the Soviets had not yet acquired an adequate
delivery capability for their modest nuclear stockpile; United
States arms expenditures had risen sharply due to the Korean
War; and NATO's conventional forces promised to grow
vigorously during the next few years.[85] The fact that no
negotiations were initiated only shows once more that military
strength may not readily lend itself to conversion into political
influence or bargaining strength; negotiation, as a means of
accommodating[86] wills, presupposes not only negotiable issues
but also the political will to exert pressures as well as to make
compromises.

A particular set of circumstances however made most of the
virulent issues increasingly non-negotiable. The "loss of China"
left bipartisan foreign policy, universally regarded as a
precondition of effective maneuvering on the international plane,
in a virtual shambles. Senator McCarthy gained more and more
popularity with his mythical vision of "a conspiracy so immense

and an infamy so black as to dwarf any previous such venture in the history of man."[87]

Things were not much better on the other side since Stalin's fear of a "zionist conspiracy" had reached pathological proportions, causing even the slightest attempt at accommodation with the West to be branded as a betrayal of "revolutionary vigilance." After having received the fabricated "confessions" of the "doctor plotters," Stalin told the other Politbureau members: "You are blind like kittens; what will happen without me? The country will perish because you do not know how to recognize enemies."[88]

Thus the anxiety created by domestic events—the present-day observer is struck by the fear of a monstrous "conspiracy" on both sides—reinforced the mythical conception of politics that had become dominant after the war. On the Soviet side, "activists" demanded an "intensification of the offensive against the positions of reaction and not concessions to reaction and the reactionary classes."[89] Slogans like "liberation" and "roll back," on the American side, were hardly more conducive to a diplomatic settlement. The new administration's election platform, which had been drafted by its later Secretary of State, promised to

end the negative futile and immoral policy of "containment" which abandoned countless human beings to a despotism and Godless terrorism which in turn enables the rulers to forge the captives into a weapon for our destruction. . . . The policies we espouse will revive the contagious, liberating influences which are inherent in freedom. They will inevitably set up strains and stresses within the captive world which will make the rulers impotent to continue in their monstrous way and mark the beginning of the end.[90]

Such hyperbolic statements were, in moments of greater sobriety, balanced by attempts to distinguish "liberation" from armed insurrection. "We do not want a series of bloody uprisings and reprisals," Dulles stated in an article in Life magazine. "There can be peaceful separation from Moscow as Tito showed, and enslavement can be made so unprofitable that the master will let go his grip."[91]

Whatever the intentions of this "liberation" strategy might have been, the bluff was soon called when Soviet tanks quelled disturbances in Eastern Germany in June 1953. Consequently, what emerged from discussions within the Eisenhower administration during the summer and fall of 1953 was a reaffirmation of containment as the appropriate strategy for dealing with the communist world, with the understanding that in the future American power might play a somewhat larger role, actively or as a deterrent;[92] the "liberation" strategy consisting of vigorous psychological, economic and paramilitary measures was, after review, explicitly rejected.

Nevertheless, Dulles persisted in using the rhetoric of "liberation" for a variety of reasons. First of all, he seems to have believed that only by characterizing every issue as a critical one for "democratic universalism" could the West master the Soviet challenge. As he once confided to a State Department official:

> If there's no evident menace from the Soviet Bloc our will to maintain unity and strength may weaken. It's a fact, unfortunate though it be, that in promoting our programs in Congress we have to make evident the internationsl communist menace. Otherwise such programs as the mutual security one would be decimated. The same situation would probably prevail among our allies.[93]

Thus, it was not so much his particular brand of moralism that led Dulles to an ideological conceptualization of the conflict of interest between the U.S.S.R. and the United States, as it was his conviction that ideology was a powerful mobilizing factor that the West could not forego in its struggle with an opponent whose ideological prowess was much feared and admired.[94] One might take issue with Dulles' particular strategy, but the danger of Western disunity, should the conflict with a clearly identifiable mythical opponent lose its compelling character, was far from imaginary. It remained for a far less ideologically oriented statesman, Harold Macmillan, to find the fitting metaphor for such dangers. When the French Parliament failed to endorse the European Defense Community, he wrote in his diary, "It looks as if Europe was breaking up under Malenkov's sunshine. Stalin's icy blast kept it together."[95]

A second reason why Dulles clung to the rhetoric of "liberation" was apparently his feeling that a merely passive containment policy would endow the status quo in Europe with legitimacy, and relinquish the political initiative to the other side. Te opponent would then have not only "the advantage of the offensive" but also the chance to "push the redivision of the world, picking the time and place for its offensive and knowing that it can consolidate its gains at leisure."[96]

Indeed, the denial of legitimacy to the status quo increased in importance for Dulles as time passed and as actual changes became less and less likely. Negotiations therefore focused more and more on what one calls "side effects" in bargaining theory, rather than on the substantive issues[97] for which negotiations were supposedly undertaken. Before the Geneva summit meeting in 1955, Dulles drafted four short papers which show that he deemed the substantive conflict over Germany non-negotiable. His bargaining goals therefore stressed the prevention of a Soviet propaganda advantage. Paper I, entitled "United States Goals," stated the overriding objective as: "Progress toward the unification of Germany under conditions which will neither 'neutralize' nor 'demilitarize' a united Germany nor subtract it as the most important Soviet goals:

> 1) An appearance that the West concede the Soviet rulers a moral and social equality which will help the Soviets maintain their satellite rule by disheartening potential resistance and help them increase neutralism by spreading the impression that only "power" rivalries and not basic principles create present tensions. (U.S. against, U.K. and France indifferent.)
> 2) A general relaxing of the military and Cold War activities of the Western nations providing the Soviets with a needed "moratorium" to use for bettering their internal position, economically and governmentally. (U.S. and U.K. against, France for.)[99]

Thus the "liberation" and "roll back" policies seemed to hold out to the American electorate, as well as to the "captive peoples" abroad, the prospects of "other, less painful and far more moral ways of obtaining the objectives of American foreign policy than contemplating any settlement with Russia, even one negotiated from a position of strength."[100] The underlying assumption of this reasoning, in accordance with the mythical conception, was clearly that Soviet power must not be taken at face value: the monolithic posture of the Kremlin covered up serious internal weaknesses which could be exploited by the "adroit and vigilant application of counterforce."[101]   This assumption was not new. It was basically an elaboration of the "domestic change" thesis. But wishful thinking—together with the favorable shift in the East-West balance of forces following the Marshall Plan and the military buildup in 1950—had transformed the domestic change thesis into a theory of the imminent virtual collapse of Soviet power. Long before Dulles' Congressional testimony to that effect,[102] a book by James Burnham, published in 1950 and entitled *The Coming Defeat of Communism,* developed the "disintegration" theseis in full detail.[103]   Burnham   stressed,   like   Dulles   after   him,   the importance of "refugee liberation movements."[104] He also emphasized the importance of what he called "the political offensive"[105] against an "outwardly strong" but internally weak, because "overextended," communist regime.

> There is an additional and profound potential weakness, which I have briefly touched on, inherent in what might be called the dynamics of communism. A totalitarian enterprise is by nature highly unstable. Once well under way it cannot stand still, it cannot even move equably. *It must* retain the initiative . . . if the fierce rhythm is broken, if the opponents are not unbalanced but cool and determined, then the totalitarian current can reverse and with the same impetus sweep smashingly back through the whole monstrous structure.[106]

Burnham's book, an instant success, was widely read and discussed in Washington circles. Needless to say, its analysis is rather superficial and the image it projects of the opponent fits a mythical archetype more closely than the actual "enemy." It pictures the oppressive present as a prelude to the decisive struggle, which can only be won by a certain type of knowledge that "unmasks" the enemy in a moment of crisis, revealing his true nature to all. But this knowledge is not based on objective analysis or dispassionate insight; it is practical knowledge[107] embodied in a "plan of action" that foreshadows the sequence of events in a dramatic story.[108] Liberation   is then as   much "self-liberation" from one's own exaggerated fears of the opponent as it is liberation from his actual power. What makes this scheme for interpreting the course of events so compelling is not only the promise of final success but the thesis that a decisive reversal of the grim situation can be brought about without large scale violence against the enemy. On the contrary, the opponent can be defeated simply by taking a new attitude towards him, as his ever-present influence is due not so much to his objective strength as to one's own weakness. Nowhere does the relationship between psychodynamics and the construction of "objective" reality become so clear as here.

In keeping with these considerations, Dulles tried "to build upon the national mood of anxiety a sense of moral urgency and missionary zeal."[109] Only the gambit that Soviet power was overextended and therefore weak seemed to provide a ray of hope.

Events following Stalin's [110] death in March 1953 seemed to confirm the correctness of this outlook. Malenkov's announcement of peaceful coexistence and his shift of emphasis from heavy industry to consumer goods, which Eisenhower called a "startling departure from the ways of his predecessors",[111] were called by Dulles mere "tactical retreats."[112] Later he told the President: "What they are doing is because of outside pressures and I do not know anything better than to keep up those pressures right now."[113] When Beria's execution was announced in Moscow in July, Dulles saw a sign that "freedom is again in the air. A new convulsion is under way."[114] A cabinet meeting was told "this is the kind of time when we ought to be doubling our bets, not reducing them—as all the Western Parliaments want to do. This is a time to crowd the enemy—and maybe finish him once for all."[115] Despite the opinion of Ambassador Bohlen, who had stressed to Dulles "that the Bolshevik system" could probably "withstand the stress of Beria's arrest because all the leaders understood the dangers of internecine warfare,"[116] Dulles believed—as many Soviet experts did—that a bloody struggle for power among Stalin's successors might topple the Soviet regime.

In Dulles' recommendation for "doubling our bets" we have a nearly classical example of the situation[117] in which one player signals his willingness to move from the minimax cell to a more cooperative strategy. This announcement, however, does not induce cooperation by the other because it is seen as a sign of weakness that justified raising the level of aspiration, and therefore the choice of uncooperative strategies, during the next rounds. In the same vein, Eisenhower, in his address to the American Society of Newspaper Editors on April 16, 1953, raised the stakes by listing several rather unrealistic preconditions of any real detente. [118]

What Soviet intentions at that time actually were is difficult to judge. The conclusion of a Korean armistice and rumors that Malenkov and Beria might accept a deal on Germany [119] suggest that the Soviets might have been willing to make significant concessions. Yet, given Soviet and American preferences, it is hard to imagine that a solution to the European dilemma deviating significantly from the status quo could have been found. As Molotov's moves during the next months of 1953 showed, Soviet foreign policy was still directed at removing American influence from Western Europe. The Soviets rebuffed Austria's feelers about an agreement to end the occupation in return for an Austrian promise to maintain a "Swiss type" of neutrality; Molotov told Krishna Menon, the Indian ambassador who served as a go-between, that "neutrality alone was insufficient." [120] Besides, a Soviet foreign policy directed explictly at the relaxation of tensions as a precondition for domestic reforms offended various party factions: Malenkov was swept out of power.

Although Nikita Khrushchev later reintroduced many of Malenkov's policies that he had once attacked, it is rather obvious that for any Soviet leader of that period the margin for foreign maneuvers must have been extremely limited. This made an extensive revision of the status quo through diplomatic bargaining very unlikely. The Soviet leadership had to stress "continuity" [121] with the previous policy line for domestic reasons; but it also had to maintain a rather unyielding negotiating posture, because any significant relaxation of its position might have been interpreted as a new sign to double the bets on the Western side. Consequently, Soviet leaders not only rejected the West's intimation that the new direction of Soviet foreign policy was due to Russian weakness, [122] but also felt bound to display their own militancy, thereby demonstrating their firm rejection of the "domestic change" thesis. [123] Thus, Soviet preconditions for the lessening of tensions were in turn impossible for the West to accept. At a press conference on November 13, 1953, Molotov had outlined the Soviet position: it included demands for United States' withdrawal from Europe, the abolition of NATO and all "bases abroad", the diplomatic recognition of China, North Korea, Mongolia and North

Vietnam, and the explicit recognition of Eastern Europe as an exclusive Soviet sphere of influence, backed by a "hands off the socialist countries" [124] policy in the West.

The crucial point for Western as well as Soviet foreign policy remained the status of Germany. Each party wanted to change the status quo to its advantage but deemed its position on the German issue for all intents and purposes non-negotiable. In fact, Soviet diplomacy during 1954 and 1955 up until the Geneva summit conference was directed toward preventing the ratification of the Paris and London agreements, which integrated Germany fully into the Western defense structure.

One might take exception with this interpretation of the period between 1953 and 1955, which stresses the non-negotiability of the German issue for both sides. After all, Beria seems to have made some plans for a German deal. But, as we have seen, this was part of his bid for power; and the fact that neither he nor the far less hated Malenkov could find enough support for a more moderate policy makes it seem very unlikely that any contender for power could have accomplished such a foreign policy turnabout. Even in the Soviet Union, the power position of a Stalin, who could pursue a Machiavellian foreign policy without regard to domestic opposition, is, historically speaking, the exception. A second objection to the thesis developed above could be based on the dramatic Soviet shift on the Austrian question, which seems at first to be a valid counterfactual example. But a closer look shows that Austria was the price the Soviets were willing to pay in order to prevent Germany from joining the Western military bloc. As Bulganin freely admitted, it was the *German* problem that led to a revision of the previous Soviet stance, which had rejected a Swiss type of neutrality as unacceptable. Noting that for the Russians the Austrian problem had been closely linked to the German issue, on which agreement was impossible, Bulganin stated: "It was only the newest development—West Germany's joining NATO—that brought about a new situation." [125] But even this concession, which appears minimal in the context of the overall distribution of power, met strong opposition within the Central Committee; Khrushchev took pains to convince the comrades that not even the Soviet zone of Austria had been part of the socialist camp and that therefore no improper concession had been made. [126] Nevertheless, Molotov doubted "whether the agreement on neutrality (of Austria) was a sensible one . . . It would be a great blunder, he said, if the German issue were to be solved on a similar basis."[127]

During preparations for the summit talks, Soviet officials did their best to dispel the illusions with which the Americans seemed to be approaching the Geneva meeting. Dulles had sounded his "disintegration thesis" again by testifying before Congress that the Soviet economy was "at the point of collapsing,"[128] to which Khrushchev answered, "We are not going with broken legs to Geneva."

On the other hand, the Soviets seem to have had their share of illusions, too, in trying to undo the Paris agreements. Soviet leaders probably assumed that France had accepted German rearmament only with great reluctance—an assumption actually not far off the mark—and that the French might be open to new proposals for a European "collective security system" that would inevitably weaken Germany. Ratification of the Paris agreements in the French National Assembly, the common front of the Western powers at the Geneva conference, and the quick degeneration of the conference itself into a public relations exercise inserted a new tone of realism into Soviet analysis.

From then on, the Kremlin pursued a "two-Germany" policy.[129] The division of Europe was final, as the Hungarian uprising and Western acquiescence in its suppression were soon to show. Sets of rules had emerged that clearly defined intra-and inter-bloc relationships.[130] Accommodation, which was thought to be dependent upon either significant domestic changes or diplomatic adjustment, came about mainly through acquiescence. "It is a melancholic fact," writes Coral Bell, "that both what we believe about ourselves and what we believe about the Russians militated against our ever having been able to negotiate from strength."[131] But acquiescence was not only the result of the Western self-image of reasonableness and obedience to law (which sharply contrasted with the West's image of reckless and irrational Soviet leaders). Acquiescence was also the natural response to an increasing susceptibility to total destruction, which made attempts to negotiate from strength not only unrealistic but suicidal for both superpowers. The mythical conception of World Politics had to be revised. It is to these factors, which became increasingly important in the late 1950's and which led to an accommodation by *default* rather than by a formal declaration of will, that we turn our attention in the next chapter.

VI Doctrines

1. Introduction

The set of inference guidance devices that directed our investigation of Soviet-American relations in the postwar era has been explicated, except for "doctrines." According to Webster's dictionary, doctrine is a "principle . . . or the body of principles in a branch of knowledge or system of belief." When applied to international politics, doctrine is defined as "a statement of fundamental governmental policy." Both definitions, the general as well as the more specific, square well with our earlier discussion of doctrines as a particular sort of inference guidance device. In our effort to distinguish political commitments, as expressed in doctrines, from rules of law, we stated that policies communicated by doctrinal pronouncements are rules "designed to guide inferences toward fixed results, or to use Dewey's term, toward ends in view,"[1] allowing the decision-maker a great deal of latitude as to the means employed and their application.

An emphasis on ends brings into sharp focus the problem of translating available power potential into usable political power for the pursuit of an announced policy, particularly in an environment where goals are largely shaped by the means available. In this context the importance of strategic doctrines becomes visible. To put it differently, "a strategic doctrine must define what objectives are worth contending for and determine the degrees of force appropriate for achieving them."[2] A strategic doctrine is therefore much more than the mere

149

selection of a weapons system (although a hypertrophic concern with the technical components of modern hardware often threatens to overshadow the fundamentally political nature of the strategic debate). Considerations of the opponent's motives as well as estimates of his capabilities, including his ability to mobilize his resources, must enter into strategic calculations. Judgments of "who counts" on what issues must rest on more than military factors. Nevertheless, perceptions of and predictions about what is usually called the "military balance" are major determinants of the state of the international system. As such a system consists basically of patterns of interdependent decision-making among states, and as these interactions in turn are based upon expectations about future interactions, the close connection between strategic doctrines and the international system is not surprising. Stanley Hoffman, for example, delineates international systems by the radical breaks that appear in strategic calculations.[3] A "new" system emerges when "there is a new answer to the question what are the units in potential conflict . . . when there is a new answer to the question what can the units do to one another in a conflict—i.e., when there is a basic change in the technology of conflict . . . when there is a new answer to the question what do the units want to do to one another."[4]

Although, quite obviously, a new weapons technology fundamentally influences the strategic choices available to the players, Hoffmann's stress on the goals of the interacting units correctly emphasizes the political component in strategic calculations, which are not simply deducible from the state of the technological art. Consequently, a doctrine is needed to relate technological givens to political goals.

When we try to apply some of these insights to an investigation of the origins and demise of the Cold War, we see that two factors were of decisive importance in the global system that evolved after the Second World War. There was first the nuclear bomb, which became the "dominant" weapon in that it promised to be decisive in any large-scale show of force. Second, the emergence of new players on the periphery of the two power blocs transformed the prevailing bipolar pattern of world politics, and undermined the perception of the international system in the mythical terms elaborated above.

Both factors, however, display the importance of doctrinal

developments. Thus, despite a revolutionizing military
technology and the nuclear monopoly the United States
enjoyed for some time, that country did not acquire
overwhelming political influence upon postwar international
affairs. This was partly because prevailing strategic doctrines
did not successfully integrate the new weapons into the
diplomatic-strategic calculus, and partly because the Soviet
Union included in its strategic response factors that could not
easily be countered by a preponderance of destructive power.
The illusion of an "atomic diplomacy," perhaps entertained by
Byrnes and Truman, soon came to naught and was replaced by
attempts to "contain" the communist colossus.

   The new peripheral actors that emerged, quickly attained an
importance in the calculations of the dominant powers which was
totally out of proportion to the new states' strategic potential.
This came about because both East and West shared the belief
that stalemate on the European front could only be broken by
bringing the new states into one's own camp. Not until the
mid-sixties did the superpowers realize that the internal
weakness of nearly all Third World regimes, as well as the
volatile character of their politics, meant it would be futile to
make the Third World the decisive arena for competition.
Besides, a more serious challenge meanwhile faced both bloc
leaders. Recognition of the system-transforming character of
nuclear weapons produced, in both blocs, serious challenges by
powers unwilling to be relegated to the status of vassals rather
than full players.[5] Significantly, it was the problem of nuclear
sharing, and the insistence of France and China on their
independent power status, that undermined the traditional
bipolar configuration of power. True, France never
developed—despite all her efforts—the "force valable" de
Gaulle sought, and China may still have far to go before it
achieves this goal. But the deepening Sino-Soviet rift and the
Sino-American rapprochement clearly show that the United
States, China and the Soviet Union are now continuously
engaged in diplomatic-strategic relations. This fact distinguishes
China's status in the international system from that of other
nuclear powers like France and Great Britain: neither France's
nor Britain's policies toward the Soviet Union or China have an
autonomous nuclear dimension.[6] Thus, even in the present
international system which puts a high premium on appearance

rather than intrinsic strength, the atomic bomb has failed to be the great equalizer it was feared and expected to be, due to the implausibility of using nuclear weapons for political advantage.

The following sections intend to develop these thoughts more fully and trace relevant historical developments more extensively. The second section will deal with the problem of nuclear weapons and their impact upon the strategic calculations of the Soviet Union and the United States from the time of the American monopoly to the era of "parity." In section three we will take up the problem of nuclear sharing and the difficulties that arose within each bloc in regard to this problem. Finally, the emergence of new peripheral players will be treated in the fourth section.

2. *The Advent of Deterrence*

When on July 19, 1945, the first nuclear device was exploded at Alamagordo, New Mexico, a new age dawned that was to have revolutionary implications for the future of the international political order. A strategist whose analysis later shaped American strategic policy decisively tried to assess the impact of this new weapon. He came to the following conclusion:

> The first and most vital step in any American security program for the age of atomic bombs is to take measures to guarantee to ourselves in case of attack the possibility of retaliation in kind. The writer in making that statement is not for the moment concerned about who will *win* the next war in which atomic bombs are used. Thus far the chief purpose of our military establishment has been to win wars. From now on its chief purpose must be to avert them. It can have almost no other useful purpose.[7]

Here is the first inkling of an age when, in Churchill's words, "by a process of sublime irony, safety will be the sturdy child of terror and survival the twin brother of annihilation."[8] But at first the new weapons had astonishingly little impact on strategy and on the newly emerging political power equation. True, Japan surrendered after the shocks of Hiroshima and Nagasaki. But it is still a matter of debate whether she had not already reached her capitulation point. Peace feelers had been extended via Moscow, and the Emperor had been willing to surrender.[9] It is this latter point that motivated revisionist historians to charge that the first nuclear bombs were directed not at Japan but at the

Soviet Union,[10] in that they were intended above all to provide an impressive lesson for the Soviets.

Whatever Truman's, Byrnes', or Churchill's hopes might have been, Stalin failed to be impressed although he knew of the new weapon. When informed about "a new weapon of unusual force," he told Truman calmly that he hoped the United States would "make good use of it."[11] Alperovitz's thesis is therefore hardly convincing. Gabriel Kolko aptly points out:

> To postpone the Potsdam meeting mainly for reasons of completing a weapon, a political as well as military tool, was not irrational, but it is plausible as a primary explanation only if the Americans hoped to keep Russia out of the war against Japan, only if they knew the full power of the bomb, only if the Russians were unfamiliar with its development and most important, only if the United States was ultimately willing to employ it against a recalcitrant U.S.S.R. None of these factors prevailed.[12]

The fact that neither Stalin nor Truman seems to have thought the exact timing of the conference to be of crucial importance undermines Alperovitz's argument that American decision-makers were responsible for Stalin's later hostility. His case is also critically weakened by his assumption of Soviet ignorance about the development of nuclear weapons. Betrayed, so the story goes, by allies who were secretly producing a weapon intended to terrorize the Soviet Union, Stalin had good reason for suspicion. In fact, Churchill interpreted Stalin's controlled reaction at Potsdam in such a way.[13] But there is overwhelming evidence that the Soviet Union was well aware of American research developments and had already made substantial progress with its own weapons program.[14] Former Secretary of State Stettinius reported that he "gained the definite impression" from Soviet intelligence activity before the Yalta conference that "the Russians certainly had an idea of what took place"[15] in American nuclear research. Besides, Soviet scientists like Pertzhak, Flerov and Kapitza had done pioneering work in nuclear physics before the war, a special committee on the "problems of uranium"[16] had been set up by the Soviet Academy of Science in 1941, and the decision to build an atomic bomb had been reached in Moscow in the summer of 1942.[17] Furthermore, Marshall Zhukov wrote in his memoirs that Stalin "indeed appreciated the significance of Truman's Potsdam revelation about the American atomic bomb and that Stalin remarked to Molotov that evening that he was going to tell Kurchatov (the physicist in charge of Russia's atomic program) 'to step things up'." [18] Finally, the higher yield of the Soviet "Joe I" bomb indicated that the Russian weapon was not a simple copy of the Los Alamos design but a product of advanced research into high explosives and thermodynamics. [19] This lends some credibility to Dimitrov's statement to Djilas in 1948 "that the Russians had the atom bomb and even a better one than the American one that exploded over Hiroshima"; [20] it also puts to rest the widely held belief that the only way the Soviets could have obtained the secret of the atomic bomb was by treason. [21] However, it also raises doubts about the revisionist assertion that a genuine American offer to share nuclear knowledge, in return for Soviet domestic liberalization or greater freedom for the Eastern European States, could have interested Stalin. He had long ago decided that the Soviet Union needed those "powerful things," [22] and the end of the American nuclear monopoly was already in sight. Despite acrimonious debates in the United Nations and Soviet propaganda invectives against the "atomic diplomacy" of the United States, Stalin's own thinking seems to have been well in tune with a cold-blooded assessment of the strategic situation as a whole. Asked about the impact of the bomb upon international relations, Stalin answered in October 1946:

> Atom bombs are designed to scare those with weak nerves, but they cannot decide wars because there are not enough of them. To be sure, atomic monopoly is a threat, but against it are two remedies: (a) monopoly of the bomb will not last, (b) the use of the bomb will be forbidden. [23]

Western commentators have usually played down such utterances as mere propagandistic cant, but there is good reason to take this statement more seriously, as it offers several important clues as to future Soviet positions. First, predicting the end of the monopoly implied that Soviet research was being vigorously pursued. Furthermore, there is a hint that the Soviet Union might have been well aware of the limited American supply of nuclear bombs. (Only 100 by 1949!) [24] Finally, one can find an indication that the Soviet Union planned to exploit the widespread revulsion against the use of such weapons, inhibiting their utility as a bargaining threat short of a Soviet move against a vital American interest. To that extent, the "Ban the Bomb" movement was a vital check on any attempt at "atomic diplomacy."

That such an assessment of the international strategic situation was by no means fanciful is borne out by Secretary of State Marshall's characterization of the American bargaining position during the March-April Moscow conference of 1947.

> When I was Secretary of State I was being pressed constantly, particularly when in Moscow, . . . by radio message after radio message to give the Russians hell. . . . When I got back, I was getting the same appeal in relation to the Far East and China. At that time, my facilities for giving them hell—and I am a soldier, and know something about the 'ability to give hell—was 1⅓ divisions over the entire United States. That is quite a proposition when you deal with somebody with over 260 and you have 1⅓.25

Most significant of all, however, was the doctrinal lag. The tremendous destructive power of the new military technology was not translated into politically useful strategies. At that time, the new bomb was treated like a typically military factor set apart from any political context, a device that would guarantee "victory" should war break out but that was of no use in deciding the pressing issues of the "peace" to be built. Indicative of this attitude is, for example, the fact that George Kennan as head of the Policy Planning Staff was never told the exact number of nuclear devices available as a potential back-up.26

The predominant image of a future war was still that a strong navy would keep fighting away from the homeland until mobilization and America's superior economic plant could bring its power to bear upon the enemy. Thus in 1949, after the explosion of a Soviet atomic bomb, an American Chief of Staff could still declare: ". . . if there is any single factor today which would deter a nation seeking world domination it would be the great industrial capacity of this country rather than its armed strength."27

American contingency planning during that time shows there was little appreciation of the imperatives of an effective deterrence strategy: deterrence would have emphasized large forces in being rather than mobilization, protection of the retaliatory force rather than the defense of populated areas, and a strike against the enemy's air force rather than against his industrial plant or population centers. But no such measures were taken. The Strategic Air Command had only a few crews trained for nuclear delivery, and its discipline, vigilance and equipment were not well enough developed for a strategy of intimidation rather than defensive war fighting.[28] It was only a series of events in 1949/50 which challenged this image of war. First, the Czech coup and the "loss" of China seemed to signal Soviet expansion despite the deterrent effect of nuclear weapons; the same point was reinforced by the outbreak of the Korean War. Second, uncontrovertible evidence of Soviet nuclear capability obtained in 1949 started within the administration pressures for research and development of a fission bomb. The new quantum jump of this new "dominant weapon" was assessed by Bernhard Brodie in the following terms:

> . . . fission bombs were sufficiently limited in power to make it appear necessary that a substantial number would have to be used to achieve decisive and certain results. That in turn made it possible to visualize a meaningful even if not wholly satisfactory air defense, both active and passive. It was also still necessary to apply the lore so painfully acquired in World War II concerning target selection for a strategic bombing campaign. Even with fission weapons numbering in the hundreds, there was still a real—and difficult—analytical problem in choosing targets that would make the campaign decisive rather than merely hurtful . . . Finally, the functions of ground and naval forces still appeared vital. [29]

Thus thermonuclear bombs, because of their enormous destructive power and their hideous radioactive fallout, made a meaningful "defense" impossible. "There is," declared Winston Churchill in 1955, "an immense gulf between the atomic and the hydrogen bomb. The atomic bomb with all its terror did not carry us outside the scope of human control or manageable events in thought or action, in peace or war."[30] The thermonuclear revolution in military affairs made it clear that these weapons were useless as classical military hardware and at the same time indispensable. By emphasizing deterrence rather than defense as the goal of security policy, thermonuclear weapons shaped decisively the future strategic programs of both sides. They led to the development of new delivery systems (thus starting the ballistic missile race), spurred research in the field of electronic surveillance equipment placed in satellites, and gave new impetus to the notion of "limited war."

True, in the early fifties those developments lay in the future. The stragegic debate in both countries still seems to have focused at that time on the possibility of active defense measures. The Soviet Union perfected its radar system and civil defense, thus considerably downgrading the potential effectiveness of the SAC bomber fleet, which still relied on obsolescent propeller-driven aircraft like the B29 and the B36.[31] In the United States, several studies—such as Project Charles in 1951 and the Civil Defense Summer Study in 1952—also stressed the need for early warning systems and anti-aircraft defense as well as the mass evacuation of the civilian population from large urban centers in crisis situations.[32] Thus, the emphasis on nuclear weapons during the Eisenhower era resulted more from the expected economy of such a military posture than from the clear recognition of the revolutionary implications of the new weapons system. Fearing that the exceedingly costly Korean War had disturbed the country's "great equation"[33] between its military and economic strength, the "New Look" of the Eisenhower administration opted for the idea of deterring future conventional probes by relying on overwhelming retaliatory power. In the words of Dulles' famous "massive retaliation speech"[34] of January, 1954:

> The way to deter aggression is for the free community to respond vigorously at places and with means of its own choosing. We have locks on our doors; but we do not have an armed guard in every home. We rely principally on a community security system, so well equipped to punish any who break in and steal that in fact the aggressors are generally deterred. That is the modern way of getting maximum protection at bearable cost. What the Eisenhower administration seeks is a similar international security system.[35]

The storm of protest that followed this announcement produced several retractions that weakened the intended psychological impact of Dulles' statement. But the debate was characterized by confusion on both sides. Dulles' critics usually tried to demonstrate that he wanted to turn every brushfire-war into an atomic encounter, a strategy without credibility and therefore disastrous for American interests abroad. But, contrary to the prevalent impression, Dulles had never discounted the importance of local defenses and was quick to point out that the threat of strategic retaliation would be very carefully handled. For example, Dulles maintained that the peculiar circumstances of the ongoing Indochina conflict made massive retaliation ''inoperative.''[36]

Also, the impression of an emphasis on more offensive air power, with which the New Look and massive retaliation are commonly identified, needs some correction. Budget outlays for strategic air power were not greater than those of the Truman years. Their increased share in the defense budget was due to the reduction of overall military expenditures.[37] Thus the principal innovation of the New Look was not air power, but oddly enough, continental defense, i.e. the building of an effective radar warning system by which the Eisenhower administration tried to counter the feared Soviet bomber build-up.

It was one of the ironies of evolving strategic thought that these measures proved useful *not* for the protection of the civilian population but for the security of America's second strike force, exactly as the Air Force had predicted a few years earlier.

Those revolutionary implications of a continental defense system emerged as a byproduct of a RAND Corporation study conducted by Albert Wohlstetter and Carl Rowen. In 1951 the Air Force had commissioned a study limited to the question of the cost-effective selection of overseas bases for American bombers. But the longer Wohlstetter worked on this problem, the more apparent it became that ''in the last half of the 1950's the Strategic Air Command, the world's most powerful striking force, faced the danger of obliteration from enemy surprise attack under the then programmed strategic bombing system.''[38] Study R-266, which dominated the internal strategic debates of the Air Force in 1953-54, not only showed the superiority of a United States-based Strategic Air Command, with refueling rather than stationing bases overseas, but also demonstrated that a vital part of any deterrent policy had to be the protection of the deterrent forces rather than the defense of the civilian population. The distinction between a first and a second strike capability emerged as the most important doctrinal innovation of this study.

Still, deterrence did not yet mean "mutual assured destruction." Aside from the understandable resistance to such a strategic innovation, hope persisted that a continental defense system would help protect the civilian population and the industrial plant of the United States as well.

This latter assumption became irrelevant only when the Soviets succeeded in the late 50's with its "Sputnik" in marrying a hydrogen warhead to an intercontinental ballistic missile, making an effective defense of the American homeland rather fanciful. It was this strategic innovation that finally shifted the focus of attention away from defense to the survival of the striking force as the best deterrent element.

Given the Sputnik shock which drove home those unpalatable truths, it was not surprising that cries for higher defense expenditures and greater outlays for a missile-technology superior to that of the Soviet Union were heard. The idea that a missile "race" had to be "won" was shared overwhelmingly by the influential public, an attitude which was in sharp contrast to official policy. Despite alarmist predictions of Soviet military capabilities—e.g. as contained in the Gaither Report[39]—and fears of a "missile gap," the administration opted for a minimum deterrence strategy. In a series of public announcements Eisenhower tried to reassure the public that the "over-all military strength of the free world was distinctly greater than that of the Communist countries"[40] and that therefore it missed the point "to say that we must now increase our expenditures on all kinds of military hardware and defense."[41]

By late May, the United States had positive intelligence about only two missile bases in Russia, the reason for this surprising fact being that the Kremlin had not embarked upon a crash missile program, as originally assumed.[42] By the end of its first year in office, the Kennedy administration[43] — somewhat dumbfounded—tried to place the missile gap controversy in the wider context of American attempts to upgrade its strategic capabilities by means of new control and command procedures[44] as well as by hardening and increasing production of ICBMs. At the same time, European NATO partners were told to contribute more to the conventional force posture of the North Atlantic defense community. All these actions were in line with the imperatives of the newly announced strategic doctrine of "flexible response."

The main outlines of this strategy emerged from President Kennedy's message to Congress on the defense budget (March 28, 1961) [45] and from Defense Secretary McNamara's two speeches in Athens [46] and Ann Arbor [47] (June 16, 1962). The unifying theme of all these official announcements was the interdependence between diplomacy and force, a relatively new development in American strategic thought. This meant creating a second-strike capability, in order to prevent a deliberate nuclear attack, but also conventional and guerrilla forces for contingencies that did not justify the employment of nuclear weapons. [48] The implications of total mutual vulnerability became obvious.

Nevertheless, there were still considerable conceptual difficulties in the new doctrine. First, McNamara's attempt to approach "general nuclear war...in much the same way" as "conventional military operations in the past" [49] was hardly in tune with the officially expounded requirements of a stable deterrence since conventional strategy was mainly a counterforce strategy presupposing the vulnerability of the enemy's retaliatory power. If it was true, as some "of the earlier denunciations of SAC vulnerability had asserted, that it was bad not only for the United States but for the world as a whole," [50] then it is hard to see why the same rationale should not apply to Soviet vulnerability. Furthermore, a city-avoidance strategy can never be a feasible option for an inferior opponent, as the vulnerability and inferiority of his striking power will make a preemptive strike and countervalue targeting necessary. If this is so, then there seems to be a difference between a counterforce and a city-avoidance strategy. McNamara's later conclusion that mutual assured destruction, or the exposure of one's population centers to enemy attack, is the only rational alternative when counterforce capabilities cannot be achieved, need not necessarily follow. [51]

The second problem of the flexible response doctrine was the emphasis on conventional capabilities especially for the defense of Western Europe; it attained new impetus in 1962 when new evidence uncovered by McNamara's sophisticated systems-analysis showed that the image of unlimited Soviet manpower pitted against a few NATO divisions was a gross exaggeration. [52]

Many Europeans had misgivings about the Pentagon's new
"numbers game", which challenged some of their most deeply
entrenched convictions. But McNamara's argument for a drastic
conventional build-up in Europe was open to a more fundamental
objection even if his calculations of Russian strength were
correct. It is not at all obvious that a large-scale conventional war
capability, which would delay the threat of nuclear escalation for
thirty days, should enhance deterrence in Europe. Since such a
battle would be exceedingly destructive, it is not clear what the
employment of nuclear weapons, introduced after a month of
fighting and an appropriate pause, could accomplish.
Khrushchev was also quick to learn that increased Western
conventional forces could be offset without difficulty by
increasing Russian manpower concomitantly or by delaying
scheduled troop reductions. Last but not least, it seems
unreasonable to assume that thirty NATO divisions have to
battle Warsaw Pact troops for 30 days before both sides realize
that a serious situation has arisen.[53]

When the Soviet Union decided to challenge the United States,
it was significantly not by some version of the "Hamburg grab,"
which worried Pentagon planners so much,[54] but by placing
strategic delivery vehicles with nuclear warheads in Cuba. Faced
with an obvious clash of interests, neither side fell back on
large-scale conventional capabilities in order to force a decision.
President Kennedy threatened a "full retaliatory blow" against
the Soviet Union if any missile on Cuba were fired against any
target in the Western hemisphere,[55] and Premier Khrushchev
obviously feared escalation and chose not to retaliate in Berlin, a
neuralgic spot where the Soviet Union held an overwhelming
superiority of conventional forces. Thus the pure capability
analysis underlying much of McNamara's strategic thinking
proved to be of little use for guiding a decision-maker in an
actual crisis situation. His dictum during the development of the
Cuban crisis that "a missile is a missile,"[56] and the implication
that its position is therefore of slight importance, was typical of
his approach and neglected exactly those political considerations
which Kennedy thought decisive. The President focused on this
point in his television address to the nation when he stated:

> For many years both the United States and the Soviet Union
> . . . have deployed strategic nuclear weapons with great care,
> never upsetting the precarious status quo which insured that

these weapons would not be used in the absence of some vital
challenge . . . American citizens have become adjusted to living
in the bull's eye of Soviet missiles located inside the USSR or in
submarines . . .

But this secret, swift and extraordinary buildup of communist
missiles in an area well known to have a special and historical
relationship to the United States . . . this sudden clandestine
decision to station strategic weapons for the first time outside of
Soviet soil is a deliberately provocative and unjustified change in
the status quo which cannot be accepted by this country if our
courage and our commitments are ever to be trusted again by
either friend or foe.[57]

It is here that the effect of the rules of the game on strategic
calculations becomes visible. As the Soviet response showed,
Soviet leaders did not deceive themselves as to the decisive
impact of nuclear weapons upon every direct superpower
confrontation. These weapons are part of every crisis, even if
their role is muted and their use not actually threatened, so that
the final outcome of a particular crisis does not seem to reflect
solely the relationship of conventional forces available in a
particular theater. Because some of McNamara's strategic
thinking rested on extremely questionable assumptions about
Soviet intentions, treating far-fetched possibilities as politically
relevant probabilities, and because the Soviet strategic literature
never fully incorporated the arguments of the "flexible
response"[58] doctrine, it seems fitting to trace more fully the
course of the Soviet strategic debate.

If it is appropriate to describe American strategic planning as
displaying a doctrinal lag, a similar charge can be made against
Soviet procurements. The heavy Soviet expenditures for air
defense radar and interceptors, as well as the purchase of only
medium-range bombers, indicated a similar emphasis on
defense and the expectation of a long war of attrition.[59] Stalin,
"the greatest strategic genius," provided the doctrinal
justification. Drawing lessons from the Great Patriotic War, he
reiterated the importance of the "permanently operating
factors" that were supposed to be decisive in any war. This
particular theory had been announced first in 1942 when the
failure of the German campaign in Russia became evident.
According to Stalin, these decisive factors were the stability of
the rear, the morale of the army, its armament, the quantity and

quality of the army, and the organizational ability of the army commanders. [60]

Thus, if surprise blows at the onset of a war could not be ultimately decisive, then neither could nuclear weapons force an early decision. Although such a doctrine might have been self-serving, it was not entirely at odds with the strategic realities of the immediate post-war era, as we have seen. Capitalizing upon the limited prospects for translating nuclear capability into usable strategic power, a Soviet historian in 1947 developed a scenario intended to deter the United States from using its superior strategic position in a possible military clash in Europe. [61] In such a case, Soviet troops would sweep across Western Europe, and bombing Soviet or occupied European cities would accomplish nothing. Although nuclear bombs naturally would play a role, the decisive force in this contest of wills would be the Red Army. Quite realistically, Soviet strategic thinking focused mainly on the peculiar features of the theater of possible conflict rather than on the abstract implications of nuclear weapons for the nature of future warfare. As a war with the United States was probable only over Europe, the ejection of American troops from the continent and the neutralization of British power—only a shadow of its former strength—could indeed have led to the envisioned stalemate.

Furthermore, Soviet procurement patterns during these years show that purchases of military hardware were well in line with this image of a future conflict. The thirty Soviet divisions stationed mainly in East Germany and throughout Eastern Europe were fully mechanized and equipped with armored vehicles and self-propelled guns designed for quick tactical maneuvers. [62] The Soviet Air Force stressed jet fighters (Mig 15's) and medium-range bombers limited to actions on the Eurasian continent. [63] Despite Stalin's pronounced interest in long-range bombers and missiles [64] — he had initiated a program for the further development of the German V-2 rocket—economic strain and technological lag in several areas forced him to limit his programs to those important in the most likely contingency. Under such circumstances, the strategy of holding Western Europe hostage promised to be an effective and economical way to influence the otherwise unfavorable balance of power to the advantage of the Kremlin. Years later, when most of Stalin's strategic heritage had been utterly discredited, the new leadership under Khrushchev nevertheless retained the hostage concept by limiting the buildup of intercontinental missiles but not that of medium-range rockets that could only threaten Europe.[65]

A re-evaluation of Stalin's tenets, rapidly being overtaken by the technological advances of the era of "nuclear plenty," came only after his death, for he had stubbornly refused during his last years to modify his dogma of the "permanent operating factors." Only a few months after Stalin's death, the first oblique criticism of the value of some of Stalin's "lessons" appeared in an article by Major General Talenski. Talenski's rather restrained criticism prepared the way for a much more principled dissent from the official line by General Rotmistrov on March 1955.[67] He raised the vital question of surprise in the nuclear era and emphasized the need for large forces-in-being rather than the broad mobilization base that Stalin had stressed.

Meanwhile, the Soviet leadership undertook to reorder its priorities by announcing its interest in a lessening of international tensions and a degree of domestic liberalization. This new line, by no means universally accepted, surfaced in a strategic debate in which Malenkov and Mikojan advocated a finite deterrence posture while Khrushchev, Bulganin, and Kaganovich emphasized the continuing necessity of large military outlays and investments in heavy rather than consumer industries.[68] Malenkov doubted the inevitability of a clash between the West and the Soviet Union, and he resolutely opposed the Cold War, "for this policy is a policy of the preparation of a new holocaust which, with the present means of warfare, means the destruction of world civilization."[69] The violent Soviet reaction to this unorthodox view, which acknowledged the uncertainty of the "final victory" of socialism on a global scale, forced Malenkov to make several retractions during the next few months. The orthodox wing of the party, which insisted that a future war would only mean the end of capitalism, was clearly in the ascendant.

As Bulganin and Khruschev themselves made similar statements about the "end of civilization" in 1955, 1957, and 1958, their vitriolic attacks against Malenkov have sometimes been interpreted as mainly a domestic ploy to gain power with the help of the military. But such an interpretation, although plausible in view of Khrushchev's opportunism, is too simplistic

and leaves out many important factors. A closer look at the
internal Soviet debate during this time rather seems to suggest
that there were important and genuine differences among the
leaders as to the appropriate military posture. Thus the twelve
percent increase in the military budget of 1955 did not represent
so much a "side payment" to the traditional military elite as a
commitment of large resources to strategic delivery means, then
at the developmental stage. The purpose of these rather large
outlays becomes even more obvious if one considers the
concomitant troop cuts of 1955, 1956, and 1957, which amounted
to about 1.8 million men. The fact that the Soviet strategic
debate was not conducted in the same abstract terms as in the
West, but was phrased as an ideological struggle between
consumer and defense advocates, indicates neither a lack of
sophistication nor a doctrinal lag in these matters, nor does it
prove that the strategic issues were used as a smokescreen
merely in order to advance the political fortunes of particular
contending factions.

The Soviet journal *Kommunist* pointed out rather clearly one
of the reasons for the Khrushchev-Malenkov feud: the image of
recklessness, so well conveyed by Khruschev's hammering with
his shoe on the speaker's platform in his United Nations speech,
was crucially important for the weaker Soviet Union in its
ongoing test of wills with the United States.

> However grievous the consequences of atomic war might be it
> must not be identified with the destruction of world civilization.
> Such an identification willy nilly brings grist to the American
> imperialist mill; it can create the incorrect concept among the
> partisans of peace that, as they say, the atomic threat is such that
> the instigators of war will not dare to use their own bombs, since
> they will not decide to commit suicide. Such a concept blunts the
> vigilance of the people toward those who, in the preparation of
> atomic war, would like to take the people by surprise. [70]

The last sentence in particular shows the appreciation of the
orthodox wing of the Soviet party for the psychological
requirements of an unstable balance of terror, in particular, the
necessity to project a certain image of irrationality.

This emphasis on the psychological implications of strategy
explains two further Soviet actions often misunderstood in the
West. One was Khrushchev's innovation of the avoidability of

war and the second was his missile diplomacy, which backfired
with the exposure of the imaginary character of the "missile
gap" and the Cuban showdown. That these two policies were
closely linked can be gathered from the following passage:

> There is of course a Marxist-Leninist precept that wars are
> inevitable as long as imperialism exists. This precept was evolved
> at a time when first, imperialism was an all embracing world
> system and second the social and political forces which did not
> want war were weak, poorly organized and hence unable to
> compel the imperialists to renounce war.
> People usually take any one aspect of these questions and
> examine only the economic basis of wars under imperialism. This
> is not enough. War is not only an economic phenomenon.
> Whether there is to be war or not depends in large measure upon
> . . . political forces . . . and . . . the resolve of the people . . .
> At the present time, however, the situation (which formerly
> made imperialist wars inevitable) has changed radically. Now
> there is a mighty force . . . (which has) the material means to
> prevent aggression. [71]

At the XXI. Party Congress, [72] Khrushchev elaborated on his
earlier remarks and concluded that the "new correlation of
power" meant that, even "before the complete victory of
socialism on earth" while capitalism still remained, "there
exists the actual possibility to exclude world war from the life of
society." [73]

Applying the deterrence concept not only to incursions into the
Soviet Union but also to conflicts affecting directly or indirectly
the global balance of power was possible only after the Soviets
had acquired a new feeling of confidence. Khrushchev's
description of the ICBM as an "absolute weapon" fits well into
this strategy. Similarly, Soviet doctrine tried to maximize the
deterrent effect of the new missiles after the Sputnik shock by
discarding the concept of limited war, so fashionable in the late
fifties in the American strategic debate, and stressing instead
the inevitability of escalation, at least for the European
theater. [74]

A reformulation of Soviet doctrine occurred only when Soviet
leaders realized, after the U-2 affair, that American fear of the
missile gap, upon which their strategy depended, had been
dispelled as soon as more accurate intelligence became

available. Indeed, deployment of the volatile liquid-fueled SS-6 ICBM had been sluggish, as the Soviets apparently decided to rely on a second generation land-based ICBM that utilized storable fuel and possessed a more accurate guidance system.[75] Consequently, Soviet claims became more modest after the bluff was called on Khrushchev's missile diplomacy. Instead of insisting on the superiority of the socialist camp, Khrushchev and other spokesmen now stressed "parity" with the West.[76] It is in this light that Khrushchev's theories about "wars of liberation" have to be read. In January 1961, Khrushchev distinguished between "world wars" which involved the Soviet Union and imperialist countries, "local wars" in which imperialist countries and socialist states other than Russia were facing each other, and "wars of liberation" which resulted from uprisings in which people fought for self-determination and independent national development.[77] Khrushchev called these last wars "sacred,"[78] which alarmed the Kennedy administration and fueled fears of a communist third world strategy.[79] But the distinction between local and liberation wars was due exactly to Khrushchev's refusal to include anticolonial uprisings in the category of *necessarily escalating* wars. The whole tone of the speech was much less confident in regard to Soviet ability to deter war in general, wherever it might occur: on the contrary, Khrushchev reverted to the old theory that war will only be avoidable "after the victory of the working class throughout the world."[80] Therefore, the main intent of the speech may have been a reformulation of exaggerated Soviet claims in order to bring doctrine into line with actual capabilities. Khrushchev gave a similarly cautious answer to Kennedy a few months later in Vienna when the American President expressed apprehension about revolutionary activities in the Third World that might affect the global balance of power. Khrushchev objected to Kennedy's interpretation and added that "he did not know whether the balance of power was exact but no matter, each side had enough power to destroy the other." "If some African countries," he continued, "were to go communist, it might add a few drops to the bucket of Communist power were the balance of power as a bucket on each side."[81]

The West's preoccupation with limited and subconventional war may well have contributed to its reading Khrushchev's statement in an "aggressive light" and to its general misunderstanding of Soviet doctrinal development, which often followed a different path from that of the West. Although Soviet strategists considered nuclear weapons to have implications of quite a different magnitude than those of other weapons, such as tanks or machine guns, Soviet military doctrine "clearly differed from the Western pattern in its early acceptance of the implications of the nuclear age."[82]

3. The Implications of Total Mutual Vulnerability

The events that followed the detection of Soviet missiles on Cuba in October 1962 are well known and need not be recounted here. What is more important for our purposes is the impact of the realization of total mutual vulnerability upon decision-makers. As we have seen in Chapter IV, crisis situations can lead to extensive redefinitions of the "game" due to mutual role-taking, whereby the exchange of perspectives leads to a sharing of aspirations, fears, and weaknesses and thus reassures the opponents. A limitation of demands becomes possible as perceptions of the opponent as well as of the stakes change. For example, Kennedy is reported to have opposed an ultimatum to Khrushchev because

> There is one thing I have learned in this business and that is not to issue ultimatums. You just can't put the other fellow in a position where he has no alternative except humiliation. This country cannot afford to be humiliated and neither can the Soviet Union. Like us, the Soviet Union has many countries which look to her for leadership and Khrushchev would be likely to do something desperate before he let himself be disgraced in their eyes.[83]

Thus a closer look at some of the decisive moves of the Cuban missile crisis drives home several points made in our analysis.

There was first of all Kennedy's superb handling of the situation: he clearly understood what kinds of pressures would limit rather than expand conflict. His choice of a blockade, despite both Acheson's and Fulbright's advice to bomb Soviet installations in Cuba,[84] indicates that Kennedy was well aware of the necessity of leaving options open, rather than reacting to the crisis by racing to commit himself, a point elaborated earlier. Secondly, there was Kennedy's important decision to focus on the hopeful aspects of the October 26 letter rather than on

Khrushchev's hardline message of October 23.[85] Analysis of these inconsistent messages for clues as to an ongoing power struggle between various Kremlin factions alerted American decision-makers to new opportunities to change the adversary's perception of the crisis and of the payoffs he could expect. They thus avoided forcing a decision according to a strategy of escalation originally devised in case no satisfactory answer was received. And, third, there was the skillful use of a third party, the United Nations, as a forum for rallying support as well as a device for facilitating the final bargaining through the intervention of Secretary General U Thant.[86] Finally, there was Khrushchev's contribution to the solution. Knowing that he had overstepped his limits, he accepted the definition of the situation as a major superpower confrontation and tried to de-escalate the conflict by successively disclosing his willingness to avoid an armed confrontation. In his letters he took pains to point out that despite serious differences he shared the President's perspective; by pointing to areas of cooperation he agreed to the definition of the situation in terms of a mixed motive rather than a zero sum game. He wrote his American opponent:

> You can regard us with distrust, but in any case you can be calm in this regard, that we are of sound mind and understand perfectly well that if we attack, you will respond the same way . . . This dictates that we are normal people that we correctly understand and correctly evaluate the situation . . . We however want to live in peace and do not at all want to destroy your country . . . we quarrel with you, we have differences on ideological questions. But our view of the world consists in this that ideological questions as well as economic problems should not be resolved by military means, they must be solved on the basis of peaceful competition. . . .[87]

One might at first be inclined to dismiss these assertions as cheap rhetoric, but such a judgment hardly does justice to the function of those signals in the resolution of conflict. Irrespective of whether these or similar utterances express the sincere preferences of the opponent, the offer of such a reading of the situation sets limits to the conflict by invoking a shared interest and by holding out hope for an adjustment without recourse to large-scale violence. Thus while such a signal might well be advanced mainly to improve one's position in a difficult bargaining situation, an offer of this kind is nevertheless the pre-condition for either player to redefine the situation and search for de-escalatory measures.

It was Khrushchev's emphasis on the common interest in imposing limits upon an explosive situation which convinced the Kennedy administration that a solution might be in sight. Khrushchev had communicated his intention by using the metaphor of a "knot of war" that might be pulled tighter and tighter "until it will be so tight that even those who tied it will not have the strength to untie it." [88] The October 27 message elaborated the same point: Cuba was again placed in the wider context of a nuclear confrontation that endangered the peace and imposed a special responsibility on the antagonists far beyond the solution of the crisis at hand. It is significant that Khrushchev at this point included in his bargaining agenda a proposal for a nuclear test ban. Aside from its obvious propaganda value, the nuclear fact had obviously contributed to the superpowers' discovery of a common interest, especially in the face of stiff Chinese opposition to Soviet accommodation in the matter of Cuba.[89] Khrushchev asked rhetorically in his letter,

> Why would I like to achieve this? Because the entire world is now agitated and expects reasonable actions from us . . . I attach a great importance to such an understanding (on Cuba) because it might be a good beginning and specifically facilitate a nuclear test ban agreement. [90]

Thus the Cuban missile crisis not only heightened the superpowers' perception of a common interest, but at the same time strengthened their conviction that increased security for one power did not require a concomitant loss of security for the other. As a matter of fact, certain unilateral measures to avoid accidents were recognized to be mutually beneficial, since only the tightest control had made crisis management possible. The record of sixty near accidents involving nuclear weapons since World War II, including the firing of two actual missiles with nuclear warheads, impelled Kennedy to disclose to the Russians several measures the United States had taken to keep nuclear weapons at all times under strictest control. [91] At an Arms Control symposium in December 1962, John McNaughton was entrusted with divulging a substantial amount of information on devices that inhibited accidental or unauthorized triggering of nuclear arms. [92] American scientists lobbied at Pugwash meetings for the same arms control concerns. Meanwhile, the Soviet Union reportedly "developed similar accident proofing devices." [93]

Another outcome of the Cuban crisis was a rather dramatic shift in the images the opponents held of each other. Faced with the fact that the American "paper tiger" had "nuclear teeth," as Khrushchev aptly remarked in refuting Chinese accusations of "capitulationism," he maintained that "in the relations with the imperialist states it is possible to agree to mutual compromises." [94] As opposed to the mythical vision of conflict between two exclusive "ways of life," resulting in an absolute struggle with a cunning and reckless enemy, Khrushchev advanced a considerably modified version of the nature of the opponent.

> Among the U.S. ruling circles are politicians who are rightly called lunatic . . . Is it not clear that if we had taken an uncompromising stand we would only have helped the "lunatic" camp to utilize the situation in order to strike at Cuba and unleash a world war?
>
> To be just it should be pointed out that among the ruling circles of the United States there are also persons who appraise the situation more soberly and, proceeding from the existing balance of forces in the world arena, realize that the United States, if it unleashed a war, would not win it and would not achieve its aim. [95]

The recognition of the existence of reasonable men in the other camp, so important for the decline of the operational significance of myths, had already begun to emerge in the pre-Cuban period. But, as William Zimmerman correctly pointed out, "reasonableness" and "realism" referred mainly to American acquiescence in, and recognition of, the shift in the global distribution of power in favor of the Soviet Union.

> Gradually the notion of realism was transformed. Especially after the Cuban missile crisis it came increasingly to refer to those who recognized a common stake in the avoidance of nuclear war and who consequently were disinclined to resort to war as an instrument of policy . . .
>
> The realists among the American decision makers . . . were

(now) those intelligently pursuing American interests under
conditions of mutual deterrence. Realism had come to mean a
commitment to the milieu goal of system maintenance. [96]

Seen in this light, we can conclude that the old Communist
theory of "coexistence" had undergone a decisive change.
Conceived originally in order to provide a breathing spell for the
embattled Soviet state, it had become a long-term strategy
"implying a continued acceptance of the necessity for an indirect
and more political way of advancing Soviet interests than the
militant advocacy of revolution and the use of force." [97] Again,
elaborating the mythical account by elongating its time frame
points to an important change in the myth's operational
significance.

A similar process of modifying the American image of the
adversary, and one more fundamental than the recurrent
atmospheric detentes accompanying "summit meetings," began
with President Kennedy's American University speech of June
10, 1963. Using the forum of a commencement to give new
impetus to the sluggish negotiations on a test ban, President
Kennedy focused upon the change in attitudes necessary on both
sides if agreement on several crucial issues was to be reached.

> History teaches us that enmities between nations as between
> individuals do not last forever . . .
> No government or social system is so evil that its people must
> be considered lacking in virtue . . .
> Let us reexamine our attitude toward the Soviet Union. It is
> discouraging to think that their leaders may actually believe what
> their propagandists write . . . But it is also a warning—a warning
> to the American people not to fall into the same trap as the
> Soviets, not to see only a distorted and desperate view of the other
> side, not to see conflict as inevitable, accommodation as
> impossible and communication as nothing other than the
> exchange of threats. [98]

After that speech, which Khrushchev called "the greatest . . . by
any American President since Roosevelt," [99] it took only nine
more days for Harriman, Lord Hailsham, and Gromyko to initial
a test ban agreement. In light of the previous "hotline"
agreement and the Declaration on the Peaceful Uses of Outer
Space (December 5, 1962), one could see that the perception of a

common interest between the superpowers, so essential for the demise of mythical antagonism, had made considerable headway. China's angry denunciation of the CPSU [100] demonstrated that the Soviet interest, shared by the West, in correctly appraising the "radical qualitative change of war" was superseding Soviet concern for ideological unity with Peking.

Although United States defense policy in the aftermath of Cuba was characterized by a good deal of wishful thinking, [101] a certain similarity of strategic outlook developed which laid the groundwork for the doctrine of assured destruction upon which the later SALT agreement was predicated. Nevertheless not all repercussions of the Cuban crisis were as beneficial. Having been forced to back down the Soviets lost no time in making up for their perceived military weakness during the following years.

The Soviet achievement of a secure second strike force, as well as the steadily increasing supply of Russian intercontinental missiles, naturally had serious implications for American strategy in that they made a counterforce strategy increasingly fanciful. [102] The administration therefore introduced in 1965 the concepts of "assured destruction" and "damage limitation" in order to explain its strategic posture. As the assured destruction of one opponent is the result of the degree of damage limitation of the other, "defensive" weapons used to minimize the damage inflicted by an adversary were now considered destabilizing for the evolving deterrent relationship. By a supreme irony, McNamara who had come into office criticizing the previous administration's massive retaliation posture and who had insisted on a war fighting capability on the conventional as well as nuclear level by stressing a counter force strategy, somehow returned to a pure deterrence strategy at least on the nuclear level. This strategy was now, because of the expanded stockpile and modern weapons systems, truly based on the idea of "massive retaliation". Indeed, there might not have been much choice in these matters, given the unfavorable exchange ratios between the strategic offense and the defense, [103] as the ABM debates showed. Having convinced himself that the American fear of a missile gap had caused the purchase of more destructive capability than necessary, McNamara now feared a new cycle of competitive armaments that would sooner or later, after the expenditure of billions of dollars, produce a stand-off on a higher plateau. Thus the ABM became, in McNamara's mind, the symbol of an arms race whose "mad momentum" had to be broken. His preoccupation with stable deterrence based upon assured destruction led McNamara not only to use delaying tactics on ABM but to two strategems that became important in the strategic debates of the next few years. [104] These were first the assertion of a clear pattern of interaction between the strategic programs of the United States and those of the Soviet Union, or the so-called action-reaction phenomenon of military budgets, and second the stress on a community of interest between the United States and Russia in preventing serious challenges to their dominant positions, which were based on nuclear superiority. It is significant in this context that the more business-like Soviet-American relations became, the more China seemed the disturber of international peace *par excellence*. But with the increasing alarm over China's threat, enhanced by its behavior during the Cultural Revolution and the mounting tension with the Soviet Union, it seemed strange indeed to explain the Soviet strategic posture as a response to United States defense efforts. On the other hand, the "common interest" argument together with the anti-China position expounded by the United States during the ABM debates [105] provided a convenient rationale for later Soviet attempts to enlist American support for a "joint action" in the event of provocation by a "third nuclear power", i.e. China. [106] Such contingency plans were apparently not new; similar plans had been advocated by some American officials earlier but had then been rebuffed by Moscow. [107] The fact that at the end of the sixties the United States remained cool [108] toward such overtures, while Moscow seriously considered action directed against its former ally, shows that a decisive shift in perceptions of the nature of the international system had occurred. This shift allowed United States' decision-makers to exploit the Sino-Soviet rift for their own strategic advantage.

As this latter problem will be dealt with more extensively in the fifth section of this chapter, we now turn to the problem of nuclear sharing, which was instrumental in altering the bi-polar pattern of postwar international politics.

4. *The Problem of Nuclear Sharing*

The set of hypotheses advanced at the beginning of Section Two of this chapter dealt with the influence that a "dominant" weapons system has on decision-makers' expectations and thereby on the characteristics of the international system. [109] We stressed that the impact of the nuclear revolution upon diplomatic-strategic behavior occurred much later than usually assumed. Nevertheless, our analysis of these events provides useful insights about how the advent of total mutual nuclear vulnerability set in motion a process of diffusion in the bipolar system. The fact that vulnerability, or the sufferance of "pain," no longer depended mainly on the previous destruction of one's own defensive forces required a strategic shift from defense to deterrence and also made one of the most valuable defense arrangements, alliances, a source of weakness rather than strength. Alliances risked to become a liability, for alliance leaders as well as for their "junior partners," since the presumption of a commonality of interest increasingly became the subject of heated political debate. [110]

In the final analysis, the nuclear revolution appeared to pose the question of the meaning of sovereignty as the dominant organizing principle of international relations, because within the realm of strategic calculations only a state with independent access to nuclear weapons seemed able to determine extensive foreign policy goals autonomously. True, the possession of nuclear weapons alone, without other superpower paraphernalia such as economic strength, population, territory, and so on, does not confer superpower status, as Great Britain and France amply demonstrate. But given the centrality of such a weapons system in strategic considerations, a country could hardly aspire to superpower status without a substantial nuclear capability. From Great Britain's Douglas-Hume, who considered the British nuclear force a "ticket to the top table," [111] to France's Pierre Messmer, who stated categorically that "one is nuclear or one is negligible," [112] to China's leadership, who stressed the importance of nuclear weapons for true independence and castigated Moscow's nuclear monopoly as a means of "lording it over the socialist camp," [113] there seems to have been universal agreement that independent nuclear forces are the precondition of great power status.

Conversely, nuclear weapons established a common interest between the two bloc leaders. Naturally, the two alliance leaders would have preferred to maintain their respective blocs, at least for strategic purposes; and in the West there were indeed various attempts to devise "sharing" arrangements—agreements intended to stem the tide of dissolution. But when it became clear that nuclear command authority cannot be shared, these attempts came to a naught, as did Moscow's collaboration with Peking in nuclear technology. Countries either had to accommodate themselves to the unilateral guarantee of their protector and content themselves with minor influence in strategic planning or they had to embark upon the arduous and dangerous effort of creating a national nuclear force. ·

The present section analyzes the process of dissolution in the two opposing alliances, which led to the introduction of China as a third player in the world strategic debate and to the accommodation of France, after her ambition to lead a "third force" had been crushed by internal instability and by the power realities evidenced in American-Soviet accords. The actions of both France and China as challengers of the two superpowers are highly interesting. Despite differences in style, timing, and ideological justification, the parallels between the Chinese and French positions often surprise the attentive observer. Indeed, such parallels are not entirely fortuitous, as a student of Chinese affairs emphasized:

> Long before the Chinese were prepared to discuss openly conflicts with the Communist Bloc over nuclear strategy, however, they had debated this issue in the guise of considering the contradictions arising within NATO over nuclear strategy . . . the implication of their remarks was quite clear . . . Thus the Chinese had sought to make their case for a Chinese nuclear capability by analogy by stressing France's need for such a force and the United States' attempt to dominate the Western Alliance by being the only nuclear power in it . . .114

In both cases, the first and rather subdued policy differences arose over the question of influence in the management of international affairs.

As we have seen, Mao was an ardent supporter of the "socialist camp" theory for quite some time. China's weakness and the hope for an eventual *"translatio imperii"* from Moscow to Peking made a close association with the "socialist fatherland" imperative. Nevertheless, Mao had not come to power by means of the Red Army, a circumstance that strengthened his bargaining position, e.g., in 1949/50 when the

Sino-Soviet Alliance treaty was negotiated. [115] Furthermore, China's growing influence over some Asian communist parties, its potential as a spokesman for what Mao called the "intermediate zone" (as exemplified by its participation in the Geneva settlement on Vietnam), [116] and the drain China represented on rather slim Soviet resources increasingly worried Soviet leaders. British Prime Minister Macmillan [117] reported that Russian leaders mentioned this latter point in private conversations at the Geneva summit and Adenauer witnessed the same preoccupation on Khrushchev's part during negotiations in Moscow in the fall of 1955. [118] However, a clear divergence of interest between Moscow and Peking became apparent only during the two Taiwan Straits crises of 1954 and 1958. In both cases Soviet support for the Chinese position seems to have been less than lukewarm. Thus in spite of boasts of strategic superiority in the aftermath of the Sputnik-shock, Khrushchev was ready to back Chinese claims to Taiwan only when the danger of war over Quemoi and Matsu had dissipated. [119]

> The Taiwan Straits Crisis had the effect—and perhaps the intention—of clarifying the Soviet attitude towards independent military initiatives by China . . . It can hardly have failed to strengthen the Chinese leaders' determination to seek their own nuclear deterrent. It must have served to underline the dubious value of the Soviet nuclear guarantee and to have raised serious questions about the continuing viability of the whole Sino-Soviet alliance. [120]

Whether this assessment of the Kremlin's failure to provide timely support is entirely correct is still debatable, particularly because the Soviet riposte mentions a letter signed by Mao expressing gratitude for Soviet assistance. [121] What is less a matter of debate is the fact that the problem of control and command must have become the focal point of Sino-Soviet tension. According to a statement by Mao in September 1962, Khrushchev proposed establishing a joint war fleet. "This proposal was rejected by the Chinese leaders who, according to Mao, regarded it as an attempt by the U.S.S.R. to control the Chinese coast and facilitate an eventual blockage of China." [122] Furthermore, there are some indications "that the Chinese resisted Soviet proposals for cooperation in military nuclear affairs that would have involved stationing Soviet nuclear forces under Soviet control on Chinese territory." [123]

By mid-1958, China already seems to have decided to start its own nuclear weapons development. Having failed to influence the Soviet policy line on international affairs, China rejected the "unreasonable demands" of the Soviet Union, which were "designed to bring China under Soviet military control." [124] Nuclear sharing proved to be incompatible with national independence, while independence precluded a division of military functions. In the stormy Lushan meeting of 1959, the worst indictment against the "revisionist" Minister of National Defense was his opposition to Mao's insistence on an "independent and complete network of national defense industries." Instead, P'eng Te-huai had advocated an arrangement with the Soviet Union that provided for China to contribute "troops and the Soviet Union atom bombs." [125]

A policy of self-reliance was all the more advisable for China in that on March 31, 1958, the Soviet Union had sent Washington and Peking a note that included the following observation:

Today only three powers—the U.S.S.R., the U.S.A. and Great Britain—possess nuclear weapons; therefore, agreement on the discontinuance of nuclear weapons tests can be achieved relatively easily. If the tests are not stopped now, within a certain time other countries may have nuclear weapons, and in such a situation it would, of course, be much more difficult to obtain an agreement. [126]

The Soviet Union's obvious willingness to make an arrangement with the West, even if this meant for all intents and purposes the abrogation of all commitments to China under the October 1957 agreement, [127] was later confirmed by Suslov in his presentation on the Sino-Soviet dispute to the Central Committee of the CPSU (February 1964).

Underlying tensions between the Soviet Union and China, which escalated continuously during the period from 1960 to the beginning of 1963, finally came to a head when Moscow entered into discussion of a nuclear test ban following Kennedy's American Unviersity speech.

The seriousness of the rift was then openly recognized on both sides: the Soviet Union saw in China's stance proof that "the Chinese leaders are transferring ideological differences to interstate relations,'' [128] and China charged that the Soviet claim that all socialist countries have to depend upon the Soviet Union for their survival struck ''an out and out great power chauvinistic note.'' [129] The system-transforming implications of nuclear weapons had found official expression.

As mentioned above, the leader of the Western bloc experienced similar difficulties with one of its members that could not accommodate itself to the power realities that emerged with the advent of nuclear vulnerability of the superpowers. As was true for China, France's dissent from the policy preferences of its alliance leader evolved over a long period of time. Interested in maintaining her colonial empire and her superiority vis-a-vis a weakened Germany, France was bound to clash with the United States' policies, as Dulles' threat of an ''agonizing reappraisal'' during the European Defense Community debate amply demonstrated. [130] But it was the frustration of her aspirations to be a world power, especially in the ill-fated Suez affair, which convinced her that the effort to maneuver American power towards support for French policies was doomed to failure. Though the Suez affair also clouded British-American relations for some time, particularly with the Federal Reserve's increased pressure on the pound by heavy selling of its holdings, [131] a reconciliation took place at Bermuda in March 1957, restoring the Anglo-American entente. [132] Britain agreed to the stationing of four squadrons of Thor missiles and received assurances of continued nuclear collaboration. The United States, already exploring the possibilities of a future test ban, knew that Great Britain, with a nuclear force of its own, would cooperate in such an enterprise only if American help for her weapons program made extensive testing superfluous. Thus the Bermuda Conference was soon followed by the Plowden-Strauss agreement, which provided for the exchange of technology and weapons design. The McMahon Act, which prohibited the sharing of weapons technology, was easily overcome when Congress voted in 1958 to amend this law to permit the transfer of weapons technology to an ally that had made ''substantial progress'' toward a nuclear capability of its own. [133]

The French were quick to sense the implications of the wording of the McMahon Act amendment. Already suspicious of American intentions, they saw this move as new proof of a policy of deliberate discrimination. Barred from a transfer of British technological know-how in regard to the manufacture of fissionable materials—it seems that the United States had objected to such ,a sharing of information—France began to construct its own isotope separation plant in July 1957. [134] Apparently, France tried to interest the Germans and Italians in such a project, proposing to share some technology in return for financial contributions. The main purpose was naturally the development of a French atomic bomb.

Meanwhile, the "great debate" had started within the Atlantic Alliance. Only a month after the successful launch of the Soviet Sputnik, a Belgian-Dutch report on NATO strategy tried to assess the implications of Soviet missiles and stated bluntly that "the Continental members of NATO do not feel adequately protected by strategic nuclear weapons which are not available either to these individual nations or to the NATO community..." [135] This raised squarely the issue of nuclear sharing in the Atlantic Alliance. The United States, in order to reassure its allies, wanted to store Intermediate Range Ballistic Missiles on European soil. When France was approached to grant permission for stationing such forces within its territorial boundaries the delicate problem of control arose. Apparently the French government—like the Chinese on the Eastern side—was willing to make such an agreement only if part of the rocket force would thereby be placed under exclusive French control, and/or France would be furnished with technological know-how for its incipient nuclear arsenal. The United States seems to have promised some help by holding out the prospects of furnishing data for Polaris propulsion [136] systems, provided Congress would agree, but France's later soundings were not favorably received. In view of the fact that France became increasingly embattled in her Algerian "provinces", the transfer of nuclear technology as well as the lack of American support for the French position attained ominous proportions. As in the case of China, escalation of the conflict resulted from the divergence of interest between the bloc leader and its ally, together with the problem of the control of nuclear missiles stationed on the ally's territory. Michel Debré, de Gaulle's first Prime Minister, wrote about that time in the Gaullist paper *Carrefour*:

The official position of the United States can be summarized as follows: It does not want France to be an atomic power. It does not

wish France to remain an African or Saharan power. It does not
hope that France will recover her political independence. 137

Ironically, at the time when the second Taiwan crisis strained
Sino-Soviet relations, de Gaulle, in a way, posed the same
problem for the Western Bloc. On September 25, 1958, the claim
to independence and super-power status was spelled out in a
letter to Great Britain and the United States:

> The French Government does not consider that the security of
> the free world, or indeed France itself, can be guaranteed by the
> North Atlantic Treaty Organization in its present form. In its view,
> political and strategic questions of world, as opposed to regional,
> importance should be entrusted to a new body consisting of the
> United States, Great Britain and France. This body should have
> the responsibility of making joint decisions on all political matters
> affecting world security, and of drawing up and, if necessary,
> putting into action strategic plans, especially those involving the
> use of nuclear weapons . . . The French Government regards such
> an organization for security as indispensable. Henceforth the
> whole development of its present participation in NATO is
> predicated on this. 138

This triple-directorate proposal would not only give France a
voice in strategic decision-making, but would also secure French
influence on *any* decision concerned with the use of nuclear
weapons. Despite some disclaimers, this seems to have been
de Gaulle's position, or, in the words of Couve de Murville,
"France should share in the decision before the United States
could use nuclear weapons anywhere in the world." 139 It was
clear that such an extensive interpretation of French interests
would be unacceptable to the United States. 140 Nor could de
Gaulle's proposal please the other European states.

The period from 1959 to 1965 saw a proliferation of proposals
that tried in one way or another to come to terms with the
problem of nuclear sharing. But the problem of control seemed
intractable, even when some proposals envisaged NATO, rather
than any particular country as the "Fourth" atomic power. After
the Nassau disaster, in which an unprepared American President
half-heartedly endorsed the idea of a Multilateral Nuclear
Force 141 — a proposal which found little enthusiasm on the other
side of the Atlantic—the American foreign policy priorities

changed. Like the Soviet Union the United States pursued from
1963 on a policy which was increasingly geared to the
preservation of the American-Soviet monopoly of nuclear
weapons rather than towards a genuine sharing within the
Alliance. True, for a time there seemed to have been renewed
interest in a MLF, but this was motivated more by the fear that
Germany might otherwise prefer bilateral nuclear cooperation
with France, [142] than by a genuine interest in solving this
Gordian knot of the Alliance. [143] The proposed arrangement
demonstrates this clearly: European say was limited to the
financial burden-sharing and a veto capacity. The decision to
utilize nuclear weapons, however, remained under the sole
authority of the American military and therefore the President of
the United States. By 1965 [144] the shadow-boxing was over and
the changed United States priorities found their official
expression in a variety of statements. [145] Thus, the Head of the
US Arms Control and Disarmament Agency suggested in an
article in Foreign Affairs in July 1965 that a "high degree of
U.S.-Soviet cooperation should be pursued" for finalizing a
nuclear non-proliferation treaty, even if one of its "heavier
costs" could be "the erosion of alliances."[146]

5. *The New Players*

After considering the "nuclear issue" and its influence in
creating and dissolving the bipolar pattern of post-war world
politics, what remains to be shown is the impact of newly
emerging players upon the structure of interstate relations.

As our above discussion showed, the fundamental difference
between a two-power world and a three-power world is that
"systemic" characteristics emerge as a critical influences upon
the expectations of decision-makers.[147] But, as we also saw, our
Gedankenexperiment was predicated upon the assumption that
indices of independent power status are commonly accepted and
the emergence of a viable new player is thus easily recognized.
However in the "real" world, some time may pass before a
peripheral player is accorded full power status. This is because a
considerable alteration of the image of reality is required for the
shift from a one-and-a-half power world to a two-power world or
from a two-power world to a three-power world. Our discussion
in the previous chapter suggested some of the reasons why this
is so. As reality is a social construct, the "correctness" of action

must be socially ascertained and reinforced. Therefore a competing image of reality usually acquires social support only after a new set of leaders comes to power. Formed by a different set of biographical experiences than their predecessors, new leaders might be less inclined to accept the predominant definition of reality. They might perceive new opportunities that were hidden by the previous frame of reference.

These theoretical considerations applied to our particular historical problem suggest that, given the new players' military weakness, the opportunities they provided the superpowers did not fit the classical strategic calculations concerned with the military "exchange ratio." These opportunities were rather the result of a concomitant revolution in the nature of the power that could be used for diplomatic advantage. [148] The stand-off on the strategic level required the superpowers to have recourse to other means of exerting influence, means more appropriate to the realities of the emerging countries. On the one hand, this explains the fact that Eastern as well as Western interest in these countries was always part of a larger concern with the nature of modern war: Khrushchev's advances in the Third World were part of his emphasis on "peaceful coexistence" and the evitability of central war (as opposed to wars of national liberation); and Kennedy's fascination with these countries was tied to a whole set of ideas concerning the dangers of underdevelopment, subversive ventures, and unconventional warfare.[149] On the other hand, the setting of these particular issues also explains the largely transitory nature of the superpower contest for the allegiance of the Third World, which entered the world political scene as the "nonaligned" or "neutralist" bloc. This "neutralism" did not entail the careful observation of the traditional principles of neutrality. Rather it stressed independence and non-participation in one of the established blocs. So the emergence of these new players frontally challenged both superpowers' "mythical" view of Soviet-American antagonism as the central organizing principle for all international issues.

Thus by their very success in defusing Cold War issues, the non-aligned countries lessened the superpowers' incentive to compete for the favors of these new forces in world politics. This was borne out not only by the downward trend in American foreign assistance in the second half of the sixties and by

Moscow's reassessment of its policy following the ouster of Khrushchev,[150] but also by the reversal of the adversary role in the Vietnam conflict. Originally, United States involvement in Indochina was motivated by the perceived necessity to "stop Communism," whether instigated by Moscow, as alleged until the early sixties, or by Peking, as later asserted. But the longer this conflict lasted and the more questionable many of its underlying premises became, the more the United States was willing to draw on its newly acquired credit in Moscow (and later Peking) in order to extricate itself from the Vietnam quagmire. The balance of the "old world" had to redress that of the new, and not vice versa as originally maintained. Given these facts, it will be the task of this section to examine more closely the system transforming impact of the emergence of this "third force" in world politics.

Soviet and American policy vis-a-vis the former colonial areas exhibited some identical features despite otherwise great differences in interests and ideology. Above all, both countries were for quite some time on record as being against "colonialism" and in favor of indigenous emancipation, an ideological tenet that soon had to be subordinated to the compelling requirements of maintaining the central balance of power. This meant, on the side of the United States, that the anti-colonial stance against Great Britain and France, so vigorously defended by President Roosevelt, had to be modified as policy differences with the Soviets became more ominous. In the case of the Soviet Union, it meant the subordination of revolutionary aspirations to considerations of its own reasons of state, as Stalin's lack of enthusiasm for liberation movements in the colonies from the late. thirties on showed. As Roger Kanet points out:

> Throughout the Second World War Soviet support for liberation movements in the colonial areas was almost nonexistent, unless such a movement was connected to the successful conclusion of the war.[151]

This was naturally to change after the war, but Soviet encouragement of nationalist movements was spectacularly devoid of revolutionary overtones. The Soviets praised African and Asian resistance leaders who had all been part of the national "bourgeoisie" rather than communist cadres.

Given the overwhelming power disparity between the Soviet

and American colossi and the rest of the world at the end of the war, no genuine multi-power game could emerge. With the deepening Soviet-American conflict in Europe, a widespread tendency developed to view events in other parts of the world as a reflection of East-West antagonism. The strategic significance of the colonial and post-colonial areas was therefore limited to that of what we called a "vassal" rather than an "ally." The Korean War convinced the American government that "containment" had to be extended to Asia and that the required manpower would have to come from indigenous sources in order to free American resources for the strategic deterrent and for increased private spending at home.

Preoccupied with the possibility of a repetition of its Korean experience, the United States undertook to form a complex alliance network around the Sino-Soviet periphery. Indeed, participation in one of these ventures became the decisive criterion for a country's membership in the club of the "free world," and neutralist tendencies aroused deep American suspicions. "Neutrality," stated Dulles in 1955, has "increasingly become an obsolete conception and except under very exceptional circumstances it is an immoral and short-sighted conception." 152 There is substantial evidence however that Dulles himself was more flexible in these matters than is usually assumed. He exempted even India, the leader of the "neutralist" movement, from his blanket indictment, and he actively supported foreign aid for Yugoslavia. But there is no question that his assertion of the "immorality" of neutralism described "the dominant conviction of the American people and the prevailing sentiment in Congress." 153 The fear that the neutralist countries were naive and blind to the dangers emanating from communism's "global conspiracy," or that their leaders were simply communist "stooges" was widely shared. It provided the frame of reference for assessing the often erratic foreign policy course steered by Third World leaders.

Ironically enough, Soviet comments about most leaders of national emancipation movements were equally negative. With the announcement of the two camp doctrine, Soviet tolerance vis-a-vis the "national bourgeoisie" in colonial and post-colonial countries was replaced by unmitigated hostility. The efforts of the nationalist leadership to attain independence were unmasked as a "fraud." Ghandi, Nehru, Sukarno and U Nu suddenly became "lackeys" of foreign imperialism. The Soviets discovered that "Ghandi has always been the principal traitor of the mass national liberation movement;" Sukarno and Hatta had oriented themselves "from the very beginning" toward the attainment of a "decent compromise with imperialism;" General Nagib of Egypt and his group of "reactionary officers" were connected with the United States; while U Nu of Burma was closely allied with the Buddhist clergy and was ruling a state dependent upon "British monopoly capital."[154] As Kanet notes: "The logical extension of the Soviet attitude to the newly independent states of South and South East Asia was a policy of nonrecognition and subversion."[155]

The only "liberation" movements the Soviets seemed to tolerate were those following the Chinese pattern, although they simultaneously downplayed the importance of the Chinese revolution. Mao's victory over the Kuomintang was depicted as the logical offspring of the Soviet revolution and the Soviet victory over Fascism in World War II.[156] The mythical image of international politics held such a powerful grip upon the minds of Moscow's followers that even China followed the Moscow line on these issues in publications destined for foreign circulation, while allowing her own domestic literature to celebrate her victory as a source of inspiration for other peoples.[157]

Moscow's intransigence sometimes led to absurd results, as in the case of Mossadegh's nationalization of the Anglo-Iranian Oil Company. While Great Britain and the United States conjured up the specter of a communist takeover as Mossadegh's policies led to domestic turmoil and the flight of the Shah, Moscow together with the Iranian Communist Party denounced Mossadegh, charging that he "aimed at winning over the landlords, the bourgeoisie, and American oil magnates against the British."[158]

Two changes during the early fifties had a decisive impact upon Soviet attitudes towards the emerging nations. First, Stalin's death brought about a domestic thaw and a search for new ways to deal with the rest of the world. The war in Korea may well have convinced the new Soviet leaders that frontal challenges around the Soviet periphery were futile and costly, and that new opportunities to extend Soviet influence lay in the exploitation of the strong anti-colonial sentiment of the emerging nations. Thus, while the United States seemed to have derived the lesson of extending alliances from its Korean experience, the Soviets apparently perceived the utility of more subtle instruments for meeting the challenges of these areas. The second event of momentous consequence was the meeting of twenty-nine Afro-Asian countries at Bandung in April 1955. [159] Contrary to popular belief, the Bandung Conference was not the first of its kind, [160] but it was Bandung that provided the world with the first clear self-representation of the emerging countries: in espousing "anticolonialism" and "nonalignment" they challenged the ordering of the international universe along the axis of East-West antagonism.

The impact of the Bandung Conference could be felt far beyond the former colonial nations, as Hungary's attempts to come to terms with Stalin's legacy showed. Removed from power and expelled from the party, Imre Nagy tried to find a way to implement a communist program without Stalinist coercion. The critical variable was naturally the problem of international politics, for without genuine independence, domestic reforms would suffer from outside intervention in both party and state affairs. Observing a major change in international politics, especially since the Bandung Conference and the softening of the Soviet stance against Yugoslavia (which constantly emphasized its non-affiliation with any bloc), Nagy hoped that the five basic principles of international affairs could solve the Hungarian problem and with it that of East Europe as a whole. As the "building of socialism" requires national independence, but such independence, particularly for small countries, is constantly threatened by the existence of two mutually exclusive blocs, Nagy concluded:

> The most practicable plan, seemingly, is the active coexistence of progressive democratic socialist or similar countries with those of other countries having a different system, through a coordinated foreign policy and through cooperation against the policies of the power groups, through neutrality or active coexistence.[161]

This experiment in "socialist independence" ended in failure as Soviet intervention was directly related to Nagy's intention to withdraw from the Warsaw Pact. But the breaking of the mythical mold encouraged a greater variety of paths to socialism, freeing the Eastern European countries from slavish imitation of the U.S.S.R., and strengthened polycentric tendencies within the communist movement.

The United States, which had been less dogmatic although often highly critical of the neutralist countries, also felt the repercussions of the rising nonaligned tide. In particular, it had to modify some of its foreign policy premises in the aftermath of the Suez crisis.

The years 1956 to 1958 saw several attempts to reformulate American foreign policy premises concerned with these areas. A Development Loan Fund was created in 1957, funds for the "soft loan window" of the World Bank were allocated, and Nixon's disastrous reception in Latin America created some administration pressure for the creation of the Inter-American Development Bank. But all in all, "American policy toward development remained," in the words of Walt Rostow, "grossly inadequate to its strategic purpose of offering a powerful constructive incentive to nationalism . . ." [162] It remained for the Kennedy administration to translate into policy the new proposals generated by the controversies of the fifties over the appropriate approach towards the new players.

Perhaps the clearest indication of the changed priorities of the incoming administration was contained in Kennedy's State of the Union message, which focused mainly on the problems of the developing world, displacing Europe from the central position of concern it had held for so long. The impression that Kennedy had given "top priority . . . to America's programs for the new and developing nations" [163] was strengthened by his Special Message to Congress on May 25, 1961. There he stated:

> The great battleground for the defense and expansion of freedom today is the whole southern half of the globe—Asia, Latin America, and the Middle East—the lands of the rising people. Their revolution is the greatest in human history. [164]

The conceptual apparatus that guided this policy was characterized by such technical terms as "self-sustained growth," "take-off stage," and so on. These phrases had an aura of academic respectability and had been developed by Walt Rostow and other "Charles River" (MIT and Harvard) economists who had joined the administration. But behind all these sophisticated technical terms lay a rather simple set of assumptions. Rostow and Max Milliken had pointed out in their programmatic statement on developmental policy in 1957 that

the communist threat, deterred at the strategic level, had shifted
to the exploitation of other means of influence, to unconventional
warfare, and to economic competition. [165] While increased
conventional and unconventional capabilities on the part of the
West were to take care of the military threat, economic aid was to
engage the energies of the new nations in internal modernization
rather than foreign "adventurism." This idea sprung from
Rostow's image of the "revolutionary romantic." For him the
appearance of "leaders obsessed by ambitious maps of their
region (or of the world) which they tried to bring to reality" was
an anachronistic response to the stresses of development. [166]
But as Rostow indicated in his Sir Montague Burton lecture:

> Resistance to the achievement of these visions, combined with the
> growing demand of people throughout the world for economic and
> social progress, has eroded both ideological and nationalist
> aggressive romanticism . . . Given the rhythm of modernization
> with vast continents entering the early stages of modernization
> after the Second World War, it is natural that we should have
> seen a phase of regional aggression. From the record of history
> we should be in reasonbly good heart about this phase. For these
> early, limited external adventures, associated with late
> preconditions or early take off periods, appear generally to have
> given way to a phase of absorption in the adventure of
> modernizing the economy and the society as a whole. [167]

According to this image of reality, the "struggle in Vietnam"
neatly fitted the description of "the last great confrontation of
the postwar era." On a more general level, Rostow's frame of
reference was related to the belief in an "end to ideology," [168]
so prevalent in the late fifties. The assumption that pragmatic or
"pocketbook" politics constituted the only "real" politics, as
opposed to "aggressive," "adventurous," and "irresponsible"
behavior, was based on the common mistake of taking the
distributive aspect of politics (who gets what, when, and how) for
the whole of politics. This image of "normal" politics reveals, on
closer inspection, a second underlying assumption: a type of
"second image" theory of international conflict. It is somehow
believed that a family of democratic and "satisfied" nations,
each devoted to its own material progress, will be at peace and
will allow for the preservation of the American way of life. But as
Hungary and many of the developing nations have learned,

concentration on domestic problems is often impossible because international factors continuously impinge upon such concerns.

The policy imperatives derived from this vision of "pragmatic" politics were rather simple. It was necessary to initiate the process of development through a transfer of capital, and meanwhile to frustrate revolutionary adventures until economic development would generate the right kinds of social pressure and eliminate the "old fashioned leaders."

> In the perspective I have presented, what is old fashioned about Vietnam is the effort by the leaders in Hanoi to make their lifelong dream of achieving control over South East Asia come to reality by the use of force. It is their concept of "wars of national liberation" that is old fashioned. It is being overtaken not merely by the resistance of the seven nations fighting there but also by history and by increasingly pervasive attitudes of pragmatism and moderation. [169]

Convinced that without extensive American involvement the Third World would sooner or later join the adversary, the United States became involved in attempts to exert influence upon the domestic structures of the new societies,[170] with all its concomitant frustrations, as the fate of the Alliance for Progress reveals.

Ironically, the Soviet Union, which at first tried to avoid all involvement in the domestic politics of the Third World, soon found itself in the position of bolstering regimes favorable to its foreign policy line. The disappointments of the mid-sixties showed the limitations of such a strategy, as Soviet disenchantment with Third World politics paralleled that of the United States.

The Soviets' reassessment of policy toward the developing nations began after the settlement of the leadership crisis, Nehru's visit in Moscow in the aftermath of the Bandung Conference, and the return visits of Khrushchev and Bulganin to the Indian subcontinent in November/December 1955.[171] Gone was Stalin's suspicion of the fraudulent character of the national bourgeoisie: the new mood was one of exuberant optimism. On the occasion of the Twentieth Party Congress Nikita Krushchev spelled out the doctrinal significance of the "anti-imperialist" movement.

> These countries . . . although they do not belong to the socialist

world system, can draw on its achievements in building an independent national economy and in raising their peoples' living standards. Today they need not go begging to their former oppressors for modern equipment . . .

The very fact that the Soviet Union and the other countries of the socialist camp exist, that they are ready to help the underdeveloped countries with their industrial development on terms of equality and mutual benefit, is a major stumbling block to colonial policy. The imperialists can no longer regard the underdeveloped countries as merely potential sources for the extraction of maximum profits. They are compelled to make concessions to them. [172]

But this description of the national liberation movement invited a challenge to Moscow's leadership of the world revolutionary process. Indeed, some African and Asian leaders soon claimed that their countries were already embarked upon building "socialism." "These claims were predicated on the underlying assumption that socialism was a general category, within which Marxist-Leninist socialism in the U.S.S.R., various African socialisms and Burmese socialism . . . were specific manifestations, all equally valid as socialism, but differing in form due to the socio-historical particularities of each area." [173] Furthermore, as the events of 1958 and 1959 in the Middle East showed, "socialist" Egypt was on a direct collision course with "socialist" Moscow because of a variety of foreign and domestic policy issues. Moscow had opposed the union between Cairo and Damascus, and the growing influence of communists in Iraq had definite anti-Nasser overtones. Nasser recalls:

> While the Communists have been attacking me, I have been attacking them.
> ...We had to expose the tactics of the Syrian communists who had formed a strange alliance with the feudalist landowners ... [174]

This controversy squarely posed the question of the appropriate role for the communist parties within national liberation movements. Having hoped to avoid entanglement in the internal affairs of the post-colonial countries, the Soviet Union suddenly found itself crucially involved. At this point Khrushchev seems to have asked Nasser to accept the responsibility of protecting Arab communists but Nasser's answer was negative.

The practical difficulties made changes in the pertinent

"theory" necessary, and the subsequent doctrine of a "national democracy" tried to establish the necessary criteria.[175] Basically, this theory suggested that democratic liberties had to be extended to the suppressed communist party before a country could qualify for the status of a "national democracy". A second problem remained: that of reconciling the "socialist" revolutions in the Third World with Moscow's claim to leadership of the Communist movement. Concerning the necessity of communist leadership in the transition to socialism, the new Party Program adopted by the XXII Party Congress stressed the significance of the Soviet experience as a model of socialist revolution.[176]

The exigencies of the political situation (or Khrushchev's opportunism, as his opponents might charge) soon required another modification of this new formula. The Chinese offensive in the Third World beginning in 1963 pressured the Kremlin into competition for the favors of the new leaders. Well aware that professing the socialist character of their revolutions was the proper way to obtain Soviet aid—as "nationbuilding" rhetoric was in the case of requests addressed to the West—Third World leaders insisted on the socialist implications of their policies even when at odds with actual practice. In addition, there was nearly always the problem of the communist party whose leaders more often than not were safely locked away in jail. This was naturally a blatant violation of the "national democratic" code, and left the Kremlin in the unenviable position of either refusing aid, thereby losing influence, or overlooking such practices, leaving itself open to charges of opportunism. Although such an accommodation to the facts of international life was not contrary to Soviet tradition, an ideological reformulation of the pertinent doctrine was again needed. Consequently, by early 1963 Khrushchev endorsed the concept of a "revolutionary democracy," which had emerged from the scholarly discussion of Soviet developmental policy.

> The earlier concept of national democracy was based on the unrealistic assumption of organizational freedom as well as a united front between communists and national democrats. The leaders of a "revolutionary democracy" by contrast, were merely supposed to let communists out of jail so that they could dissolve themselves and join the leading party as individuals . . .
> . . . The transition to socialism could now be achieved whether the leadership was in the hands of the working class or not. By

clear implication, the fate of Communist parties in states ruled by revolutionary democrats now assumed marginal importance. [177]

The reason for such a step was not hard to perceive when Khrushchev bestowed the title of "comrade" on both Ben Bella and Nasser in the spring of 1964, overlooking the latter's rigorous imprisonment of communist party members. Moscow's strong interest in the Middle East had once more won out over its desire to maintain ideological purity.

Khrushchev's ouster and the disappointments of the strategy of "revolutionary democracy" in following years led to a critical reappraisal of Soviet involvement in the Third World. The overthrow of Ben Bella in October 1965 and that of "revolutionary" democrat Nkhrumah in February 1966 showed that the "progressive" character of the regime was no insurance against the vagaries of Third World politics. Soviet economic strains, furthermore, counseled a more modest aid program, particularly because a more critical attitude toward aid uncovered serious shortcomings in an approach that had relied nearly exclusively on political criteria rather than on some considerations of economic feasibility, leading to frustrations on both sides. The new Soviet rulers, who took pride in a "more businesslike approach" to world affairs, increasingly favored an emphasis on long-term gains for the Soviet Union as a world power. This meant strict *quid pro quo* deals that allowed economic feasibility criteria to be included in the decision premises. [178] In addition, improving relations with the United States and coping with the rapid deterioration of the Sino-Soviet dispute compelled a reordering of the Kremlin's foreign policy objectives. The Soviets' adroit diplomacy on the Indian subcontinent, mediating rather than exploiting the Indo-Pakistani conflict, served as an early indication that the "containment" of China (and therefore the neutralization of her potential ally Pakistan) had superseded Soviet concern with classical Cold War issues in this area. The doctrinal manifestations of these shifts were the emphasis on Soviet domestic development, the distinction introduced by Suslov between "non-capitalist" and "socialist" patterns of development (formerly used interchangeably), [179] and Brezhnev's proposal for a "collective security system" in Asia. [180]

The emphasis on Soviet development as "the chief contribution to the development of the world revolutionary movement," and the careful disengagement of Soviet interests from revolutionary activity are well captured in a *Pravda* editorial that commented upon the Brezhnev-Kosygin line towards the Third World. Under the heading "The Supreme Internationalist Duty of a Socialist Country," the paper maintained:

> . . . the socialist countries, in deciding revolutionary tasks, cannot substitute for other detachments of the liberation struggle. They cannot take the place of the peoples of the young national states in solving the tasks of the national liberation movement, nor can they take the place of the working class and the working people of the capitalist countries in the struggle for the overthrow of capitalism. . . . such actions could lead to the unleashing of a world thermonuclear war, with all its grave consequences for all peoples. This would mean not the fulfillment by the socialist countries of their internationalist obligations to the working people of the entire world, but the infliction of irreparable harm on the cause of the social and national liberation of the peoples of other countries and on the entire world revolutionary process. The peoples of the socialist countries are concentrating their main efforts on the building of socialism and communism in their own countries, seeing in this the decisive precondition for intensifying their help to the other detachments of the liberation struggle and their chief contribution to the development of the world revolutionary movement. [181]

That this was not a casual analysis by some editorial writer but the official new line can be seen from the basically similar statements Soviet spokesmen made during the next few years.

Brezhnev's proposal for an Asian collective security system, finally, has to be seen in the light of the Soviet Union's new self-assertiveness in laying claim to super-power status, as well as in the context of a desire to contain China. [182] Significantly enough, the pursuit of "milieu goals" was no longer based solely upon the revolutionary tradition. Foreign Minister Andrei Gromyko indicated in June 1968 that the orthodox Marxist-Leninist "class analysis" of international affairs might not be a particularly helpful guide for the decision-maker:

> One encounters in international life certain actions which cannot be easily classified as either purely foreign political or purely ideological. They are mostly of both, one and the other. [183]

And in his report to the Supreme Soviet on July 10, 1969, he based his explanation of the extensive foreign policy interests of the U.S.S.R. as much on the status of the Soviet Union as a global power as on her revolutionary heritage.

> It is natural . . . that the Soviet Union, which as a major world power has extensive international ties, cannot adopt a passive attitude toward events which might be territorially remote but affect our security and the security of our friends. [184]

Whatever the true reasons for Soviet expansion into the Indian Ocean, it becomes clear that the emergence of a new pole of strategic significance had once more altered the nature of the international game.

6. *"The Structure of Peace"*

The enormous changes that had taken place in the international arena by the late sixties compelled a critical reassessment of the major decision-premises upon which American foreign policy had been based. Proposals for a new frame of reference were many indeed, as we have seen, but they were mainly advocated by scholars or other individuals outside the government. The administration, despite its efforts at "bridge building" [185] and its genuine interest in the limitation of strategic weapons, was still identified in the public mind with the traditional definition of political reality. Thus its attempts to initiate new departures and escape from old conceptual traps only heightened public impressions of a widening gap between policy and its professed objectives. Meanwhile the dollar came under increasing pressure, and the Vietnam conflict continued to resist the cures advanced by Washington decision-makers who had taken pride in their doctrinal prowess and in their superior analytical techniques. What was required, in short, was more than an *ad hoc* revision of the once self-evident principles that had interpreted and motivated international events in the postwar era. Rather than mere pragmatic adjustments, a conceptual reorientation was imperative in order to establish a meaningful context for future choices, rally domestic support to them, and restore international credibility.

It remained for the new Nixon administration to attempt such a comprehensive new reading of international reality and to transform in a fundamental way the strategic calculations that help to structure the international system. The need to come to terms with the changed parameters of the "world political conversation" was plain enough: Moscow had achieved strategic parity with the United States and the widening Sino-Soviet split undermined the premise that the Eastern bloc had to be contained, if necessary, by wars with its proxies. But because Vietnam had been made a test case of American resolve to resist "communist aggression," extrication from the Asian quagmire was inordinately difficult. Exactly because Vietnam had always been seen as part of a larger picture, its solution raised the question of the future relationship between the United States and the communist powers.

An article by Richard Nixon, published in *Foreign Affairs* in October 1967,.[186] focused upon this set of problems. Defending America's original involvement in Vietnam as a "proof" that "Communism is not necessarily the wave of Asia's future" and as a largely successful attempt to divert Chinese subversion from other Asian countries, Nixon pointed to two new developments that would rule out similar interventions by the United States in the future. First, he doubted that the American public or the Congress would support a future military intervention "even at the request of the host government" [187] and even in case it were directed against an insurrection receiving outside communist support. But aside from drawing the rather obvious historical lesson from Vietnam, Nixon also pointed out that "Asia can become a counterbalance to the West": he perceived "an increasing disposition to seek Asian solutions to Asian problems through cooperative action" [188] that would make major American interventions unnecessary in the future. Here the basic outline of the "Nixon Doctrine" is already clearly visible. In much the same fashion the President told reporters in a background briefing in Guam in July 1969:

> First, the United States will keep all of its treaty commitments.
> Second, we shall provide a shield if a nuclear power threatens the freedom of a nation allied with us or of a nation whose survival we consider vital to our security.
> Third, in cases involving other types of aggression, we shall furnish military and economic assistance when requested in accordance with our treaty commitments. But we shall look to the nation directly threatened to assume the primary responsibility of providing the manpower for its defense. [189]

Thus emerged the *Leitmotiv* of the American retreat from the high watermark of global interests.

The *Foreign Affairs* article, however, was important for still another reason, quite apart from the first inklings it offered of the Vietnamization policy. In another paragraph Nixon indicated that a new approach to American foreign policy would also have to come to terms with the problem of China:

Taking the long view, we simply cannot afford to leave China forever outside the family of nations, there to nurture its fantasies, cherish its hates and threaten its neighbors. There is no place on this small planet for a billion of its potentially most able people to live in angry isolation. [190]

But what was still missing was a frame of reference that would give conceptual coherence to such a reordering of American priorities. Elaborating upon the requirements of an adequate conception of world politics, Nixon shortly after taking office told the British journalist Henry Brandon that the boldness appropriate in the postwar era, when policy differences were understood as conflicts between two contrasting ways of life, no longer served a purpose.

Boldness is not the quality one needs. Today one has to be more subtle, more careful, more circumspect. Others sometimes call it devious or deceptive . . .

Churchill at the end of World War II saw great forces in the world developing. Many of his geopolitical ideas are now fully accepted. But in those days it was easier even than in the Eisenhower days to be decisive and to rally people . . .

He (the President) should have a basic idealistic concept . . . What is needed is a sense of history, an enormous capacity to keep up to date and to be able to contemplate problems without getting tied down in nitpicking irrelevancies. [191]

This "idealistic concept," or what a later presidential report on United States foreign policy called "the vision of the world we seek," [192] as well as a "sense of history," would be provided by the man who became Nixon's national security advisor, Henry Kissinger. "Nixon shrewdly recognized," writes Brandon, "that Kissinger would not only be an asset to him as the only recognized and respected intellectual in his presidential environment, but that he would also provide him with a kind of raw and finished material and the concepts policies are made of." [193] Thus Nixon's and Kissinger's talks during their first month in the White House, which aimed to clarify America's long-range objectives, were, in Brandon's words, "seventy percent historical or philosophical." [194] Indeed, the stress on an adequate frame of reference for policy runs through all of Kissinger's writings. In his doctoral dissertation, which dealt with the establishment of a new international system after the Napoleonic wars, Kissinger approvingly quoted Metternich's dictum "because I know what I want and what others are capable of I am completely prepared." [195] In his later work on *Nuclear Weapons and Foreign Policy*, Kissinger's most severe indictment is reserved for the *ad hoc* character of American policy initiatives. In the last chapter, significantly entitled "The Need for Doctrine," Kissinger wrote:

> Thus at a moment when the capacity to think conceptually was never more important, technical problems have become so complicated that they tend to preempt all attention . . . Each problem is dealt with "on its own merits;" a procedure which emphasizes the particular at the expense of the general and bogs down planning in a mass of detail . . . [196]

Bringing these considerations to bear on the global problems America faced in the late 'sixties, Kissinger identified the elaboration of conceptual framework to guide policy initiatives as the central task for American foreign policy. A closer investigation of his last major article before joining the administration shows further similarities between Nixon's and Kissinger's outlook. Agreeing with Nixon in the rejection of a formerly undifferentiated globalism, Kissinger voiced the same concerns as were at the heart of Nixon's *Foreign Affairs* article.

> The United States is no longer in a position to operate programs globally; it has to encourage them. It can no longer impose its preferred solution; it must seek to evoke it. In the forties and fifties we offered remedies; in the late sixties and in the seventies our role will have to be to contribute to a structure that will foster the initiative of others . . . We can continue to contribute to defense . . . but we must seek to encourage and not stifle a sense of local responsibility . . .
>
> Regional groupings supported by the United States will have to take over major responsibility for their immediate area, with the

United States being concerned more with the overall framework of order than with the management of every regional enterprise. [197]

Thus for Nixon and Kissinger alike the historical lesson of Vietnam was clear: America's retreat from hegemony was not to end is isolationism, as the United States still had to play a vital role in maintaining international order. Stability could no longer be based soley on American preponderance, but different means of ensuring the minimum conditions of order could be found by giving every major power a stake in the preservation of the system. President Nixon later addressed the same idea when he wrote in his 1971 foreign policy report about the changes in America's mission:

> Two centuries ago our mission was to be a unique exemplar of free government. Two decades ago it was to take up world-wide burdens of securing the common defense, economic recovery and political stability. Today we must work with other nations to build an enduring structure of peace. We seek a new and stable framework of international relationships. [198]

But the "structure of peace" was no longer seen as the self-evident result of universal acceptance of democratic values; rather, it was seen as the outcome of a long process of interaction that endows particular methods of adjusting conflicts with an aura of legitimacy. The second image theory of international order so prevalent in "containment" policy, particulary in its "domestic change" version, was now replaced by an emphasis on a "third image" theory of international politics. Redefining the scope of American policy goals, Nixon declared in his 1970 report:

> The internal order of the USSR, as such, is not an object of our policy, although we do not hide our rejection of many of its features. Our relations with the USSR as with other countries are determined by its international behavior. [199]

Consequently, America's task was to draw other powers, irrespective of their ideological preferences, into a process of interaction. This meant not only a new emphasis on negotiation—the era of negotiation had been invoked at Nixon's first inaugural speech [200] —but also the inclusion of powers that had participated only marginally in the established international order. Thus, Nixon's declaration that "the United States is prepared to see the People's Republic of China play a constructive role in the family of nations" [201] was more than a subtle hint at his interest in a new China policy as it was indicative of a fundamental reorientation of the image of the international system upon which foreign policy decisions are based.

It was as an attempt to win support for this idea, called somewhat fancifully a "structure of peace," that Nixon's remarks about the pentagonal structure of the present international system had to be understood. Far from a revival of the idea of a classical balance of power system, the Kansas City speech that broached this image should be understood as an attempt to integrate new centers of power into a conceptual framework in an era when power could no longer be assessed unequivocally.

> The President himself . . . specifically spoke of newly emerging *economic* centers of power . . . Moreover, he specifically distinguished China and the USSR on the one hand from Europe and Japan on the other; in classifying China and Russia as "superpowers" Mr. Nixon almost invariably makes it clear that actual or potential military capability constitutes the primary—though not the only—power referrent. [202]

This interpretation seems appropriate particularly because Kissinger, despite his fascination with Castlereagh and Metternich and the European state system, took great pains to point out that a return to a classical balance of power system was impossible due to several factors.

> Many of the elements of stability which characterized the international system in the 19th century cannot be recreated in the modern age. The stable technology, the multiplicity of major powers, the limited domestic claims, and the frontiers which permitted adjustments are gone forever. A new concept of international order is essential. . . . The traditional criteria for the balance of power were territorial. A state could gain overwhelming superiority only by consent. . . . In the contemporary period that is no longer true . . . major increases in

power are possible entirely through developments within the territory of a sovereign state. 203

Although a revival of the old balance of power system was impossible, modern decision-makers faced the same task as confronted European statesmen at the Congress of Vienna. It is here that Kissinger's writings throw a good deal of light upon the professed goal of the Nixon administration to "build a structure of peace." In the introduction to *A World Restored* Kissinger described the link between peace and international order in the following fashion:

> Whenever the international order has acknowledged that certain principles could not be compromised even for the sake of peace, stability based on an equilibrium of forces was at least conceivable. Stability, then, has commonly resulted not from a quest for peace but from a generally accepted legitimacy. "Legitimacy" as here used should not be confused with justice. It means no more than an international agreement about the nature of workable arrangements and about the permissible aims and methods of foreign policy. It implies the acceptance of the framework of the international order by all major powers, at least to the extent that no state is so dissatisfied that . . . it expresses its dissatisfaction in a revolutionary foreign policy. 204

In a searching investigation of Kissinger's conception of a stable international order, the "stable structure of peace" of later days, Frank Burd shows that a balance of power is only one and perhaps not even the most important ingredient of Kissinger's "legitimate order." Equally important is a "psychological equilibrium" among the powers "formed by the reconciliation of historical aspirations," an agreement on the necessary conditions for the effective use of diplomacy, a reduction in the use of violence, at least in the sense of specifying the "extent and type of war which is legitimate," and an acceptance of the order as legitimate (which enables parties in conflict to roughly assess the "justice" of their respective claims within the established framework). The last point is of particular importance, as it is a distinctive feature of classical equilibrium theory to exclude such considerations.

> The deficiency of calculations based on power alone and the subsequent need for acceptance is developed in Kissinger's

treatment of Bismarck, who ignored the effort of the Metternich system "to endow change with the legitimacy of a European consensus in spite of the fact that the legitimacy of the major outlines of the Vienna settlement was a key aspect of its stability." [205]

The acceptance of an international order as legitimate has several advantages: it sets limits to conflicts and institutionalizes international interaction, thus freeing statesmen from the need to make constant and masterful calculations of power. Interaction becomes routinized and the legitimizing principles become embodied "in a gradually created network of agreements" [206] that harden into "objective" social facts, as outlined in Chapter IV.

This view allows us to assess another key concept of the Nixon-Kissinger "structure of peace," the idea of "linkage." By the late 'sixties, the superpowers had already achieved some reconciliation of their aspirations, at least in the sense that mutual assured destruction removed any incentive for surprise attacks, and thus prevented sudden decisive shifts in the distribution of power. This meant that the common interest embodied in the nonproliferation and test ban treaties could be used to facilitate an understanding on still unresolved issues. Concretely, the Soviet interest in strategic arms limitation (which could only lead to official American recognition of the Soviet Union as a coequal superpower) as well as the United States' new link to Peking could be employed to help resolve other conflicts, particularly the Vietnam war.

The steps the new administration took were quite interesting. First, significantly enough, Nixon, who had campaigned vigorously on a platform of "strategic superiority," promptly dropped this term in one of his first official announcements and substituted the concept of "sufficiency." [207] As a second step, Soviet interest in SALT was placed in a larger setting. Nixon and Kissinger both stalled on the SALT talks because a precise negotiating position had not been agreed upon by the various Washington bureaucracies and because Kissinger judged the time not yet ripe for a "right balance of interest" that would "tempt Moscow toward cooperation in resolving a variety of issues." [208] Nixon made the same point during his first press conference, when he tied SALT to progress in the resolution of the Middle East conflict. [209]

It remained for Kissinger to promulgate and interpret the concept of linkage. But neither the administration's critics in Congress nor the Soviets liked the idea: Ambassador Dobrynin is said to have considered "linkage" as something like arm-twisting or extortion. [210] The Soviet Union was increasingly preoccupied with its containment of Peking, which meant that it had to play its cards in Hanoi very carefully; consequently, Moscow was less cooperative than the administration had expected. Some understandings emerged governing Soviet and American conduct in the Middle East, but the Jordanian crisis in September 1970 and the Soviets' renewed attempt to make Cuba a strategic base by building a nuclear submarine facility at Cienfuegos showed that Moscow was not really impressed by the new tone in Washington.

During the second half of 1970, however, new developments occurred of great future importance. First, the American attempt to establish a dialogue wth Peking, ordered by Nixon immediately after his move to the White House, [211] began to show some progress. During the August 26-September 6, 1970 meeting of the Chinese leadership, the faction advocating a "double adversary strategy" under Lin Piao lost out against the moderate wing under Chou En-lai. Mao's support for a Sino-American rapprochement was reflected in the interview he gave Edgar Snow in December 1970. Professing to prefer Nixon "to social democrats and revisionists," Mao issued an invitation:

Nixon could just get on a plane and come. It would not matter whether the talks would be successful. If he were willing to come, the Chairman would be willing to talk to him and it would be all right. It would be all right whether or not they quarreled, or whether Nixon came as a tourist or as a President. He believed they would not quarrel. [212]

Peking was therefore on record as interested in a rapprochement with Washington going beyond limited ambassadorial contacts in Warsaw, a fact whose significance could not have been lost on the Kremlin. That the United States had similar aspirations had become obvious from some of the measures taken during the previous year. Kissinger's background briefings, moreover, focused on the deterioration of Sino-Soviet relations. On August 24, 1970, he told his audience:

> The deepest international conflict in the world today is not between us and the Soviet Union but between the Soviet Union and Communist China . . . therefore one of the positive prospects in the current situation is that whatever the basic intentions of the Soviet leaders, confronted with the prospects of a China growing in strength and not lessening in hostility they may want a period of detente in the West not because they necessarily have changed ideologically but because they do not want to be in a position in which they have to confront major crises on both sides of their huge country over an indefinite period of time.[213]

The successful resolution of the Cienfuegos crisis, after Kissinger insisted that the Soviet's submarine base construction be stopped, and the surprising performance of the Jordanian Army is repelling the assault of Soviet-backed Syrian and Palestinian forces had re-established some ground rules that made similar probes less attractive than they had originally seemed. Second, the labor troubles that broke out in Poland in December 1970 inspired a Nixon message to Brezhnev in which an offer of economic help was linked to greater flexibility on political issues such as SALT.[214]

The result of these efforts was that the deadlock on SALT was broken by secret talks between Kissinger and Dobrynin. In March, Brezhnev, at the Twenty-fourth Party Congress, threw his support behind a policy of detente with the West. Thus the gambit of using the Sino-American detente as well as economic incentives to establish "linkages" seems to have worked.

The developments of the following months that led to the historical meetings between the American President and Chinese leaders and to the Moscow summit are well known and need not be repeated here. More significant for our purpose is the fact that the visits to Moscow and Peking substantially transformed the "international system," i.e. that image of the world political process which informs the choices of decision-makers interacting with each other. The importance of the "summits" does not lie in the "atmospherics" — indeed the naiveté of some American reporters in Peking was embarrassing and irrelevant, as were the "man in the street" reports from Moscow. What was important was that some agreement on the nature of the international game could be reached. The "Basic Principles of Relations between the United States of America and the Union of Soviet Socialist Republics," [215] signed on May 29, 1972, embody therefore a "concrete definition and the conditions conducive to the transformation of the cold war system to a new international system." [216] The new legitimizing principle as well as the claim to pre-eminence and joint responsibility is reaffirmed in the second and third Principles. [217] This does not guarantee that the powers will follow automatically the new set of rules, as Kissinger correctly remarked: "But it lays down a general rule of conduct which if both sides act with wisdom, they can, perhaps, over a period of time, make a contribution." [218] By the same token, Mao's point that a philosophical discussion might have some value even if it did not lead to the resolution of concrete issues, as well as Chou's interest in the "pentagonal world" outlined by Nixon in his Kansas City speech, were well to the point. Similarly, the importance of SALT I, which was the main achievement of the Moscow meeting and whose substantive provisions may justifiably cause some concern, lay in the fact that it somehow institutionalized the strategic dialogue between the superpowers, which up until then had been carried on mainly in the echo chamber of threats and propaganda.

SALT surely was not a solution to our strategic problems: indeed the predicament of mutual assured destruction embodied in the treaty is more than grim. But SALT recognized not only Russian parity but also the joint responsibility of the superpowers for maintaining the central balance without recourse to strategic conflict. Thus the common interest in avoiding nuclear exchanges due to total mutual vulnerability has been embodied, as some sort of legitimizing principle, in a network of commitments. It has also given rise to a substantively similar strategic outlook on the part of both superpowers and to their acceptance of "national means of verification." True, this by itself does not dispose of the various and genuine conflicts of interests between the powers, but it nevertheless avoids some of the "dysfunctions of secrecy" discussed in an earlier chapter. The real problem of this approach is not so much whether any particular agreement was as beneficial as it was made to appear—the nature of political bargains is always an issue—but whether the strategic dialogue between the established great powers can accommodate the challenges of modern times. In this respect SALT already seems outmoded. Transnational factors are constantly undermining the state-centered view upon which these strategic treaties are built. New technology makes the number of ballistic missiles less and less important and gives rise to a technological race which undermines the assured destruction strategy which is essential to SALT. Last but not least, the dissatisfaction of new peripheral actors and their potential for upsetting the slowly established equilibrium of the international system through the unconventional means of terrorism and economic pressure make it doubtful that a structure of peace is likely to develop. Thus, a final evaluation of this particular strategy to establish a new international system will have to wait until some crucial tests have been weathered. First of all, nobody is yet sure of what will happen when China has attained full superpower status and the triangle of Washington, Peking and Moscow truly exhibits the features of a three power world. Second, such challenges as OPEC and the cry for a new economic order will have widespread repercussions upon the confidence in our ability to establish a stable structure of expectations and, thereby, an international order which minimizes violence and provides for a wider sharing of the Earth's wealth. Finally, a set of rules of the game can be successful only if it attains the status of "social facts," as pointed out above. Thus, the test will be whether these new "regles du jeu" will survive the change of one or more sets of political actors. New "generations" of leaders might see things in a different light and might embark on a strategy of reformulating and re-negotiating the nature of the set of rules that we call the international system.

Conclusion

The reader who has had the patience to follow our investigation to this point might wonder what could be the purpose of such a study in particular and of such an attempt to think coherently about international order problems in general. After all, no "solution" to the pressing international political problems of our time has been given: the threat of nuclear war is still with us, cynically embodied in rules upon which our system of order relies and which derive their stability from the effective threat of "mutual assured destruction." Even aside from these unpleasant thoughts which we all try to suppress in order to carry on a "normal" life, the prospects for ensuring minimum order, in the sense outlined in the first few chapters, through the establishment of "rules of the game" seem slim enough. First, the establishment of rules does not guarantee the avoidance of violent conflict, be it through miscalculation or through deliberate action, as it was shown that "following a rule" also entails in its grammar the "making of a mistake." It is in this context that a most disturbing paradox emerges: if it is true that the management of conflict depends upon the growth of conventions, or, as we called it, the growth of an assumed knowledge, it is also clear that the incentives for acting contrary to the expectations created by such a background knowledge increase proportionately as the rules of the game become accepted and begin to influence the behavior of the participants. Practically, this means that exactly at a time when such rules "harden" and attain the status of "social facts" by molding

207

decisions, the "defection" from rule-regulated behavior is most profitable. This paradox naturally derives from the fact that it is impossible to construct a communication system which cannot be misused by sending "wrong signals." To that extent statesmen will always face situations which are ill-defined. Insecurity, continuous "probes," and requests for reassurance will always be a crucial part of the international game.

Second, at a time when the present "international game," as defined by the super powers and imposed by them upon the lesser actors of international politics, comes increasingly under pressure from outside challengers, as OPEC has amply demonstrated, it might seem that the chosen approach taken here, which focuses upon the stability of interactions between the super-powers, is open to a variety of criticisms. On the one hand, the emphasis on stability may suggest that the preservation of the status quo is the implicit guiding notion of such an enterprise, making short shrift of grievances and pleas voiced by less powerful nations in the name of international "justice." Thus, it appears that the stress upon "international order" is fundamentally at odds with the quest for international "justice." [1] Our investigation may have overcome this dilemma only at the cost of a certain obtuseness towards *"world order"* problems which had been excluded from this book by definition. The limitation of our inquiry into the minimum conditions of social coexistence *among states* may therefore have succumbed to the "statist" imperatives of the present international system which prevent the analysis and solution of world order problems, since their transnational scope and "unorthodox" character would require a dramatic reorientation of policy priorities among nations. From the world order perspective, the meager results attained by the present international system to come to terms with the problem of a more equal sharing of the world's wealth and resources as well as with the threat of an ecocide through global pollution is not so much due to the ill will of particular states or decision-makers as it is the outcome of the irrationality of the statist imperatives and the lack of a "central guidance system." [2] Thus the painful division between collective and individual rationality as brought out by classical game theory or the collective goods debate is reflected here in the split between the reformist advocates of "world order" and "statists" concerned more narrowly with the security dilemmas of the society of states. This leads us to our third point which needs further clarification in these concluding remarks: given the dismal facts mentioned above, what can be learned from such a study of international order? After all, the paradox mentioned in the context of the establishment of rules of the game made it clear that no "solution" of the dilemmas of international politics can be found.

As these three issues will need further elaboration, let us start with the last point and work our way backward. What contribution has this rather lengthy essay on post-war international relations made? Without wishing to exaggerate, I think the argument has helped to clarify certain basic concepts without which a coherent discussion of the pertinent problems degenerates into either wishful thinking or a morass of ideological argumentation. Second, by bringing to the analysis of Cold War problems some of the insights developed in symbolic interactionism and bargaining theory, a new perspective has emerged which allows us to better appreciate the debate between two conflicting schools of historiography. Thus we neither have to take one side nor the other uncritically, nor do we have to withdraw to a position of "golden mediocrity" in granting each opponent half of his case. To that extent, this investigation has helped to revive the discussion and pursue it on a more rigorous plane than has been the fashion up to now. Furthermore, if it is true that correct analysis has to precede a possible therapy, then this work could be useful for the evaluation of policy alternatives and for the distinction of real from merely imaginary possibilities. Third, a set of hypotheses was offered concerning the influence of particular historical experiences, a particular weapons system, and certain new players in the international system. These hypotheses seem to warrant further investigation beyond the scope of the present study, for they appear to be heuristically fruitful.

Having defined crucial terms and justified a particular approach, our discussion showed that social conflict can be managed best—and thus violence minimized—when a common assumed knowledge is available. The opponent's actions can then be understood as "moves" within a game, analyzable in terms of some of the models of strategic interaction. But we also saw that social reality is more complex than that: often actions cannot be explained by reference to the rules of a particular game because most social situations are "rule flexible." Particular actions, although allowed within a game, cannot be deduced from any set of rules. Thus, for example, a boxer's left hook, in a particular boxing match, is "permissible" according to the game's rules but not "deducible" from the structure of the game. Participants in such games will therefore need other aids in order to predict particular actions. Here the role of analogies, metaphors and historical experiences *that serve as inference warrants* becomes visible. The following chapters were devoted to the study of four types of such inference guidance devices that played a role in regulating the interactions of the super powers in the post-war era.

We offered some explanatory sketches for the perceptual change that accompanied the super powers' realization of mutual vulnerability, which also led to their realization that they had a common interest in avoiding major clashes and in preserving their nuclear monopoly against challengers. The institutionalization of methods of avoiding clashes that could lead to nuclear conflict then appeared as a potentially legitimizing principle for the new "structure of peace."

But these contributions, as helpful as they might be, do not dispose of the more principled criticism that one could make considering the restricted focus of our inquiry. Thus the objections raised above deserve some further attention. One criticism can be shown rather easily to be based on a misconception: i.e., the assertion that the focus on stability of expectations contains an intrinsic "status quo" bias. As our exposition of rule-guided behavior should have made clear, what is at issue is not any particular distribution of values which has to be preserved—that is, any particular status quo which is considered inviolable—but rather the ability of the participants interacting with each other to make "sense" out of each other's moves. It is entirely conceivable that vast changes in the distribution of values can take place without the escalation of conflict due to the disappointment of expectations. What is required in that latter case is that all participants change their expectations in a mutually compatible way. "Stability" of expectations thus refers to the ability of the participants in an interaction to continue their relationship without major disruptions—here our remarks about "metacommunications" as outlined in Chapters Two and Three are of importance—rather than to the "identity" of the environment in which interaction is taking place. Another variation on this criticism which has somewhat more validity is the assertion that by making "stability" of expectations our analytical focus of interest, we might therefore implicitly condemn some participants to an "inferior" position as social relationships are usually hierarchically structured and imply asymmetrical "rights" and/or duties. Without denying the last observation, it simply does not follow that the choice of mutually compatible role expectations as the main focus of interest implies the approval of and/or neglect of relationships of subordination. The function of this analytical point of departure is merely to give the conditions under which conflict is likely to arise, escalate or de-escalate, and subside. This leads us to the second point mentioned above: the problem of "order" vs. "justice."

While conventional world order speculation usually assumes that justice and order, equality and liberty are achievable simultaneously "and that the achievement of any of them is essentially independent of the achievement of the others,"[3] some critical recent works emphasize the possibility that order and justice could be classified as "competitive goods," i.e., the achievement of larger quantities of one value is only possible at some opportunity costs. For example, Richard Falk expresses this thought when he assesses the dilemma between "law" (order) and "justice":

> Law tends to support stability of expectations inherited from the past, upholding that which has been vested in assuring the reliability of international and transnational agreements and relationships; justice involves changing expectations about what needs to be done in the future, giving priority to claims for revising inherited rights and duties in light of altered circumstances. Therefore, law is connected with the societal drive toward stability, justice with the drive toward change.[4]

Although this passage captures an important insight, it is important to see that in actual international politics the dilemma may be more tractable than it seems at first. As we tried to show above, "order" is not only the result of legal prescriptions but of various sets of rules with great ambiguity as to when "sanctions" of one sort or another apply. Thus, in order to gain an adequate picture of international reality, we must see interactions between actors as largely "rule-flexible," as the above discussion of the "boxing game" showed; in addition, deviations from accepted rules are rather common. All this makes for a good deal of "change" in actual transactions, although the set of rules governing the behavior of the various actors need not have undergone a transformation. Examples taken from recent international events come readily to mind. Not only the super powers but small nations as well have been able to circumvent formal and informal rules. Cuba, for example, not only successfully withstood the pressures resulting from the application of the "Monroe" doctrine but could also lend her active military support to revolutionary movements in Latin America and Africa. Furthermore, few will deny that with the appearance of OPEC and the intense efforts of the Third World countries concerning their sovereign right over resources within their territorial limits, the bargaining power of the less developed nations has dramatically increased irrespective of whether the proposed far-reaching changes in the structure of international law will be universally accepted. Nevertheless, the full recognition of what was at first only a claim, perhaps initially begrudgingly accepted as a "right," has important implications for conflict resolution. Our above discussion of the function of "perceptual" shifts concerning the nature of the game is relevant in this context. The willingness to be "exploited" crucially depends upon the expectation of predictable behavior in future rounds and thus on the availability of a common background knowledge and reassuring symbols which make mutually empathetic role-taking possible. Thus "justice" and "order" might not be so far apart as it at first seemed. Although "order" most certainly can exist without justice, it is hardly conceivable that justice can be achieved on any sustained basis without an agreement on the procedures ensuring everyone his "due." Unless one assumes that what is due to someone can easily be derived from the inspection of some transcendental order of being, the command of God, or "right reason"—and the problem of natural law theories has exactly been that such a 'natural order of things' could not be constructed by critical reason—"justice" does not refer to any particular distribution of values but to a process of adjusting claims. Whereas the natural law or "dogmatic" theories of justice in general argue with the *intrinsic* just character of acts when measured against a transcendental yardstick, the other class of theories of justice focuses upon the process in which aspirations can be shared through the invocation of principles like equity, proportionality, equality, and altruism, so that conflict is not only settled but future trust can be gained. David Hume made a similar distinction when he separated "justice" from virtuous acts, and when he pointed out the crucial role which common perceptions of mutual "advantage" play in sustaining an institutionalized regime of justice:

> The only difference betwixt the natural virtues and justice lies in this, that the good which results from the former rises from every single act, and is the objective of some natural passion; whereas a single act of justice, considered in itself, may often be contrary to the public good; and it is only the occurrence of mankind in a general scheme or system of action which is advantageous . . . Judges take from a poor man to give to a rich; they bestow on the dissolute the labour of the industrious . . . The whole scheme, however, of law and justice is advantageous to the society . . . After it is once established by these conventions, it is naturally attended with a strong sentiment of morals which can proceed from nothing but our empathy with the interests of society. [6]

It is now clear why the present international order only marginally satisfies the conditions of justice.

Due to the "episodic" character of international interactions, no overarching goal such as "national survival" informs the political process. Competing national claims are therefore adjusted with only minimal regard for equity, proportionality, and altruism. Exactly these factors, however, assure in the domestic arena that the interest of groups which lost in a particular bargain may be taken into account in a future round. It is here, then, that world order thinking tries to come into its own by postulating matters of global concern that could provide the international political process with an overarching goal and thus restructure the bargaining process. Noting that "law" and "justice" are sufficient coordinates for action and judgement only within a system whose "over-all tendencies can be taken for granted," Richard Falk points out the following:

> At present the whole question of law and justice is rendered problematical by the belief that neither stability nor change can be satisfactorily achieved within the framework of the state

system. The new agenda of international concerns arising from population pressure, pollution, resource depletion, and intense economic interdependence requires a series of feats that the international political system cannot readily perform without a significant increase in procedures and institutions of cooperation, what I have elsewhere called a capability for central guidance.[7]

Thus, what distinguishes world order thinking from the investigation of international order problems is the belief of world order advocates that the enumerated concerns are salient enough (or can be made salient enough) to serve as rallying points for the transformation of the international political process. But since the state actors have been oblivious to such concerns, the state as the sole or at least predominant actor in international relations is supplanted by "elites" who make this new "agenda" the cornerstone of their policies. Seen from this angle, world order thinking is thus "reformist" and, more often than not, anti-statist in character. Its style is hortatory and value laden rather than positivistic and historical. Rather than taking the present givens of international politics as the basic building blocks for further speculation, world order thinking starts with the need for a new consciousness and tries to illuminate the conditions necessary, attitudinal as well as institutional, for such a change to come about. Stanley Hoffman's remarks concerning the need for "relevant utopias" which have to be linked to the political present is an appropriate characterization of this type of order speculation.

Our choice of a different focus starting from the present "givens" of international politics, i.e., the state, and for that matter, the dominant states that define the character of the international game, was not motivated by the belief that the problems dealt with by world order inquiries are trivial or unworthy of close attention. Rather, it was based on the recognition that for an adequate mapping of international reality, the understanding of the strategic relations of nations is of central importance. Thus, the emergence of new issues and the phenomenon of the "changing essence of power"[8] can be appreciated only against the background of a strategic analysis which iluminates the reasons for the relative depreciation of military power in the nuclear era, at least for the "dominant" states. To that extent the historical reconstruction of the chain of events which led to such a state of affairs serves an important function.

Furthermore, world order analysis usually does not deal adequately with the problem of the aggregation of interests in the international arena. After all, even if we assume that satisfactory "transformation functions" can be found for the competing goods of justice and order, there still remains the awesome problem of aggregating the interests of the various actors. The postulation of a "world interest," be it ecological stability, dignity, or simply "peace"—values usually introduced as ultimate goals in world order analysis—assumes that this problem has already been solved and the main political task is now to help elites who hold such preferences to gain power in all important countries. But since such preferences are not the outcome of genuine political deals with other relevant political interests but rather the pure distillations of "likeminded" people in several countries, they "provide even less in the way of an authoritative guide to the interests of the world as a whole than do the views of sovereign states, even unrepresentative or tyrannical ones, which are at least the authentic expression of the perceived interests of some part of the globe." [9] World order analysis usually circumvents this problem by simply declaring the "state system" unrepresentative and overtaken by actual historical developments.

Several factors, however, suggest that such a strategy is problematic. First, despite the growth of transnational relations, so well highlighted by the "interdependence" literature, and in spite of the challenge posed to the state system by subnational and non-state actors, it seems in my opinion, exaggerated to conclude that the state system's demise is currently in the offing. The increase in domestic violence and the largely internationalist rhetoric of dissenting groups attacking the present international system seem to be less a function of the predicted decline of the nation state than a disagreement about who shall rule within a given state and what shall be done with the national independence, for which most revolutionaries purportedly fight. Second, even if it is true that the state system is under pressure and might eventually be overcome by some other form of social organization, it does not follow that such a future organization will exhibit the features characteristic in a "one power world." Practically speaking, this means that the policy process that is likely to prevail after the nation state has been effectively circumvented as an aggregator of interests may look quite similar to the present interaction process. Advocates for the multinational corporations, for example, have pointed out that sovereignty would be at bay [10] in an era when these corporations would become the future international actors. But I find little excitement in the prospects of IBM fighting ITT or Unilever on such a worldwide basis, nor does it seem likely that under such circumstances a "higher" or collective rationality concerning global value choices will emerge from the laissez faire of business firms. World order theorists will object that this is naturally not the world they seek, rather, their image of the future is a situation in which a common purpose unites mankind.

Without denying the importance of a change in consciousness which undoubtedly has to follow from such an agreement on a common goal, we would do well not to draw hasty conclusions from such premises.

After all, we know from experience that disagreements and conflicts arise with respect to the proper strategy to follow, even if all people agree on a common goal. "Hyperpolitization" is the result (e.g., in developing countries when strategies of attaining the universally agreed upon goal of increasing the GNP are discussed), exactly because no single compellingly obvious strategy follows from the agreed upon goal. Similarly, a model in international politics which tries to capture the decisive features of international interactions cannot assume that, given one goal, the international political process will be susceptible to analysis in terms of the "rational action" model in which questions of strategy can be decided according to the principle of goal maximization. For these reasons, such a model must be at least "rich" enough to allow for interdependent decision-making. This point naturally has been elaborated in our discussions concerning the "one power" vs. the "two power world," etc. Although "power" in our discussion represented the classical nation states as international actors, I submit that most of the theoretical insights developed above would be applicable to situations which need not entail state to state interactions, as long as a decision process between autonomous decision-making centers is being analyzed. Thus, our final justification for choosing an international order focus emerges: whereas it seems possible to comprehend a political process which shows the features of the rational action model—or to put it differently, the "one power world"—as a special case of a more complicated n-person game, the reverse is not true and may thereby discourage a stringent examination of the dynamics of international politics.

With these considerations in mind, we can now tackle the last and most important issue raised above, i.e., the question of how the study of international and world order problems can contribute to our understanding and perhaps offer some solutions to the dilemmas of contemporary international politics. Above all, our preceding discussion showed that the "solutions" found will not have the same character as "technological" or mathematical solutions, for in the latter case, "correctness" can be compellingly shown. Although it might be possible under certain conditions to construct "optima" for some given set of values, e.g., when the transformation and aggregation problem can be solved, there is a more compelling reason to doubt that the social scientist will often be in the happy position of his colleagues in the "hard" sciences who not only explain and predict but can give advice. Admittedly, it is not necessary to claim that a different logic of "explanation" distinguishes these two branches of knowledge. Nevertheless, as Popper points out, there exists a basic difference in our interest which constitutes the frame of reference in which problems of social and hard sciences appear. [11] The interest of the hard sciences is focused upon classes of events for which explanations are tendered and corroboration is achieved through experiments. While it is beyond the capability of the exact sciences to predict any concrete singular event, like the fall of a leaf from a tree or even any sequence of three or more causally connected events, it is exactly this type of knowledge that we want to possess for the regulation of the social world. Thus, in a search of such a usable knowledge, people accept advice and explanations which are not necessarily of "scientific" status. After all, the person who wants to grow tomatoes in his backyard is hardly interested in the laws that can be adduced to explain the growth of his plants; the person who wants to learn how to ride a bicycle is hardly helped by hearing that he has to solve a set of simple mechanical equations. He rather proceeds by some rules of thumb that survive pragmatic tests. What serves as an "explanation," therefore, need not be solely decided according to logical criteria.

Similarly, when a psychiatrist "explains" some recurrent difficulties in the social encounters of a particular person, he does not adduce "general laws," despite the attempts of some psychiatrists to give Freudian or Adlerian insights the status of scientific laws. Louch writes:

> Psychoanalysis is a special case of a more widespread activity in which we engage with friends and relatives, students and colleagues. It is persuasive argument. We say: But look, you're behaving . . . just like a child . . . And this makes us quite uncomfortable . . . For we do not like to be told when stamping the foot that we are acting like a child. It touches us at the level of moral awareness, it rends the fabric of our self conceit, and undermines the rationale for our performances. The analytic move is explanatory in the sense that diagnosing motives is explanatory. It is addressed to questions of the propriety of action when seen in the light of moral points of view shared by analyst and patient. 12

What serves as an explanation here is the construction of a context within which an event can be understood. True, theories of the hard sciences also establish such contexts or perspectives, but the validity of their predictions is independent of their *persuasive* character. Success or failure can be comprehended within the deductive schemes of the logic of explanation, and counterfactual cases will refute the theory. In the establishment of a "perspective" in the case of human action, however, counterfactual examples do not necessarily invalidate the advanced interpretation. The persuasive skills of the person explaining an action will be exercised to place the rejection of the tendered explanation in the context of the perspective, showing why it was rejected *without* necessarily changing the perspective. We discussed this problem in connection with our investigation of what is entailed in "following a rule." Freud's discussion of "reaction formation" could also be adduced in this context. Thus, rather than being "theories" properly speaking, such explanations exhibit the characteristics of *rhetorical pleas*, which depend upon their "explanatory character" for their effectiveness in *shaping attitudes* and inducing action.

These remarks have important implications for our discussion of political action and the role of a theorist concerned with problems of international order. The role of the theorist now appears very much like that of a therapist, who pleads with his/her audience to pay attention to particular features of reality, who tries to establish a frame of reference that allows intersubjective communication, and who establishes criteria for appraisal and decision. As Rapoport reminds us, even the elegant strategic models that deduce certain decisions from the multiplication of utilities and probabilities serving as guides to "calculated risk taking" are nothing more than pleas or arguments, supported not by proofs but by "bids for attention to certain matters in preference to others."[13] Thus, a great theorist of international politics like Grotius—who convinced substantial numbers of decision-makers that certain rules could still be observed in international relations, despite the fact that the traditional frame of reference had been destroyed by the savageries of war and by religious differences—was creating international reality as much as he was reflecting upon it. If this is true, then it is the never-ending task of theory to reflect upon action, clarify its premises, and change the guides for political decisions. But it is, in the last analysis, action—sometimes well-guided, sometimes foolish, but in its most decisive forms transcending the given frame of reference—which decides the fate of the human race. Herodotus' remark, with which this book began, perhaps discerns correctly the reason for man's tragic failure: not his lack of knowledge but his inability to achieve his aspirations:

It is the most hateful of sorrows afflicting mankind to have knowledge of so much and power over nothing.

FOOTNOTES

Preface

1See Chapter V, first subsection, for the reasons in choosing 1972 as an important historical landmark. In my view the signing of the Moscow accords, as well as the introduction of China as an independent third player into the strategic calculations of the two superpowers, justify using this date as an important historical point of reference.

2Inis L. Claude, *Power and International Relations* (New York: Random House, 1962).

3See, e.g., Grenville Clark and Louis Sohn, *World Order Through World Law* (Cambridge, Mass.: Harvard University Press, 1966).

4Warren Wagar, *Building the City of Man* (New York: Grossman Publishers, 1971).

5Richard Falk, *This Endangered Planet* (New York: Random House, 1971). For a clear statement concerning the reformist "world order approach" see especially Richard Falk, *A Global Approach to National Policy* (Cambridge, Mass.: Harvard University Press, 1975) Parts 1 and 4.

6R. Buckminster Fuller, *Operating Manual for Spaceship Earth* (Carbondale, Ill.: Southern Illinois University Press, 1969).

7On the problem of "rule governed" behavior, see Chapter IV below.

8For this problem see Peter Berger and Thomas Luckmann, *The Social Construction of Reality* (Garden City, N.Y.: Doubleday, 1967).

9George Herbert Mead, *Mind, Self and Society,* ed. by Charles Morris (Chicago: University of Chicago Press, 1972).

10Erving Goffman, *Strategic Interaction* (Philadelphia: University of Pennsylvania Press, 1969); Erving Goffman, *Interaction Ritual* (Garden City. N.Y.: Doubleday, 1967).

11Herbert Blumer, *Symbolic Interactionism* (Englewood Cliffs, N.J.: Prentice-Hall, Inc., 1969).

12Berger and Luckmann, *The Social Construction of Reality,* op cit.

13Burns, *Of Powers and Their Politics* (Englewood Cliffs, N.J.: Prentice-Hall, Inc., 1968).

14Oran Young, *The Politics of Force* (Princeton, N.J.: Princeton University Press, 1969).

15Thomas Schelling, *The Strategy of Conflict* (New York: Oxford University Press, 1963); Thomas Schelling, *Arms and Influence* (New Haven: Yale University Press, 1966).

16Robert Jervis, *The Logic of Images in International Relations* (Princeton, N.J.: Princeton University Press, 1970).

221

17David Hume, "An Enquiry Concerning the Principles of Morals," in *Hume's Moral Philosophy*, ed. by Henry Aiken (Darien, Conn.: Hafner, 1970).

18Here, I follow Hedley Bull, "Order and Justice in International Society," *Political Studies*, 19 (1971): 269-83. Bull gives three criteria for any social order. These minimum criteria are (1) a restriction of the resort to violence on the part of the members of a given society; (2) a presumption that promises will be kept; and (3) a means for securing the stability of possessions. Given these criteria for social coexistence, an "international order" would require such minimum understandings which make the coexistence in a "society" of states possible.

19For an illuminating (and nearly prophetic) account of the role of the Super-powers in the post war international system see William R.T. Fox, *The Super-powers* (New York: Harcourt Brace, 1954).

20For an attempt at deriving international conflict from the structure of international society, see, e.g., Johann Galtung, "A Structural Theory of Imperialism," *Journal of Peace Research*, 8 (1971): 81-117.

21See Chapter II below, third section.

22This follows from the pay-off structure of the games; in a "chicken" game the choice of the mix of cooperative non-cooperative strategies is less costly to any one player than mutual non-cooperation. In a "prisoner's dilemma" on the other hand, mutual non-cooperation is a way of cutting one's losses which would result from a choice of the cooperative-noncooperative mix of strategy.

23See Chapter II below, third section, for an extended game matrix which models the degenerative process from a prisoner's dilemma into a daring game of chicken.

24See, for example, the substitution of a satisfying criterion for the optimization criterion as soon as a "sequential" approach to problem solving is chosen and the assumption of full and costless information is dropped. These ideas are developed in Charles Lindblom and David Baybrooke, *A Strategy of Decision* (New York: The Free Press, 1963); Richard Cyert and James March, *A Behavioral Theory of the Firm* (Englewood Cliffs, N.J.: Prentice-Hall, Inc., 1963).

25See, e.g., Cyril Black and Richard Falk, *The Future of the International Legal Order*, 4 vols. (Princeton, N.J.: Princeton University Press, 1969).

26The work of Myres McDougal could be mentioned here. For a short discussion of his approach, see Myres McDougal and Harold Lasswell, "The Identification and Appraisal of Diverse Systems of Public Order," in Richard Falk and Saul Mendlovitz, *The Strategy of World Order*, Vol. II: *International Law* (New York: World Law Fund, 1966), pp.25-75.

27See Chapter III below, second section.

Chapter I

1See, e.g., Grenville Clark and Louis Sohn, *World Peace Through World Law*, op. cit.

2Myres McDougal and Harold Lasswell, "The Identification and Appraisal of Diverse Systems of Public Order," in Myres McDougal, et al., *Studies in World Public Order* (New Haven: Yale University Press, 1960), pp.3-41.

3Richard Falk, *This Endangered Planet* (New York: Random House, 1971), p.215.

Consortium on World Order Studies, Saul Mendlovitz, Director (mimeographed), p. 1.

5See, e.g., Professor O'Connell's discussion in Stanley Hoffmann, "Report on the Conference on Conditions in World Order," *Daedalus*, 95 (1966):455-78.

6See, e.g., Oran Young's proposal, "On International Order," Princeton University, Center of International Studies, 1971 (mimeographed).

7Stanley Hoffmann, "Report of the Conference on Conditions of World Order."

8Plato, *Republic*, Bk. II, passim.

9Thomas Hobbes, *Leviathan*, Ch. 13.

10*Ibid.*, chaps. 13, 17; see also Immanual Kant, *Idea of a Universal History*, and Immanual Kant, *Eternal Peace*. For an interpretation on Kant's writing on foreign affairs, see F.H. Hinsley, *Power and the Pursuit of Peace* (Cambridge, Mass.: Cambridge University Press, 1967), pp.62-80.

11For a fundamental discussion of the problems involved, see Inis L. Claude, *Power and International Relations* (New York: Random House, 1962).

12For a critique of this theory, see Michel Barkun, *Law Without Sanction* (New Haven: Yale University Press, 1968), and H.L.A. Hart, *The Concept of Law* (Oxford: Clarendon Press, 1961).

13Hobbes, *Leviathan*, Ch. 14.

14For the concept of anomie, see Emile Durkheim, *Suicide* (Glencoe, Ill.: The Free Press, 1952).

15David Hume, *Treatise on Human Nature*, Bk. III "Of Morals," in *Hume's Moral and Political Philosophy*, ed. Henry Aiken (Darrien, Conn.: Hafner, 1970), pp.59-60.

16Hume, *Enquiry Concerning the Principles of Morals*, sect. IV in Henry D. Aiken, *Hume's Moral and Political Philosophy*, p.202.

17Arthur Lee Burns, *Of Powers and Their Politics* (Englewood Cliffs, N.J.: Prentice-Hall, Inc., 1968), p.103.

18Morton A. Kaplan, *Systems and Process in International Politics* (New York: John Wiley, 1957).

19Hedley Bull, "Order and Justice in International Society," *Political Studies*, 19 (1971): 270.

20Oran Young, *The Politics of Force* (Princeton, N.J.: Princeton University Press, 1968), p. 25.

223

21Thomas Schelling, *The Strategy of Conflict* (New York:Oxford University Press, 1960), p. 57.

22Aristotle, *Politics*, Bk. I, 1253 a 16-18.

23Aristotle, *On Interpretation*, 16a-17a.

24Kenneth Boulding, "Organization and Conflict," *Journal of Conflict Resolution*, I (1957) p. 11.

25Murray Edelman, *The Symbolic Uses of Politics* (Urbana: University of Illinois Press, 1967), p.11.

26Edelman, *The Symbolic Uses of Politics*, p. 6.

27Young, *Politics of Force*, p. 116.

28The term "structural certainties" was coined by Bertrand de Jouvenel, *The Art of Conjecture* (New York:Basic Books, 1967).

29Kaplan, *System and Process in International Politics*, passim.

30Boulding, "Organization and Conflict."

31 Schelling, *The Strategy of Conflict*, p. 57.

Chapter II

1"A partisan decisionmaker is defined in the following way: In a group of decisionmakers a decisionmaker is partisan with respect to the others if (a) he does not assume that there exists some knowable criteria acceptable to him and all the other decisionmakers that is sufficient, if applied, to govern adjustments among them; and (b) he therefore does not move toward coordination by a cooperative and deliberate search for and/or application of such criteria or by an appeal for adjudication to those who do search and apply. A partisan decisionmaker is therefore one who makes decisions calculated to serve his own goals, not goals presumably shared by all other decisionmakers . . ." Charles E. Lindblom, *The Intelligence of Democracy* (New York: The Free Press, 1965), pp.28-29.

2*Ibid.*, p. 9 and p. 3.

3See, for a good discussion of these factors, Werner Levi, "On the Causes of Peace," *Journal of Conflict Resolution*, 8 (1964): 23-25.

4Herbert Blumer, "Society as Symbolic Interaction," in *Symbolic Interactionism* (Englewood Cliffs, N.J.: Prentice-Hall, Inc., 1969), pp. 88-89.

5Anatol Rapoport, "Systemic and Strategic Conflict," in *The Strategy of World Order*, ed. Richard Falk and Saul Mendlovitz, Vol. I*Toward a Theory of War Prevention* (New York: World Law Fund, 1966), p. 256.

6Lewis Richardson, *Arms and Insecurity* (Pittsburgh: Boxwood, 1960). For an extensive discussion and critique of Richardson, see Anatol Rapoport, *Fights, Games and Debates* (Ann Arbor: University of Michigan Press, 1960), Part I, "The Blindness of the Mass," pp. 15-107.

7Rapoport, "Systemic and Strategic Conflict.."

8For an elaboration of this point, see Arthur L. Burns, "Quantitative Approaches to International Politics," in Morton Kaplan, ed.,*New Approaches to International Relations* (New York: St. Martin's Press, 1968), pp.170-202.

9See Herbert Blumer's objections to "Variable Analysis" in *Symbolic Interactionism,* Chapters I and VII.

10Douglas Hunter, "Development of a Decision-Making Model in Nuclear Deterrence Theory," Ph.D. dissertation, University of California, Los Angeles, 1969.

11Pitkin, *Wittgenstein on Justice,* pp. 166-67.

12Rapoport, "Systematic and Strategic Conflict," p. 281.

13Pitkin, *Wittgenstein on Justice,* p. 269.

14Leonard Broom and Philip Selznick, *Sociology* (New York: Harper & Row, 1963), p. 68 et seq.

15See the discussion in Uta Gerhardt, *Rollenanalyse als Kritische Soziologie* (Neuwied-Berlin: Luchterhand, 1971), especially pp. 18-42.

16Ralf Dahrendorf, "Home Sociologicus," in Dahrendorf, *Pfade aus Utopia* (München: Piper, 1967), p.145, et seq.

17Judith Blake and Kingsley Davis, "Norms, Values, and Sanctions," in *Handbook of Modern Sociology,* ed. Robert Farris (Chicago: Rand McNally, 1964), p.464.

18Ludwig Wittgenstein, *Philosophical Investigations,* trans. G.E.M. Anscombe (New York: MacMillan, 1953), p.85.

19Pitkin, *Wittgenstein on Justice,* p.165.

20See, e.g., James Rosenau, "Pre-theories and Theories of Foreign Policy," in *Approaches to Comparative and International Politics,* ed. R. Barry Farrell (Evanston, Ill.: Northwestern University Press, 1966), pp.27-92.

21Richard Falk, "The Regulation of International Conflict by Means of Law," in *Legal Order in a Violent World* (Princeton, N.J.: Princeton University Press, 1958), pp.39-79.

22Again the signaling function of law and its connection to social practice becomes visible. Rather than seeing International Law as underdeveloped law in terms of insufficient norms which could (or should) be alleviated by closing "the gaps" through treaty arrangements, the deficiency of the international legal order lies in its inability to trigger action. Because the various nation states, the classical subjects of International Law, have no interest in the maintenance of any particular international order, the basic function of such a normative order, i.e., to guarantee the existence of a particular society, has no overriding purpose.

23See, e.g., Morton Deutsch, "Conflict and Its Resolution," in *Conflict Resolution: Contributions of the Behavioral Sciences,* ed. by Clagett G. Smith (Notre Dame, Ind.: Notre Dame University Press, 1971), pp.36-57.

24Raymond W. Mack and Richard C. Snyder, "The Analysis of Conflict—Toward an Overview," in *Conflict Resolution: Contributions of the Behavioral Sciences*, ed. by Clagett G. Smith (Notre Dame, Ind.: Notre Dame University Press, 1971), p.13.

25*Ibid.*, p.3.

26George Simmel, *Conflict*, trans. Kurt H. Wolff (New York: The Free Press, 1955).

27Lewis Coser, *The Functions of Social Conflict* (Glencoe, Ill.: The Free Press, 1956), and Lewis Coser, *Continuities in the Study of Social Conflict* (New York: The Free Press, 1967).

28Dahrendorf, *Class and Class Conflict in Industrial Society* (Stanford, Calif.: Stanford University Press, 1959).

29Deutsch, *"Conflict and Its Resolution."*

30Clinton Fink, "Some Conceptual Difficulties in the Theory of Social Conflict," *Journal of Conflict Resolution*, XII (1968): 434.

31Raymond Mack, "The Components of Social Conflict," *Social Problems*, 22 (1965): 391-92.

32Mack and Snyder, "The Analysis of Conflict—Toward an Overview," p.9.

33Nicholas Timasheff, *War and Revolution* (New York: Sheed and Ward, 1965), p.63.

34Mack and Snyder, "The Analysis of Conflict—Toward an Overview," pp.8-9.

35For a general discussion of the relevance of these two games for International Politics, see Glenn Snyder, "Prisoner's Dilemma and Chicken Models in International Politics," Working Paper No. 4, University of New York at Buffalo (mimeographed).

36See Snyder, "Prisoner's Dilemma and Chicken Models in International Politics."

37The only difference between these two groups is that the "realists" point to the incompatibility of goals and accept it as "a fact of life" whereas the "mirror image" theory sees such incompatibilities of goals as a problem of perception.

38Henry Hamburger, "Separable Games," *Behavioral Science*, 14 (1969): 121-32.

39For a more extensive treatment of the problem involved, see Paul Diesing, "Types of Bargaining Theory," Working Paper No. 5, State University of New York at Buffalo, to which the present discussion is indebted.

40Needless to say, such a formalization is possible only if two or three players are involved (otherwise the matrix gets exceedingly complex) and an

226

ordering of strategies is possible according to the criterion of decreasing utility to the opponent. Furthermore, "strategy" then refers not to a complete set of contingent choices for all possible moves of the opponent but only to movements up or down the escalation ladder.

41Lewis Coser, "The Termination of Conflict," *Journal of Conflict Resolution,* V (1961): 348.

42Note that this is still a more complex process than the formalization of bargaining theory suggests, as the creation of a bargaining space is very often an intrinsic part of the process. Classical bargaining theory assumes, however, that this space is already created, or known to the opponents, and the only issue is to find a point on the "bargaining boundary" acceptable to both. See below for a further discussion.

43Coser, "The Termination of Conflict," p.352.

44For a general discussion of the role of third parties, see Oran Young, *The Intermediaries* (Princeton, N.J.:Princeton University Press, 1967), and his "Intermediaries," *Journal of Conflict Resolution,* XVI (1972):51-65.

45Thomas Schelling, *The Strategy of Conflict* (New York: Oxford University Press, 1963), and Thomas Schelling, *Arms and Influence* (New Haven: Yale University Press, 1966). For a critique of Schelling's principle of prominence see Rapoport, *Strategy and Conscience,* pp.110-115.

46The matrices for these two games may look like the following:

		Player B Chicken					Player B Prisoner's Dilemma	
Player A	CC	0 0	-10 10	CD	Player A	5 5	-10 10	
	DC	10 -10	-20 -20	DD		10 -10	-5 -5	

47Charles Lockhart, "The Formulation of Interaction Strategies in International Crises" (Ph.D. Dissertation, State University of New York, Buffalo, 1971), p.43.

48Roger Fisher, "Bringing Law to Bear on Governments," in *The Strategy of World Order,* ed. by Richard Falk and Saul Mendlovitz, Vol. II: *International Law* (New York: World Law Fund, 1966), pp.75-87.

49Louis Henkin, *How Nations Behave* (New York: Praeger Publishers, 1968).

50The process described here is very close to what Hays called "metacommunication" in social interactions (see, for example, footnote 22 above). He writes, "What I mean is that at every moment the partners in a relationship implicitly point up each other's smallest deviations from the established pattern of conduct. In the beginning of a relationship, the implicit metacommunication consists of proposals about the form the relationship might take. Person A tries out a role from his stock of program images, person B does the same and each gives the other signals which cause him to alter the roles and images whereby he analyzes himself and his partner. As this process goes on, either the partners fail and give up, or else they come reasonably close to conformity to another's image." Hays, "Language and Interpersonal Relationships," p.214.

51See the earlier section on "Determinants of Behavior," above.

52Robert Jervis, *The Logic of Images in International Relations* (Princeton, N.J.: Princeton University Press, 1970), p.142.

53Lockhart, *The Formulation of Interaction Strategies in International Crises*, pp.5-6.

54Schelling, on the other hand, seems more concerned with tactical moves within a crisis situation than with the general requirements of an overall crisis strategy as he discounts the future implications of a threatening commitment and focuses narrowly on the initial defection. For a general discussion of bargaining in crisis situations. see Charles Herman, ed., *Crisis in Foreign Policy* (Indianapolis: Bobbs-Merrill, 1969); Diesing, "Types of Bargaining Theory;" and Paul Diesing, "Notes on a Cognitive Process Model of Bargaining," Working Paper No. 5, State University of New York, Buffalo (mimeographed).

55See for a general discussion of the Cuban crisis: Eli Abel, *The Missile Crisis* (New York: Bantam Books, 1966); Graham Allison, *Essence of Decision* (Boston: Little, Brown & Co., 1971); Theodore Sorensen, *Kennedy* (New York: Bantam Books, 1965); Theodore Sorenson, *Decision-Making in the White House* (New York: Columbia University Press, 1963); Arthur Schlesinger, *A Thousand Days* (New York: Fawcett Crest, 1965); and Robert Kennedy, *Thirteen Days* (New York: W.W. Norton, 1971).

56This approach is based on Herbert Simon's fundamental reorientation of rational decision-making and its development in the work of Cyert and March. See Herbert Simon, *Administrative Behavior* (New York:Macmillan, 1948); Herbert Simon and James March, *Organizations* (New York: John Wiley, 1958); Richard Cyert and James March, *A Behavioral Theory of the Firm* (Englewood Cliffs, N.J.: Prentice-Hall, Inc., 1963).

57Lindblom, *The Intelligence of Democracy*, p. 143.

58I adopt this stage model from Paul Diesing's paper on "Decision-Making," State University of New York at Buffalo, no date given (mimeographed).

59See *Deterrence and Defense*, passim.

60See Abel, *The Missile Crisis;* also Arnold Horelick, "The Cuban Missile Crisis," *World Politics*, 16 (1964):363-89.

61For further discussion of this point, see Rapoport, *Strategy and Conscience*, Chap. 7.

62Abram Chayes, "An Inquiry into the Workings of Arms Control Agreements," in *American Defense Policy*, ed. by Richard Head and Ervin Rokke (Baltimore, Md.: Johns Hopkins University Press, 1973), p. 322.

63*Ibid.*, p. 328.

Chapter III

1See, e.g., *The Statesman*, passim; *The Laws*, passim.

2See, e.g., the "Essex Result" of the debates concerning the Massachusetts constitution in Oscar and Mary Handlin, eds., *Popular Sources of Political Authority, Documents on the Massachusetts Constitution of 1780* (Cambridge, Mass.: Harvard University Press, 1966), especially pp.447-48.

3See, e.g., Harry Eckstein, "A Perspective of Comparative Politics, Past and Present," in *Comparative Politics*, ed. Harry Eckstein and David Apter (Glencoe, Ill.: The Free Press, 1963), pp. 3-34.

4See for a critique of this movement, James Brierly, *The Basis of Obligation in International Law and Other Papers* (Oxford: Clarendon Press, 1958).

5Sir Hersch Lauterpacht, *The Function of Law in the International Community* (Oxford: Clarendon Press, 1933).

6Oliver W. Holmes, *Collected Legal Papers* (New York: Peter Smith, 1952).

7Richard Falk, "The Relevance of Political Context to the Nature and Functioning of International Law," in *The Relevance of International Law*, ed. by Karl Deutsch and Stanley Hoffmann (Cambridge, Mass.: Schenkman Publishing Co., 1968), p. 136.

8For a discussion of "law" in terms of social mapping, see Anton Hermann Chroust, "Law: Reason, Legalism and the Judicial Process," *Ethics*, LXXIV (October 1963): 1-18; Michael Barkun, "International Norms: An Interdisciplinary Approach," *Background*, 8, No. 2: 121-29; and Richard Falk, "The Relations of Law to Culture, Power and Justice," *Ethics*, LXXII (1961-62): 12-27.

9Morton Kaplan and Nicholas B. Katzenbach, *The Political Foundations of International Law* (New York: John Wiley, 1961), p. 4.

10On such and similar "avoidance techniques" used by the courts see Alexander Bickel, *The Least Dangerous Branch* (Indianapolis: Bobbs Merrill, 1961).

11Fritz W. Scharpf, "Judicial Review and the Political Questions Doctrine," *Yale Law Journal*, 75 (March 1966): 517, and Herbert Wechsler, *Principles, Politics and Fundamental Law* (Cambridge, Mass.: Harvard University Press, 1962).

12See Justice Brennan's reasoning in *Baker vs. Carr*, 369 U.S. 189, 323 (1962).

13Gidon Gottlieb, "Toward a Second Concept of Law," in *The Future of the International Legal Order*, ed. Cyril Black and Richard Falk, Vol. IV (Princeton, N.J.: Princeton University Press, 1972), p.340.

14*Ibid.*, p. 333.

15C.E. Vaughn, ed., *The Political Writings of Jean Jacques Rousseau* (Oxford: Clarendon Press, 1962), Vol. I, p. 305.

16Hans Kelsen, *Principles of International Law* (New York: Rinehart, 1952).

17Myres McDougal and Associates, *Studies in World Public Order* (New Haven:Yale University Press, 1960).

229

18For a critique of McDougal's approach, see, e.g., Knud Krakau, *Missions bewusstsein und Volkerrechssdoktrin in den Vereinigten Staaten* (Frankfurt: Metzger, 1968); Oran Young, "International Law and Social Science," *American Journal of International Law*, 66(1972): 60-77; and Richard Falk, "McDougal and Feliciano on Law and Minimum World Public Order," in Richard Falk, *Legal Order in a Violent World*, pp.80-96.

19Hoffman, *The State of War*, pp.124, 131.

20Henkin, *How Nations Behave*, op. cit.; Coplin, *The Functions of International Law*.

21Myres McDougal, *et al.*, "The World Constitutive Process of Authoritative Decision," *Journal of Legal Education*, 19 (1967): 403.

22See Hobbes, *Leviathan*, Chap. 5.

23Anthony d'Amato, *The Concept of Custom in International Law* (Ithaca, N.Y.:Cornell University Press, 1971), p. 36.

24Wittgenstein, *Philosophical Investigations*, *§224*.

25*Ibid.*, §217.

26Gidon Gottlieb, *The Logic of Choice* (London: Allen and Unwin, Ltd., 1968), p.34.

27K.T. Fann, *Die Philosophie Ludwig Wittgensteins* (München: List, 1971), p. 76.

28Gottlieb, *The Logic of Choice*, p.43.

29Wittgenstein, *Philosophical Investigations*, §85.

30Gottlieb, "Toward a Second Concept of Law," p.370.

31Such an understanding of strategy, called the "fabian approach" by Liddel Hart (because of Fabius Maximum Cunctator), was developed to perfection in the time between the Thirty Years War and the Napoleonic revolution of warfare, as the "reveries" of the Marechal de Saxe show. Unfortunately, lesser minds saw in it more a stylized version of a baroque minuet, which led to the ossification of strategic thought. Napoleon's tactical innovations finally resulted in revolutionary changes because the strategists of the Ancien Regime had mistaken the means for gaining a decisive position psychologically, through clever maneuvering, for the goal of strategy itself.

32Lenin, as quoted in Andre Beaufre, *An Introduction to Strategy* (London: Faber and Faber, 1965), p.23.

33*Ibid.*, p.22.

34Henry Kissinger, *Nuclear Weapons and Foreign Policy* (New York: W.W. Norton, 1969), pp.5, 224.

35This useful distinction was elaborated by Arnold Wolfers, *Discord and*

Collaboration (Baltimore, Md.: Johns Hopkins University Press, 1962).

36See, e.g., Stanley Hoffmann, *Gulliver's Troubles* (New York: McGraw-Hill, 1968), pp.63-64.

37Robert Jervis, *The Logic of Images in International Relations* (Princeton, N.J.: Princeton University Press, 1970), p.232.

38Gottlieb, *The Logic of Choice,* pp.40-41.

39See Pitkin's remarks in the previous chapter.

40Murray Edelman, *Policies as Symbolic Action* (Chicago: Markham, 1971), p.67.

41*Ibid.,* p.68.

42Peter Berger and Thomas Luckmann, *The Social Construction of Reality* (Garden City, N.Y.: Anchor, 1967), p. 57.

43*Ibid.,* p.58.

44*Ibid.,* p.64.

45*Ibid.,* p. 65.

46The parallel between the shaman and the psychiatrist has been drawn by Claude Levi Strauss, *Structural Anthropology* (New York: Basic Books, 1963), Chap. 7, pp. 186-205.

47Herodotus, *Histories* I, 1.

48The Greek word "historizein" from which history is derived originally meant "to search."

49Thucydides, *The Peloponnesian War,* I, 22.

50Polybios, *Histories* I, 1.

51Erik Erikson, *Young Man Luther* (New York: W.W. Norton, 1958),p.111.

52Georges Sorel, *Reflections on Violence,* trans. T.E. Hulme and J. Roth (New York: Collier, 1961).

53*Ibid.,* pp. 41-42.

54Norman Cohn, *The Pursuit of the Millenium* (London: Paladin, 1970).

55Eric Voegelin, *The New Science of Politics* (Chicago: University of Chicago Press, 1952).

56Plato, *Republic,* Bk. III.

57Cicero, *De re publica,* II.

58Livy, *Annals I*, 7.

59Henry Tudor, *Political Myth* (New York: Praeger Publishers, 1972), p. 138.

60*Ibid.*, p. 131.

61Cicero, *De re publica* I, 44-70.

62*Ibid.*, p. 131.

63Aristotle, *Rhetoric*, passim.

64See, e.g. Giambattista Vico, *On the Study Methods of Our Time*, ed. by Elio Gianturco (Indianapolis: Bobbs Merrill, 1965).

65The reason is that Bentham's proposal presupposes an interpersonal utility comparison, which cannot be "scientifically" constructed except by political fiat. For a good critique of the liberal utilitarian position, see John Plamenatz, *The English Utilitarians* (Oxford: Blackwell, 1958).

66Aristotle, *Rhetoric*, 135a, 12-13.

67Ernest Casirer, *Language and Myth* (New York: Harper, 1946), p. 37.

68Leonard Berkowitz, *Aggression* (New York: McGraw-Hill Book Co., 1962).

69See the section entitled "Social conflict" in Chapter III, above.

70Murray Edelman, *Politics as Symbolic Action*, pp. 58-59.

71George H. Mead, *Mind, Self and Society*, ed. Charles W. Morris (Chicago: University of Chicago Press, 1959).

72Edleman, *Politics as Symbolic Acts*, pp. 8-19.

Chapter IV

1Zbigniew Brzezinski, "How the Cold War Was Played," *Foreign Affairs*, 51 (1972/73): 179.

2Whereas it had been customary to date the beginning of the Cold War from the announcement of the Truman Doctrine or the Berlin Blockade, revisionist historians claimed to see the origins of the Cold War in a change of policy beginning with Truman's presidency and the cancellation of Lend-Lease Agreements with Soviet Russia. See e.g., Gar Alperovitz, *Hiroshima and Potsdam* (New York: Simon and Schuster, 1965); also, Thomas G. Paterson, "The Abortive Loan to Russia and the Origins of the Cold War, 1943-1946," *Journal of American History*, 56 (June 1969): 93-114. The most dispassionate account is probably John Gaddis, *The United States and the Origins of the Cold War, 1941-1947* (New York: Columbia University Press, 1972).

3For the thesis that the Cold War dates back as far as 1918, see Andre Fontaine, *Histoire de la Guerre Froide* (Paris: Fayard, 1965-1967). Also Arno

Mayer, *Politics and Diplomacy of Peacemaking: Containment and Counter-revolution at Versailles 1918-1919* (New York: A.A. Knopf, 1967).

4For a discussion of the various "causes of the Cold War" see, e.g., Walter La Febre, *The Origins of the Cold War, 1941-1947* (New York: John Wiley, 1971).

5This thesis is perhaps best developed by Arthur Schlesinger, Jr., "The Origin of the Cold War," in *The Origins of the Cold War*, ed. by Joseph Hutmacher and Warren Susman (Waltham, Mass.: Ginn and Co., 1970), pp.41-77.

6Some of the better known works of the revisionist school of historiography are, e.g., William A. Williams, *The Tragedy of American Diplomacy* (New York: Dell Publishing Co., 1962); D.F. Fleming, *The Cold War and Its Origins, 1917-1960*, 2 vols. (Garden City, N.Y.: Doubleday, 1961); Gabriel Kolko, *The Politics of War, 1943-1945* (New York: Vintage, 1968); Gabriel Kolko and Joyce Kolko, *The Limits of Power, 1945-1954* (New York: Harper and Row, 1972); Lloyd C. Gardner, *Architects of Illusion* (Chicago: Quadrangle, 1970).

7See a critique of this thesis by Robert W. Tucker, *The Radical Left and American Foreign Policy* (Baltimore, Md.: Johns Hopkins University Press, 1971), pp.55-145.

8See, e.g., Louis J. Halle, *The Cold War as History* (New York: Harper and Row, 1967), especially pp.xi-xiii.

9See below the arguments against the traditional view that "universalism" was the decisive guiding principle for American decision-making, a criticism which owes much to the material presented by the revisionist historiography.

10See the well documented attack on the misuse of source material by Robert J. Maddox, *The New Left and the Origins of the Cold War* (Princeton, N.J.: Princeton University Press, 1973). The revisionist perspective is critically evaluated by Robert W. Tucker, *The Radical Left*, and Charles S. Maier, "Revisionism and the Interpretation of Cold War Origins," *Perspectives in American History*, 4 (1970):313-347; also, J.L. Richardson, "Cold War Revisionism: A Critique," *World Politics*, 24 (1972): 579-612. The actions of the Soviet side contributing to the Cold War, usually neglected by the revisionist school, are dealt with in Joseph Starobin, "Origins of the Cold War, The Communist Dimension," *Foreign Affairs*, 48(July 1969):681-96.

11See the discussion of "casual explanation" and "rule governed behavior" in Chapter III.

12Milovan Djilas, *Conversations with Stalin* (New York: Harcourt, Brace, 1962), p.114.

13Raymond Aron, *The Imperial Republic* (Englewood Cliffs, N.J.: Prentice-Hall, 1974), p.33.

14Hans Morgenthau, "The Origins of the Cold War," in *The Origins of the Cold War*, ed. by Joseph Hutmacher and Warren Susman (Waltham, Mass.: Ginn and Co., 1970), p.81.

15Morton Kaplan, ed., *Great Issues of International Politics* (Chicago: Aldine, 1970), pp.17 and 189.

16See in this respect Premier Khrushchev's two messages during the missile crisis of October 26 and 28, 1962. In the latter note progress on the Cuban problem is linked to a possible nuclear test ban agreement. The text of the letters can be found in Walter La Feber, *The Dynamics of World Power: A Documentary History of United States Foreign Policy*, Vol. 2: *Eastern Europe and the Soviet Union* (New York: Chelsea House and McGraw-Hill, 1973), pp.698-705.

17Henry Kissinger, *Nuclear Weapons and Foreign Policy* (New York: W.W. Norton, 1962), pp.44-45.

18I am indebted here to the argument advanced by Arthur L. Burns, *Of Powers and Their Politics* (Englewood Cliffs, N.J.: Prentice-Hall, 1968), Chap. 5, "The Criteria of Systemic Change."

19*Ibid.*, p.102.

20*Ibid.*, p.103.

21This distinction between "vertical" or hierarchical and "horizontal" conceptions of international order has been elaborated by Richard Falk, "International Jurisdiction: Horizontal and Vertical Conceptions of Legal Order," *Temple Law Quarterly*, 32 (1959):295-320.

22From this point of view, attempts to endow the General Assembly with law making power have to be evaluated rather skeptically, not only because of the lack of realistic chances for such an enterprise to succeed but because of the theoretically questionable assumptions upon which such proposals are based.

23As quoted in Raymond Aron, *The Imperial Republic*, p.1.

24*The Public Papers of Franklin Delano Roosevelt* (Washington, D.C.: Government Printing Office), Vol. 13, p. 350.

25For a classical exposition of American foreign policy as a struggle between "realism" and "idealism" see Robert Osgood, *Ideals and Self Interest in American Foreign Policy* (Chicago: University of Chicago Press, 1953).

26G.W. Hegel, "Die Vernunft in der Geschichte," in *Vorlesungen uber die Philosophie der Weltgeschicte* (Hamburg: Felix Meiner, 1955), p.208.

27For an interesting thesis as to the awareness of the Founding Fathers of a particular configuration of power in Europe as a precondition for the political viability of the American Republic, see Walter Lippmann, *U.S. Foreign Policy: Shield of the Republic* (New York: Picket Books, Inc., 1943).

28See, e.g., Franklin D. Roosevelt's view that German troops in Africa were not merely trying to cut off Great Britain from its imperial hinterland but preparing for a jump across the Atlantic to Brazil and thus were threatening United States security, in Elliot Roosevelt, *As He Saw It* (New York: Duell Sloan, Pearce, 1946), p.54. Apparently this view was not whimsical imagination, as United States contingency planning reveals. See "Joint Board Estimates of United States Over-all Production Requirements (1941)," in Robert Sherwood's *Roosevelt and Hopkins* (New York: Harper Brothers, 1948), pp.410-418.

29Charles Bohlen, *The Transformation of American Foreign Policy* (New York: W.W. Norton, 1969), p.85.

30See, e.g., Cordell Hull's statement before Congress after the Moscow conference on November 18, 1943: "As the provisions of the four nation declaration are carried into effect there will no longer be a need for spheres of influence, for alliances, for balance of power or any other of the special arrangements through which, in the unhappy past, nations strove to safeguard their security or to promote their interests." *Congressional Record*, 78th Cong., 1st Sess., Part 7, p.9679.

31See, e.g., Ambassador Ivan Maisky's reservation on the occasion of the acceptance of the Atlantic Charter by the Soviet Union, September 24, 1974: "In accordance with a policy inspired by the above principles which have been unswervingly applied by the Soviet Union . . . the Soviet government proclaims its agreement with the fundamental principles of the declaration . . . Considering that the practical application of these principles will necessarily adapt itself to the circumstances, needs and historic peculiarities of particular countries, the Soviet government can state that a consistent application of these principles will secure the most energetic support of the Government and peoples of the Soviet Union . . ." In Louise Holborn, ed., *War and Peace Aims of the United Nations* (Boston: World Peace Foundation, 1943-1948), Vol. I, pp.356-57.

32As quoted in Kolko, *The Policies of War,* pp.470-71.

33As quoted in *Ibid.,* p.471.

34*Ibid.,* p.473.

35See, e.g., count 6 of the Stimson memorandum to Stettinius on January 23, 1945, quoted in Henry L. Stimson and McGeorge Bundy, eds., *On Active Service in Peace and War* (New York: Harper and Brothers, 1948), p.604.

36Henry Kissinger, *Nuclear Weapons,* p.78.

37Walter Mills, ed., *The Forrestal Diaries* (New York: Viking Press, 1951), p.128.

38*Ibid.,* p.72 (June 30, 1945).

39See, e.g., the rationale by Colonel House to Walter Lippmann for participation of the United States in World War I; see Lippmann, *U.S. Foreign Policy,* pp.33-34.

40Kolko, *The Politics of War,* p.425.

41Lloyd Gardner, *The Origins of the Cold War* (Waltham, Mass.: Blaisdell Ginn, 1970), pp.31-32.

42U.S. Department of State, *Foreign Relations of the United States, Diplomatic Papers: The Conferences at Malta and Yalta 1945* (Washington, D.C.: Government Printing Office, 1955), p.234.

43U.S. Department of State, *Foreign Relations of the United States,*

Diplomatic Papers: The Conference of Berlin (Potsdam) 1945 (Washington, D.C.: Government Printing Office, 1955), p.234.

45Gardner, *Architects,* p. 95.

46See, for example, Gardner's assessment of the Moscow conference, *Ibid.,* p.260f.

47See the preceding section for reference to the Gedanken experiment.

48Stalin told Secretary of State Marshall, who had complained about the pace of the conference, "what difference does it make if we can't agree now; after all, we can come back in six months and try again, and even if we don't agree then, life will still go on." As Bohlen reports, "This attitude impressed Marshall very much indeed . . . General Marshall felt that Stalin was obviously waiting for Europe, harassed and torn by the war and in virtual ruins, to collapse and fall into the Communist orbit." Bohlen, *The Transformation of American Foreign Policy,* p.88.

49See the crucial distinction between "play" and a "game" as elaborated by George Herbert Mead, *Mind, Self and Society* (Chicago: University of Chicago Press, 1972), pp. 150-164.

50See Willard Range, who reports that Franklin Roosevelt "lashed out at the critics," saying: "I get everlastingly angry at those who assert vociferously that the Four Freedoms and the Atlantic Charter are nonsense because they are unattainable. If those people lived a century and a half ago, they would have sneered and said that the Declaration of Independence was utter piffle. If they had lived a thousand years ago they would have laughed uproariously at the ideals of the Magna Carta. And if they had lived several thousand years ago they would have derided Moses when he came from the mountain with the Ten Commandments." *Franklin D. Roosevelt's World Order* (Athens, Ga.: University of Georgia Press, 1959).

51See one of the many accounts on Roosevelt's "strategy" of delaying "political questions" until after the war in Sumner Wells, *Seven Decisions that Shaped History* (New York: Harper Brothers, 1950), Chap. V. pp.123-45.

52John Gaddis, *The United States and the Origins of the Cold War,* pp.1-2.

53Walter Millis, *Forrestal Diaries* (April 25, 1947), p. 265.

54Robert Gilpin, "The Politics of Transnational Economic Relations," *International Organization,* 25 (Summer 1971): 409.

55For an excellent discussion of the British-American differences on postwar economic reconstruction, see Robert Gardner, *Sterling Dollar Diplomacy: Anglo American Collaboration in the Reconstruction of Multilateral Trade* (Oxford: Clarendon Press, 1956).

56See Gilpin, "The Politics of Transnational Economic Relations," p.409.

57See Frederick Dobney, ed., *Selected Papers of Will Clayton* (Baltimore, Md.: Johns Hopkins University Press, 1971), pp.211-218, especially the policy discussions leading to the Marshall Plan.

236

58Cordell Hull, *Memoirs*, 2 vols. (New York: Macmillan, 1948), Vol. 1, p.81.

59Molotov, before the Paris Peace Conference, August 15, 1946, as quoted by Herbert Feis, "The Conflict Over Trade Ideologies," *Foreign Affairs*, 25 (January 1947): 225-26.

60For a discussion of Soviet economic practices in Eastern Europe, see Vladimir Dedijer, *Tito* (New York: Simon and Schuster, 1953): "Immediately after the war the Soviet government endeavored to set up a sealed-off economic area in the Eastern European countries. The plan was to turn the Soviet Union into a vast market absorbing the entire production of Eastern European countries. With such a market the Soviet Union would have absolute mastery over economic life and development in these countries . . ."(p.268). "It came as a surprise to many Communists in Yugoslavia and in other Eastern European countries when after the war they saw that the economic relations between their countries and the Soviet Union were based on purely capitalist principles . . ."(p.300).

61Herbert Feis, "The Conflict Over Trade Ideologies," p.226.

62W.W. Rostow, *The United States in the World* (New York: Harper and Brothers, 1960), p.133.

63Raymond Mikesell, "Negotiating at Bretton Woods: 1944," in *Negotiating With the Russians*, ed. by Raymond D. Johnson (Boston: World Peace Foundation, 1951), p. 101.

64George Kennan, *Memoirs: 1925-1950*, 2 vols. (Boston: Little Brown; New York: Bantam Books, 1967). Vol. I, p.308.

65For an assessment of this telegram, see Kennan, *Memoirs*, pp.308-309.

66*Ibid.*, pp.568-587.

67Joseph Jones, *The Fifteen Weeks* (New York: Viking Press, 1955), p.272.

68Willard Range, *Franklin Delano Roosevelt's World Order* (Athens, Ga.: University of Georgia Press, 1959), pp.92 and 175.

69Thomas Campbell, *Masquerade Peace* (Tallahassee, Fla.: Florida State University Press, 1973), p.2.

70Dept. of State, *The Conferences at Malta and Yalta*, p. 612; see also Roosevelt's letter to Churchill on November 18, 1944, as quoted by Herbert Feis, *Churchill, Roosevelt, Stalin* (Princeton, N.J.: Princeton University Press, 1970), p.472.

71William McNeill, *America, Britain and Russia: Their Cooperation and Conflict 1941-1946* (New York: Johnson Reprint Corp., 1970), p.501.

72Arthur Vandenberg, *The Private Papers of Senator Vandenberg* (2nd ed.; Boston: Houghton Mifflin, 1972), pp.155-56

73Ernest May, *Lessons of the Past* (New York: Oxford University Press,

1973), p.15.

74Winston Churchill, *The Hinge of Fate* (Boston: Houghton Mifflin, 1950), p.201.

75William Bullitt, "How We Won the War and Lost the Peace," *Life*, 25, Part I (August 30, 1948): 84-96 at 94.

76Range, *Franklin Delano Roosevelt's World Order*, p.194.

77See the discussion of the Eisenhower administration below.

78Range, *FDR's World Order*, p.58.

79See, e.g., Mancur Olson, *The Logic of Collective Action* (New York: Schocken, 1969); Mancur Olson and Richard Zechauser, "An Economic Theory of Alliances," in *Economic Theories of International Politics*, ed. by Bruce Russet (Chicago: Markham, 1968), pp.25-49; and Norman Frohlich, et al., *Political Leadership and Collective Goods* (Princeton, N.J.: Princeton University Press, 1971).

80True, Hitler had already ordered contingency plans for the invasion of Russia (first oral orders to General Halder, Chief of the Army General Staff on July 31, 1940) and reiterated his desire to proceed with "Operation Barbarossa" the same day Molotov was negotiating in Berlin (November 12, 1940). The "Top Secret Military Directive No. 18" read: "Political discussions have been initiated with the aim of clarifying Russia's attitude for the coming period. Regardless of what results these discussions will have, all preparations for the East . . . are to be continued." Thus it can be argued that no Soviet decision would have prevented the German attack on the Soviet Union. This argument is, however, irrelevant for assessing Stalin's moves, as he did not know about Hitler's plans and determination and even later dismissed reports of an imminent attack. Thus, given his preference to avoid war at the moment, in order to gain time for rearmament, this policy was surely not helped by provoking Hitler on the Balkans. Stalin must have realized that this might at least heighten the danger of Germany turning East rather than towards England, but he still traded off this increased danger for the apparently more "concrete" gains in the Balkans. Louis Fisher, at least, thinks that a more "accommodating attitude might have changed Hitler's time-table;" Military concentrations can always be dispersed and warlike preparations suspended. No one can say whether if, instead of revealing Moscow's intention to resume the war against Finland and to debauch into the Balkans toward the Straits, Molotov had accepted the role of fourth wheel to Germany's war chariot, Hitler might not have turned toward Africa and seized Gibraltar and Suez. Such a plan existed." Louis Fisher, *Russia's Road from Peace to War* (New York: Harper and Row, 1969), p. 432.

81*Ibid.*, p.440.

82*Ibid.*, p.433. See also George Kennan, *Russia and the West Under Lenin and Stalin* (New York: Mentor, 1960), pp.311-327.

83These words were reportedly used by Hitler in the conversation with Molotov on November 13, 1940; see Fisher, *Russia's Road*, pp. 427-31.

84See, for a careful treatment of this problem, Vojtech Mastny, "Stalin and the Prospects of a Separate Peace in World War II," *American Historical Review*, 77 (1972): 1365-88.

85Mastny, "Stalin and the Prospects ...." p.1375, et seq.

86*Ibid.*, p.1376.

87"Roosevelt to Stalin," received June 4, 1943, in Mastny, "Stalin and the Prospects ...," p.1378.

88*Ibid.*, p.1379.

89There is some evidence that already at the Moscow conference Soviet authorities had lost enthusiasm for Western invasion plans. Fearing Western insistence upon an East European settlement at odds with Soviet aspirations, Vice-Commissar for Foreign Affairs Korneichuk told Alexander Werth, British correspondent in Moscow at that time: "Things are not going so well on our front that it might even be better not to have the Second Front till next spring. If there were a Second Front right now the Germans might allow Germany to be occupied by the Anglo-Americans. It would make us look pretty silly. Better to go on bombing them for another winter; and also let their armies freeze another winter in Russia; then get the Red Army right up to Germany and then start the Second Front." Werth concludes from these remarks, "Quite obviously a man like Korneichuk was anxious that the Russians should occupy Poland before the collapse of Germany or a *de facto* surrender to the West." Alexander Werth, *Russia at War* (New York: Avon Books, 1964), p.683.

90"Roosevelt to Stalin, December 1, 1943," in *Foreign Relations of the United States, Diplomatic Papers, The Conferences at Cairo and Teheran* (Washington, D.C.: Government Printing Office, n.d.), 594.

91Mastny, "Stalin and the Prospects of a Separate Peace," p.1388.

92Campbell, *Masquerade Peace*, p.36. For the slightly changed attitude of the Soviet Union towards economic activities after the death of Stalin, see Alvin Rubinstein, *The Soviets in International Organizations* (Princeton, N.J.: Princeton University Press, 1964).

93V.M. Molotov, *Problems of Foreign Policy* (Moscow: Foreign Languages Publishing House, 1949), pp.250-51, 252, 255. For a good discussion of the veto problem and its political use by the Soviet Union, see John Stoessinger, *The UN and the Superpowers* (New York: Random House, 1965).

94For a discussion of the shift from "enforcement" to "preventive" diplomacy see Inis Claude, *Swords Into Plowshares*, (4th ed.; New York: Random House, 1964), Chaps. 12 and 14. Also see Inis Claude, *The Changing United Nations* (New York: Random House, 1967), Chaps. 1-3, and Lincoln Bloomfeld, ed., *International Military Forces* (2nd ed.; Boston: Little, Brown, 1964).

95For the financing problem of the United Nations, so critical after the Congo operation, see John Stoessinger, et al., *Financing the United Nations System* (Washington, D.C.: Brookings Institution, 1964).

96Edward McWhinney, "The Rule of Law and the Peaceful Settlement of Disputes," in *Soviet and American Policies in the United Nations,* ed. by Alvin Rubinstein and George Ginsburg (New York: New York University Press, 1975), pp.178-79.

97See, e.g., the "cooling off period" recommended by Art. 12 of the Covenant.

98Lloyd George, for instance, called Hitler "a hero who had saved his people from misery and humiliation . . ." See *Daily Express,* September 17, 1963, as quoted by Alfred Jüttner, *Die Deutsche Frage* (Cologne: Carl Heymanns Verlag, 1971), p.172, n.42.

99Arthur M. Schlesinger, Jr., *A Thousand Days* (Greenwich, Conn.: Fawcett Crest, 1967), p.83.

100See, e.g., Kennedy's undergraduate thesis, "Why England Slept." According to Schlesinger, Kennedy blamed more the "general weakness of democracy and capitalism" than the political leaders; *A Thousand Days,* p.85. See also the predilection for "Toughness" in Kennedy's appointees, *ibid.,* p.142.

101Anthony Eden, *Full Circle* (Boston: Houghton Mifflin, 1960), p.578.

102Arthur M. Schlesinger, Jr., *A Thousand Days,* p.750.

103See, e.g., Dean Acheson's speech on February 16, 1950, where the idea of "negotiations from strength" was first formulated. For the text see W. McGeorge Bundy, *The Pattern of Responsibility* (Boston: Houghton Mifflin, 1952), pp.19-43; for an excellent historical account of this policy, see Coral Bell, *Negotiations from Strength* (New York: Alfred A. Knopf, 1963).

104Theodore Sorensen, *Kennedy* (New York: Bantam Books, 1966), pp.577-78.

105Harry S Truman, *Memoirs* (Garden City, N.Y.: Doubleday, 1956), Vol. 2, pp.332-33.

106*Ibid.,* p.340.

107Bohlen, *Witness to History,* p.292.

108Sherwood, *Roosevelt and Hopkins,* pp.898-99.

109Vandenberg, Jr., *Private Papers,* pp.176-77.

110See Ernest May, *Lessons of the Past,* Chapter 11, pp.19-51.

111*Ibid.,* p.36.

112Gaddis, *The United States and the Origins of the Cold War,* pp.308-312.

113Seyom Brown, *The Faces of Power* (New York: Columbia University Press, 1968), p.38.

114"American Relations with the Soviet Union" (Clark Clifford Report), in Arthur Krock, *Memoirs* (New York: Funk and Wagnall, 1968), Appendix A, p.477.

115Joseph Jones, *The Fifteen Weeks* (New York: Viking Press, 1955), p.60.

116*Foreign Relations of the United States, 1946,* Vol. 7, pp.840-42.

117Lyndon Johnson, "Remarks to American and Korean Servicemen at Camp Stanley, Korea, November 1, 1966," *Public Papers,* Vol. 1966 (Washington, D.C.: Government Printing Office, 1968), p.1287.

118Eric Goldman, *The Tragedy of Lyndon Johnson* (New York: Alfred A. Knopf, 1969). p.381.

119*Ibid.* See also Robert W. Sellen, "Old Assumptions Versus New Realities: Lyndon Johnson and Foreign Policy," *International Journal,* 28 (Spring 1973): 207-229.

120*Department of State Bulletin,* 24 (May 28, 1951):847.

121Dean Rusk, "The Containment of China," in *Containment and the Cold War,* ed. by Thomas G. Patterson (Reading, Mass.: Addison-Wesley, 1973),p.184.

122The warnings that such historical analogies are not sufficient inference warrants for a policy decision, because important differences that would require an assessment on the merits are obscured, went unheeded in the debate of 1964/5. Rejecting the analogy of Korea, George Ball emphasized in a memo (October 5, 1964), the reasons why "South Vietnam is not Korea." George W. Ball, "Top Secret: The Prophecy the President Rejected," *Atlantic Monthly,* 230 (July 1972), 35-39.

123*The Pentagon Papers* (Boston: Beacon Press, 1971), vol. 2, p.664.

124May, *Lessons of the Past,* p.100. Rusk had had the same opinion in respect to Korea as reported by Paige, *The Korean Decision,* p.178.

125Walt Rostow, *The Diffusion of Power* (New York: Macmillan, 1972), p. 12.

126*Ibid.,* p.13.

127Strobe Talbott, ed., *Khrushchev Remembers* (Boston: Little, Brown, 1970), pp.367-68.

128See Acheson's remarks on January 12, 1950, to the National Press Club in McGeorge Bundy, *The Pattern of Responsibility,* pp.199-201; also Dean Acheson, *Present at the Creation* (New York: Signet, 1970), pp.462-68.

129For a discussion of this episode, see Christopher Jones, ".Just Wars and Limited Wars," *World Politics,* 28 (October, 1975): 44-68.

130In his pamphlet, "Left-Wing Communism: An Infantile Disorder," Lenin formulated it as the "Fundamental law of revolution . . . that only when the lower classes do not want the old way and when the upper classes cannot carry on the old way only then can the revolution triumph. This truth may be ex-

pressed in other words: revolution is impossible without a nationwide crisis (affecting both the exploited and the exploiters). As quoted in Robert C. Tucker's
chapter entitled, "Marxism and Communist Revolutions," in *The Marxian
Revolutionary Idea* (New York: W.W. Norton, 1970), p.150.

131See, for example, the account of Wolfgang Leonhard, *Child of the Revolution*.

132How the perception of great opportunities did not lead to revolutionary
enthusiasm can be seen by the address of Mathias Rakosi in May of 1945.
Rakosi, an old trusted Stalinist and surely well informed about the "official
line" told party workers "that the post-war phase would be dominated by the
collapse of the British Empire and by weakened Anglo-American relations.
This would allow in turn, the gradual expansion of the Communist sphere.
However, to prevent a mobilization of capitalist resistance such expansion
would have to avoid a radical revolutionary character..." As quoted in Zbigniew
Brzezinski, *The Soviet Bloc* (Cambridge, Mass.: Harvard University Press,
1971), p. 50.

133Robert C. Tucker, "Russia, The West and the World Order," in his book,
The Soviet Political Mind (New York: W.W. Norton, 1971), p. 268.

134This particular theoretical formulation intensified Western fears that the
Soviet Union would promote the "proletarian revolution" abroad not only as
"cheap" opportunities arose but as a matter of primary importance to Soviet
foreign policy. See, e.g., the study of George A. Morgan of the State Department, which became part of the conventional wisdom during the period from
1949 to the end of the sixties. Morgan had his article published in *Foreign Affairs* under a pseudonym in 1949 (the parallels to Kennan's article are striking).
See Historicus, "Stalin on Revolution," *Foreign Affairs*, 27 (January 1949):
175-214; see also a critical review of Historicus' interpretation by Jonathan
Harris, "Historicus on Stalin," *Soviet Union*, I, Pt. 1 (1974): 54-73.

135Stalin, "The Foundations of Leninism," in Bruce Franklin, *The Essential
Stalin*, pp. 110-111. If this utterance reflected Stalin's thinking accurately, then
the revisionist assertion that his goals were solely dictated by considerations of
"national interest" or "security", and not by a much more "revolutionary"
reading of international reality, hardly deserves much credence.

136Stalin, *Works* (Moscow: Foreign Languages Publishing House, 1954),
Vol. 10, pp.140-41. The bracketed elaborations were left out in the 1954 version.
On the significance of this deletion see Robert C. Tucker, *Russia, the West and
World Order*, pp.270-71.

137Robert C. Tucker, "Russia, the West and World Order," p.270.

138Brzezinski, *The Soviet Bloc*, p. 27.

139See Leonhard, *Child of the Revolution*, pp. 318-21.

140Djilas, *Conversations with Stalin*, p. 153. Stalin's sudden confidence
could perhaps be explained by the unexpectedly weak reaction of the Western
powers in regard to Soviet actions in East Germany. A very curious incident at
Potsdam seems to indicate that Stalin not only expected the Western powers
not to withdraw from central Germany, but also, most probably, thought they

would put up more resistance to the manhandling of dissidents in the Eastern Zone. As to the first problem Robert Murphy reports: "Stalin's favorite economist, Eugene Varga, inadvertently presented us with startling evidence of the type of bargaining which the Kremlin apparently expected concerning Germany. Varga, who arrived two days late for the conference, was assigned immediately to our Economic Subcommittee while we were clarifying what was meant in the Yalta agreements by the phrase "minimum needs of the German people." We concluded that the expression indicated barely enough to keep the Germans alive and working. To our astonishment, Varga then produced much lower estimates of the food needs of the Soviet zone than our own calculations. After a confused discussion we discovered that Varga had not included the German states of Thuringia and Saxony in his figuring. When asked to explain this omission, Varga said, 'American troops occupy those sections of the Soviet zone.' He was informed that American forces had been evacuated from this and all other Soviet areas before the conference convened, and that Russians were in full control of all the territory assigned them. Varga was incredulous; he seemed to suspect we were jesting. It became transparently clear that he had made his calculations upon the assumption that Americans would remain for some time in those districts of the Soviet zone which they had conquered. When Varga finally was convinced that Americans had relinquished portions of the Soviet zone without seeking any quid pro quo, he withdrew to revise his estimates. If a man so close to Stalin expected Americans to exploit their conquests, it seems probable that Stalin himself had similar expectations." Robert. Murphy, *Diplomat Among Warriors* (Garden City, N.Y.: Doubleday, 1964), p. 273.

141Brzezinski, *The Soviet Bloc*, p. 60.

142Adam Ulam, *The Rivals* (New York: Viking Press, 1971), p. 130.

143Walter Bedell Smith, *My Three Years in Moscow* (Philadelphia: Lippincott, 1950), pp. 249-54.

Chapter V:

1Murray Edelman, *Politics as Symbolic Action*, p.15.

2Philip Geyelin, *Lyndon Johnson and the World* (New York: Praeger Publishers, 1966), p.5.

3Range, *FDR's World Order*, p.80.

4Bruner, "Myth and Identity," p.277.

5Robert Tucker, *Philosophy and Myth in Karl Marx* (Cambridge: Cambridge University Press, 1961).

6See discussion above in Chapter IV.

7John Kautsky, "Myth, Self-fulfilling Prophecy, and Symbolic Reassurance in the East-West Conflict," *Journal of Conflict Resolution*, 9 (1968): 1-18.

8This hope was not so unrealistic since Stalin himself dropped hints several times that he might one day bequeath to Tito the leadership of the international communist movement. See Vladimir Dedijer, *Tito* (New York: Simon and

Schuster, 1952), pp. 272, 303.

9Vladimir Dedijer, *The Battle Stalin Lost* (New York: Viking Press, 1971), p.150.

10Donald Zagoria, *The Sino-Soviet Conflict 1956-61* (Princeton, N.J.: Princeton University Press, 1963), p. 146.

11As quoted in Vernon Asparturian, "The Cold War, Containment of Soviet Power or Counter Revolution," in *Process and Power in Soviet Foreign Policy*, ed. by Vernon Asparturian (Boston: Little, Brown, 1971), p.262.

12See above Chapter IV, "Following a Rule."

13For a good discussion of the pertinent literature and some experimental evidence, see the article by Warner Wilson, "Reciprocation and Other Techniques for Inducing Cooperation in the Prisoner's Dilemma Game," *Journal of Conflict Resolution*, 15, No. 2 (June 1971): 167-96.

14For a good discussion of these ideas, see Ernst Troeltsch, *The Social Teachings of the Christian Churches*, 2 vols. (New York: Macmillan, 1949).

15"Generation" is used here not in a chronological sense but rather in the sense of Karl Mannheim's group specific consciousness. See for further clarification, Karl Mannheim, "Das Problem der Generationen," in *Wissenssoziologie*, ed. by Kurt Wolff (Berlin: Luchterhand, 1966), pp.509-555.

16See Brzezinski, *The Soviet Bloc*, Chap. 10, especially pp. 219-222.

17Walt Rostow, *The United States in the World Arena* (New York: Harper Brothers, 1960), p.114.

18Truman, *Memoirs*, Vol. I, pp.245-46.

19See, e.g., Gar Alperovitz's thesis of a planned "showdown," in Gar Alperovitz, *Atomic Diplomacy.*

20See Byrnes, *Speaking Frankly*, passim.

21*Ibid.*, p.121.

22For the text of this speech, see *Vital Speeches*, 12 (1946): 300-304.

23"Murphy to Byrnes, February 24, 1946," *Foreign Relations of the United States, 1946*, Vol. V, pp. 505-506.

24*Vandenberg Papers*, pp.247-48.

25Gaddis, *The United States and the Origins of the Cold War*, p.308.

26For a text of this speech, see Walter LaFeber, *The Dynamics of World Power*, pp.211-212.

27*Ibid.*, pp.216, 211.

28Vandenberg Papers, p.268.

29Richard Powers, "Who Fathered Containment?" *International Studies Quarterly*, 15 (1971): 526-43.

30Frederick Dobney, *Selected Papers of Will Clayton* (Baltimore, Md.: Johns Hopkins University Press, 1971), pp.198-99.

31Kennan, *Memoirs*, Vol. I, p.597.

32Joseph Jones, *Fifteen Weeks*, p.141.

33*Ibid.*, p.142.

34Acheson, *Present at the Creation*, p.293.

35Jones, *Fifteen Weeks*, p.142.

36For the text of Truman's message to Congress, see Jones, *Fifteen Weeks*, Appendix, pp.269-74. The quoted portion can be found on p.272.

37See Senate, Committee on Foreign Relations, *Hearings on S. 938, Assistance to Greece and Turkey*, March 24, 1974, p.13.

38Robert Tucker, *The Radical Left*, p.107. Also internally, "loyalty programs " were introduced to eliminate suspected communists.For a discussion of these programs, see Richard Freeland, *The Truman Doctrine and the Origins of McCarthyism*, p.10ff.

39This point is made by Adam Ulam, *Stalin, The Man and his Era* (New York: Viking Press, 1973), p.658ff.

40For the text, see Alvin Rubinstein, ed., *The Foreign Policy of the Soviet Union* (New York: Random House, 1966), pp.229-31.

41See Brezinski, *The Soviet Bloc*, p.58.

42See Ulam, *Stalin, The Man and His Era*, pp.658-61.

43*Ulam, Stalin*, p. 101. Symbolic of Stalin's disregard for the welfare of Russian prisoners of war was his treatment of his own son. Captured by the Germans, he was offered in exchange for the Soviet release of a captured German Army commander (most probably General Field Marshall Paulus, the commander of the Battle of Stalingrad). Stalin refused the exchange. See Svetlana Alliluyova, *Twenty Letters to a Friend* (New York: Harper and Row, 1967); see also Adam Ulam, *Expansion and Coexistence* (New York: Praeger Publishers, 1968), p. 401.

44Ulam, *Stalin*, p.636.

45Andrei Zhdanov, *Essays on Literature, Philosophy and Music* (New York: International Publishers, 1950), p.72.

46Martin Herz, *The Beginnings of the Cold War* (Bloomington, Ind.: Indiana

University Press, 1966), p.140. An indication of the free acknowledgement of Russia's dominant influence on the affairs of the Eastern European countries can be found in Jan Masaryk's remark to John Foster Dulles, "that the Soviet Union would be satisfied if Czechoslovakia became politically allied with it." Consequently, in the United Nations Masaryk voted consistently with the Soviet Union, although some of the Soviet proposals, he said, "smelled so bad that he had to hold his nose with one hand while he raised the other hand to vote for them." John Foster Dulles, *War or Peace* (New York: Macmillan, 1950), p.143.

47Rubinstein, *The Foreign Policy of the Soviet Union*, p.235.

48*Ibid.*, p.237.

49For a good discussion of "domesticism" as opposed to later forms of national communism, see Brzezinski, *The Soviet Bloc*, pp.51-58.

50See, e.g., Adam Ulam, *Titoism and the Cominform* (Cambridge, Mass.: Harvard University Press, 1950), Chap. III, pp.69-96.

51Djilas, *Conversations with Stalin*, pp.178.

52Michael Petrovich, who translated Djilas' *Conversations*, has here a version different from that of Brzezinski, *Soviet Bloc*, op. cit., p.57, given above; Petrovich translates: "Your trouble is not errors but a stand different from ours." Djilas, *Conversations*, p.176.

53See, e.g., the resolution passed by the Cominform in June 1948; the text is published in Barry Farrel, ed., *Yugoslavia and the Soviet Union, 1948-1956* (Hamden, Conn.: Shoe String Press, 1956), pp.75-82.

54Marshall Shulman, *Stalin's Foreign Policy Reappraised* (Cambridge, Mass: Harvard University Press, 1963).

55Eugenio Reale, *Avec Jacques Duclos* (Paris: Librairie Plon, 1958).

56See Philip Jaffee, "The Cold War Revisionists and What They Omit," *Survey*, 19 (Fall 1973): 123-43.

57See the treatment below in the third section of the Soviet notes from 1952 to 1954.

58In a significantly frank assessment of the dangers of a free press for the Soviet system, Stalin told Harold Stassen in April 1947: "It will be difficult for our country to dispense with censorship." He (Stalin) added that this had been tried several times but "we had to resume it and each time we repented it." *Documents on American Foreign Relations*, Vol. 9, 1947, p.615.

59See, e.g., Paul Ello's interpretation of the Soviet intervention in Czechoslovakia in 1968, in Paul Ello, ed., *Czechoslovakia's Blueprint for Freedom* (Washington, D.C.: Acropolis Press, 1968).

60George Kennan, *Russia, the Atom and the West* (N.Y.: Harper, 1958).

61See the remark by Acheson as recorded in *Foreign Policy*, 7 (Summer 1972): 53.

53.

62"X" (George Kennan), "The Sources of Soviet Conduct," *Foreign Affairs*, 25 (July 1947): 556-82, reprinted in Paterson, Containment.

63Kennan, *Memoirs*, Vol. I, p.378.

64Kennan, *Sources of Soviet Conduct*, pp.32, 34.

65See an imaginative critique along these lines by William Zimmerman, "Soviet Foreign Policy in the 1970's," *Survey*, 19 (Spring 1973): 187-98.

66Kennan, *Sources of Soviet Conduct*, p.26.

67*Ibid.*, p.25.

68See McGeorge Bundy, *The Pattern of Responsibility* (Boston: Houghton, Mifflin, 1952), Chap. 10, pp. 244-75.

69George Kennan, *Russia the Atom and the West* (New York: Harper Brothers, 1958).

70See, e.g., Coral Bell's perceptive critique of the policy of negotiating from a position of "strength" in Coral Bell, *Negotiations from Strength* (New York: Alfred A. Knopf, 1963).

71Acheson, *Present at the Creation*, p.442.

72*Ibid.*, p.447.

73See Adenauer's insistence in 1945 on European economic integration as a goal of overriding importance in Konrad Adenauer, *Erinnerungen*, Vol. I (Stuttgart: Deutsche Verlagsanstalt, 1965), pp.34-35.

74Schuman's new "gambit" to attach the problem of German industrial potential from the "point of view of Europe as a whole" is aptly summarized by Acheson, *Present at the Creation*, pp.443-44.

75Acheson, *Present at the Creation*, pp.500-506.

76Townsend Hoopes, *The Devil and John Foster Dulles* (Boston: Little, Brown, 1973), p.105.

77See *Documents on American Foreign Relations*, Vol. 14, pp.506-508, 524-25, especially p. 524

78Adenauer, *Erinnerungen*, Vol. II, p. 55, See also the Soviet notes of March 10, 1952; April 1952; May 24, 1952; and August 29, 1952; in *Documents on American Foreign Relations*, Vol. 14(1952), pp. 248-62.

79Adenauer, *Erinnerungen*, Vol. II, p.70.

80The fear that the United States might return to a "fortress America" conception was however not merely imaginary. At the end of 1950, Herbert Hoover had urged a defense concept that relied exclusively on naval and air force and opposed stationing any troops in Europe. See Acheson, *Present at the Creation*, pp.631-33.

81For a general discussion of the problem of neutralization, see Cyril Black, et al., *Neutralization and World Politics* (Princeton, N.J.: Princeton University Press, 1968).

82LaFeber, *The Dynamics of World Power*, pp.559, 450.

83See, e.g., Acheson's critique of Kennan's position, which shows that he took essentially the same position as Dulles, in *U.S. News and World Report*, January 17, 1958, p. 63. For a discussion of the whole period, consult Walter LaFeber, *America, Russia and the Cold War* (New York:John Wiley, 1972), pp. 201-210.

84See Coral Bell, *Negotiation from Strength*, pp.214-16.

85United States defense expenditures rose from $12 billion in 1949 to $41.4 billion in fiscal 1951-52, and troop strength increased from 1.5 million before Korea to more than 3.5 million in October, 1951. NATO also had gained in strength by the addition of Greece and Turkey in 1952. The ambitious "Lisbon goals" for a dramatic increase in the number of divisions had just recently been announced and the European Defense Community still looked like a feasible project.

86"Negotiation" in this context is a narrower concept than "bargaining." According to Ikle, whose definition of negotiation is quite useful, "negotiation is a process in which explicit proposals are put forward ostensibly for the purpose of reaching agreement on an exchange or on the realization of a common interest where conflicting interests are present." Fred Ikle, *How Nations Negotiate* (New York: Praeger Publishers, 1964), pp.3-4.

87As quoted by LaFeber, *America, Russia and the Cold War*, p.152.

88See Nikita Khrushchev's "Secret Speech" at the Twentieth Party Congress. For the full text see Dan Jacobs, ed., *The New Communist Manifesto* (New York: Harper Torch Books, 1965), p. 152.

89See, for example, D. Chesnokov's article in *Kommunist*, No. 2 (1953): 22: this article is analyzed by Tucker, "The Stalin Heritage," pp. 97-98.

90Brown, *Faces of Power*, pp.109-110.

91John Foster Dulles, "A Policy of Boldness," *Life*, 32 (May 19, 1952): 146-60, reprinted in Paterson, *Containment and the Cold War*, pp.75-55.

92As a result of a reassessment of American strategy, Eisenhower on May 8, 1953, ordered three groups to articulate and defend three possible strategies The alternatives were (a) to continue containment, (b) to "draw a line" at certain threatened areas—Formosa, Middle East, South East Asia—and serve notice to the Soviet Union that any crossing of the line would result in general war as an option, (c) to adopt a strategy of "liberation." For further discussion, see Chapter 42 of Walt Rostow's *The United States in the World Arena.*

93Brown, *Faces of Power*, p.92.

94See, e.g., Dulles' reasoning concerning the success of communism in *War or Peace*, Chapter 13, "Why Communism Wins," pp.165-72.

95Harold Macmillan, *The Tides of Fortune*, p.513.

96Dulles, *War or Peace*, p.165.

97See Iklé, *How Nations Negotiate*, particularly Chapter 4, "Negotiating for Side-Effects," pp.43-59.

98LaFeber, *The Dynamics of World Power*, p.250.

99*Ibid.*, p. 521. In order to prevent the Soviets from scoring a moral victory, Dulles proposed that the President should avoid being photographed with the Kremlin leaders. See Paper IV in *Ibid.*, p. 523.

100Bell, *Negotiations from Strength*, p.75.

101This was Kennan's terminology in his "X" article.

102Dulles testified on June 10, 1955, before a House Subcommittee that "the economy of the Soviet Union is on the point of collapsing," as quoted in David Dallin, *Soviet Foreign Policy after Stalin* (Philadelphia: Lippincott, 1961), p.278.

103James Burnham, *The Coming Defeat of Communism* (New York: John Day, 1950).

104See, e.g., *ibid.*, Chapter XIV, pp.208-221.

105*Ibid.*, Chapter IX.

106*Ibid.*, pp. 233,234.

107See Chapter IV above concerning the importance of different modes of comprehending situations; similarly see Clifford Geertz, "Ideology as a Cultural System," in David Apter, *Sociology and Discontent* (New York: Free Press, 1964).

108For the importance of such a comprehensive "plan," see Burnham, *The Coming Defeat of Communism*, p. 235.

109Hoopes, *The Devil and John Foster Dulles*, p. 125.

110When Stalin died there were no "plans," despite the fact that according to Cold War mythology all absolute dictatorships collapse with the death of the dictator. See Peter Lyon, *Eisenhower, Portrait of a Hero* (Boston: Little, Brown, 1974), pp.530-31. Intelligence reports submitted to the President seem to have refuted this widely shared assumption, one report stressed that the new Soviet premier would have to consolidate his internal control and consequently would not undertake new departures in foreign affairs; LaFeber, *America, Russia and the Cold War*, p. 148.

111Dwight Eisenhower, *Mandate for Change* (New York:Doubleday, 1963), p. 148.

112Hoopes, *The Devil and John Foster Dulles*, p. 171. (Dulles read from the Chapter "Tactical Retreats" of "Problems of Leninism.")

113Emmet John Hughes, *The Ordeal of Power* (New York: Atheneum, 1963), p.109.

114Hoopes, *The Devil and John Foster Dulles*, p. 179.

115*Ibid.*, p. 180.

116Bohlen, *Witness to History*, p. 356.

117See the second section in this chapter, above.

118"A Chance for Peace," address to the American Society of Newspaper Editors, April 16, 1953, *Public Papers of the Presidents, Dwight Eisenhower,* Vol. I (1953), pp. 179-88.

119Bohlen, *Witness to History*, p. 371; also Bell, *Negotiation from Strength,* μ. 216.

120Karl Gruber, *Zwischen Befreiung and Freiheit* (Vienna: Ullstein, 1953), p.309.

121See Dallin, *Soviet Foreign Policy*, Part II, Chapter I and Chapter 3, pp.117-24, 135-40.

122See, e.g., Pravda's firm rejection of any preconditions for a summit talk, *ibid.*, p. 130. Also Khrushchev is said to have grumbled: "We are not going with broken legs to Geneva."

123When French Socialists visited Moscow in the spring of 1956, Shepilov and Khrushchev took pains to point out that the "thaw" after the Twentieth Party Congress would not mean a gradual transformation of the Soviet system into a Western type of democracy. Both leaders stated firmly "that no second political party would be permitted to emerge in Russia." Dallin, *Soviet Foreign Policy*, p. 240.

124*Ibid.*, p. 139.

125*Ibid.*, p. 257.

126See, for a general report of the July 1955 Plenum of the Central Committee, Dallin, *Soviet Foreign Policy*, Part III, Chapter I, pp. 227-33.

127*Ibid.*, p. 230.

128See above, n. 119.

129See Bell, *Negotiation from Strength*, pp. 129-30.

130For the various rules applying to the relationship within the bloc and between the blocs, see Morton Kaplan, *System and Process;* see also Morton Kaplan and Nicholas Katzenbach, *The Political Foundations of International Law* (New York: John Wiley, 1961).

131Bell, *Negotiation from Strength*, p. 239.

Chapter VI

1Gottlieb, *Toward a Second Concept of Law*, p. 370; see also above discussion of "Following a Rule" in the second section of Chapter. IV.

2Kissinger, *Nuclear Weapons*, p. 5.

3Stanley Hoffmann, "International Systems and International Law," *The State of War*, pp. 88-122.

4*Ibid.*, pp.92-93.

5Compare the above distinction between vassal and ally in the second section of Chapter IV.

6I am indebted in this discussion to Arthur L. Burns, "Military Technological Models and World Order," *International Journal*, 42, No. 4 (1969): 790-806.

7Bernard Brodie, *The Absolute Weapon* (New York: Harcourt, Brace. 1946), p. 76.

8See, e.g., John Toland, *The Rising Sun* (New York:Random House, 1970),pp.806-855.

9*New York Times*, March 2, 1955.

10Gar Alperovitz, *Atomic Diplomacy.*

11Byrnes, *Speaking Frankly*, p. 263.

12Gabriel Kolko, *The Politics of War*, pp.421-22.

13Churchill, *Triumph and Tragedy*, pp.668-70.

14For a good discussion of the Soviet nuclear program, see Arnold Kramish, *Atomic Energy in the Soviet Union* (Stanford, Calif.: Stanford University Press, 1959).

15Edward Stettinius, *Roosevelt and the Russians: The Yalta Conference* (Garden City, N.Y.:Doubleday, 1949),p.43.

16For a short discussion of the indigenous character of the Soviet nuclear program (rather than the widely accepted opinion that only espionage enabled the Soviet Union to proceed with the development of these weapons), see Walter and Miriam Schneir, *Invitation to an Inquest* (Garden City, N.Y.:Doubleday, 1965), p. 17.

17In August 1966, Igor N. Golovin, a Soviet physicist, disclosed the date of the crucial decision. See Thomas Wolfe, *Soviet Power and Europe* (Baltimore, Md.: Johns Hopkins University Press, 1970), p. 35, n. 7.

18Wolfe, *Soviet Power and Europe*, p.36,n.8.

19See James Glackin, "How Secrecy Played Executioner," *Bulletin of the Atomic Scientists*, XXI, No. 6 (1975): 14-16.

20Djilas, *Conversations with Stalin*, p. 153.

21On this point see Schneir, *Invitation to an Inquest* and Glackin, "How Secrecy Played Executioner."

22Djilas, *Conversations with Stalin*, p. 153.

23Ulam, *The Rivals*, p. 103.

24George Quester, *Nuclear Diplomacy* (New York:Dunellen, 1970), p. 5.

25Huntington, *Common Defense*, p. 40.

26U.S. Atomic Energy Commission, *Transcript of Hearings in the Matter of J. Robert Oppenheimer* (Washington, D.C.: Government Printing Office, 1954), p.366.

27Huntington, *Common Defense*, p.366.

28*Ibid.*, pp.308-309; Quester, *Nuclear Diplomacy*, p.34.

29Bernhard Brodie, *Strategy in the Missile Age* (Princeton, N.J.:Princeton University Press, 1965),pp.153-54.

30Huntington, *Common Defense*, p. 89.

31See, e.g., the B-36 controversy which erupted in 1949 when some United States admirals suggested that Navy jet interceptors should be given a chance in showing their superiority over this bomber type, thereby disputing the Air Force's claim to large resources. For a discussion of this controversy, see Walter Millis, Harvey Mansfield, and Harold Stein, *Arms and the State* (New York: Twentieth Century Fund, 1958), pp.250-55.

32Huntington, *Common Defense*, Chapter 5, pp.326-41.

33On this point see especially Robert Donovan, *Eisenhower, The Inside Story* (New York: Harper Brothers, 1956), passim.

34For a text of Dulles' speech before the Council on Foreign Relations see *Documents on American Foreign Relations 1954* (New York: Harper & Brothers, 1955), pp. 7-15.

35*Ibid.*, pp.10, 9.

36Alexander George and Richard Smoke, *Deterrence in American Foreign Policy* (New York: Columbia University Press, 1974), p.255. On the other hand, Dulles seems to have offered 2 atomic bombs to the French embattled at Dien-

252

Bien-Phu; see Roscoe Drummond and Gaston Coblentz, *Duel at the Brink* (Garden City, N.Y.:Doubleday, 1960),pp.121-22.

37Huntington, *Common Defense*, p. 78.

38Bruce Smith, "RAND Case Study: Selection and Use of Strategic Air Bases," in *American Defense Policy*, ed. by Richard Head and Ervin Rokke, p. 452.

39Morton Halperin, "The Gaither Committee and the Policy Process," *World Politics*, 13, No. 3 (April 1961): 360-84.

40*Ibid.*, p. 370.

41*Ibid.*

42Roy Licklider, "The Missile Gap Controversy," *Political Science Quarterly*, LXXXCV, No.4 (December 1970): 600-615. See also U.S. Congress, House, Committee on Appropriations, *Hearings, Department of Defense Appropriations for 1961*, Part 1, 86th Cong., 2nd Sess., 1960, p.23.

43According to Sorensen the evidence from U-2 photographs had not been available to Kennedy during his campaign, but had served as a basis for the administration's downgrading of the Soviet missile threat. Sorensen, *Kennedy*, pp. 688-90.

44For a discussion of the "quick fix" measures designed to improve the reliability and effectiveness of United States forces, see William Kaufmann, *The McNamara Strategy* (N.Y.:Harper & Row, 1964),Chapter 2, pp.47-73.

45*Congressional Quarterly Almanac*, 87th Cong., 1st Sess., Vol. VII (Washington, D.C., 1961),pp.899ff.

46This speech before the NATO Council is still classified but there seems to be agreement that the subsequent Ann Arbor address is the declassified version of the Athens speech. See John Newhouse, *De Gaulle and the Anglo Saxons* (New York: Viking Press, 1970), p.162.

47For the text see *Vital Speeches*, XXVIII (August 1, 1962):622-29.

48For the fascination of Kennedy and the New Frontiersmen with guerrilla warfare and counterinsurgency, see Sorensen, *Kennedy*, pp. 709-714, and naturally the *Pentagon Papers*.

49LaFeber, *Dynamics of World Power*, p. 685.

50Quester, *Nuclear Diplomacy*, p. 228.

51This distinction between a no-city strategy and a counterforce strategy is brought out by Thomas Schelling, "Nuclear NATO and the 'New Strategy,' " in *Problems of National Strategy*, ed. Henry Kissinger (New York: Praeger Publishers, 1965), pp.169-86.

52A valuable account of the revision of Soviet strength through the new analytic techniques introduced by McNamara is Alain Enthoven and Wayne Smith, *How Much is Enough?* (New York: Harper and Row, 1971).

53See also Bernhard Brodie's critique in *War and Politics* (New York: Macmillan, 1973), p. 404.

54*Ibid.*,p. 398.

55Schlesinger, *A Thousand Days*, p. 743.

56Elie Abel, *The Cuban Missile Crisis* (Philadelphia: J.B. Lippincott, 1966), p. 52.

57Sorensen, *Kennedy*, p.793.

58See, e.g., the discussion of C.G. Jacobsen, *Soviet Strategy and Soviet Foreign Policy* (Glasgow: Robert Macleahouse and Co, 1973).

59For the pattern of Soviet procurement after the Second World War see Quester, *Nuclear Diplomacy*, pp.39-44; also see Wolfe, *Soviet Power*, Chap. 3.

60For a further discussion see Herbert Dinerstein, *War and the Soviet Union* (New York: Praeger Publishers, 1962), pp.6-7.

61Anatol Rapoport, *The Big Two*, pp. 103-104.

62Wolfe, *Soviet Power*, p. 38.

63For an interesting treatment of Soviet capabilities and the development of strategic doctrines see Young Hoon Kang, "The Relationship Between the Development of Strategic Nuclear Weapons Systems and Deterrence Doctrine in the Soviet Union and China" (Ph.D. dissertation, University of Southern California, 1973).

64See, e.g., the report of defector Colonel G.A. Tokaev, *Stalin Means War* (London: Genge, Weidenfeld and Nicholson, 1951), p. 115.

65Asher Lee, ed., *Soviet Air and Rocket Forces* (New York: Praeger Publishers, 1959).

66For the text of N. Talenski, "On the Question of the Laws of Military Science," see Nikolai Galay, "New Trends in Soviet Military Doctrine," *Bulletin, Institute for the Study of the U.S.S.R.*, Vol. 3, No. 6 (June 1956).

67Dinerstein, *War and the Soviet Union*, pp. 49-52.

68Raymond Garthoff, *Soviet Military Policy* (New York: Praeger Publishers, 1966).

69Dinerstein, *War and the Soviet Union*, p. 71. Actually the "end of civilization theme" echoed Eisenhower's statement made before the United Nations in December 1953.

70Dinerstein, *War and the Soviet Union*, p.77.

71Frederic Burin, "The Communist Doctrine of the Inevitability of War," *American Political Science Review*, 57 (1961): 343-54.

254

72For a text of Khrushchev's report to the Twenty-First Party Congress see *Current Soviet Policies* (New York: Praeger Publishers, 1960), Vol. III.

73*Ibid.*, p. 58.

74Kang, "Development of Strategic Nuclear Weapons Systems and Deterrence Doctrine," Chap. 4.

75For a study of the use of exaggerated claims made in connection with the "Missile gap," see Arnold Horelick and Myron Rush. *Strategic Power and Soviet Policy* (Chicago: University of Chicago Press, 1966).

76William Zimmerman, *Soviet Perspectives*, pp. 191-92.

77For the text of his speech see LaFeber, *Dynamics of World Power*, pp.649-61.

78Schlesinger, *A Thousand Days*, p.339.

79See, e.g., Kennedy's and McNamara's reactions to this speech as reported by William Kaufmann, *The McNamara Strategy*, pp. 60-63.

80LaFeber, *Dynamics of World Power*, p. 653.

81Schlesinger, *A Thousand Days*, pp.339-40.

82Jacobsen, *Soviet Strategy*, p. 21.

83Edward Weintal and Charles Bartlett, *Facing the Brink* (New York:Scribner, 1967), p.68.

84Robert Kennedy, *Thirteen Days* (New York:W.W. Norton, 1969), pp.32, 126.

85For the text of these letters see LaFeber, *Dynamics of World Power*, pp. 699-710.

86For the role of the United Nations as a face-saving device in reaching the final "deal" see Graham Allison, *Essence of Decision*, pp.218-28. Also see Schlesinger, *A Thousand Days*, p. 709.

87LaFeber, *Dynamics of World Power* p. 700.

88*Ibid.*, p. 703.

89Having pledged open support for the Soviet Union in the Cuban crisis China lost no time in attacking the Kremlin when Khruschchev's indication of intent to withdraw the missiles was announced. Besides, China felt betrayed by the Soviets since the Kremlin failed to take her side in the border dispute with India which led to military clashes during the time of the missile crisis. See John Gittings, *Survey of the Sino-Soviet Dispute* (New York:Oxford University Press, 1968), pp. 174-83.

90LaFeber, *Dynamics of World Power*, p. 705. See also Khrushchev's disarmament proposals in the aftermath of the crisis. *Ibid.*, p. 707.

91Bell, *Conventions,* p. 78.

92Kaufmann, *The McNamara Strategy,* Chap. 4.

93Bell, *Conventions,* p. 78.

94Report by Premier Khrushchev on the International Situation, in LaFeber, *Dynamics of World Power,* p. 720.

95*Ibid.,* p. 718.

96Zimmerman, *Soviet Perspectives on International Relations,* p. 223.

97Marshal Shulman, *Beyond the Cold War* (New Haven: Yale University Press, 1966), p.54.

98LaFeber, *Dynamics of World Power,* pp.725-26.

99*Ibid.,* p. 724.

100Gittings, *A Survey of the Sino-Soviet Dispute,* pp.184-92.

101See, e.g., Secretary of Defense McNamara's testimony at an appropriations hearing in 1965. "The Soviets have decided that they have lost the quantitative race and they are not seeking to engage us in that contest. It means that there is no indication that the Soviets are seeking to develop a nuclear force as large as ours." *Congressional Record,* 89th Congress, 1st Session, vol. III, Part 6 (April 7, 1965),p.7271.

102See, e.g., McNamara's recognition of this fact in his testimony before the House Armed Services Committee, *Hearings on Military Posture,* 1963, as quoted in Kaufmann, *The McNamara Strategy,* p. 94.

103For a discussion of the ABM problem see Herbert F.York, ed., *Arms Control, Readings from Scientific American* (San Francisco:Freeman and Co., 1973); U.S. Congress, Senate, Committee on Armed Services, *Military Implications of the Treaty on the Limitation of Antiballistic Missile Systems and the Interim Agreement on Limitation of Strategic Offensive Arms, Hearings,* 92nd Cong., 2nd Sess. (Washington, D.C.: Government Printing Office, 1972); William Kintner and Robert Pfaltzgraff, *SALT, Implications for Arms Control in the 1970's* (Pittsburgh: University of Pittsburgh Press, 1973); John Holst and William Schneider, eds., *Why ABM* (New York: Pergamon, 1969); Abram Chayes and Jerome Wiesner, eds., *ABM, An Evaluation* (New York: Harper & Row, 1969); and C.F. Barnaby and A. Boserup, eds., *Implications of Antiballistic Missile Systems,* Pugwash Monograph I (London: Souvenir Press, 1969).

104See, e.g., Robert McNamara, "The Dynamics of Nuclear Strategy," Address to the editors and publishers of the United Press International on September 18, 1967, in LaFeber, *The Dynamics of World Power,* p. 786. For a discussion of McNamara's ABM policy see Benson Adams, "McNamara's ABM Policy 1961-67," *Orbis,* XII, No. 1 (Spring, 1968): 200-225; see also Morton Halperin, "The Decision to Deploy the ABM," *World Politics,* 25, No. 1 (October 1972): 62-95, reprinted in Head and Rokke, *American Defense Policy,* pp.466-86.

105Halperin, "The Decision to Deploy the ABM,"p. 482.

106Marshal Shulman, "Toward a Western Philosophy of Co-existence," *Foreign Affairs*, 52, No. 1(1973):45-59.

107See, e.g., the references given by the German news magazine *Der Spiegel* in its title article, "Eine schwarze Wolke hängt über uns," 28, No. 7 (February 11, 1974):72-84 at p. 79.

108Newhouse, *Cold Dawn.* pp. 188-89.

109In this discussion I am indebted to Arthur L. Burns, "Military-Technological Models and World Order," *International Journal*, 42, No. 4 (Fall 1969): 790-806.

110See, e.g., Henry Kissinger, "Coalition Diplomacy in a Nuclear Age," *Foreign Affairs*, 42 (July 1964): 525-45. Also see Pierre Gallois, "U.S. Strategy and the Defense of Europe," *Problems of National Strategy,* ed. by Henry Kissinger, pp.288-312. Although the latter piece is and was very controversial in some of the conclusions, it was highly influential in structuring the debate about the changed utility of alliances in the nuclear age.

111Rostow, *The United States in the World Arena*, p. 76.

112*Journal Officiel*, January 24, 1963, as quoted by B.W. Augenstein, "The Chinese and French Programs for the Development of National Nuclear Forces," *Orbis*, XI (Fall 1967): 854.

113See the Statement by the Chinese Government on August 15, 1963, on proposals for nuclear nonproliferation, in John Gittings, *A Survey of the Sino-Soviet Dispute*, p. 192.

114Halperin, *China and the Bomb,* pp.49-51.

115For an account of this meeting see Alexander Dallin, *Soviet Foreign Policy After Stalin*, pp.77-93, and John Gittings, *The World and China 1922-72* (New York: Harper and Row, 1974), Chap. 7.

116For an elaboration of this theory see Mao's "Supreme State" speech in 1958; also see Gittings, *China and the World*, pp.232-35.

117Harold Macmillan, *Tides of Fortune*, p. 630.

118Adenauer, *Erinnerungen*, Vol. II, pp. 527-28.

119For an account of the 1954 and 1958 crisis see Alexander George and Richard Smoke, *Deterrence in American Foreign Policy*, Chap. 9; also Gittings, *China and the World*, Chap. 10.

120See "Chinese Government Statement of September 21, 1963," in Gittings, *Survey of the Sino-Soviet Dispute*, 5, p.92.

121See "Soviet Government Statement, September 21, 1963," in Gittings,

Survey of Sino-Soviet Dispute, p.92.

122*Keesing's Research Report,* No. 3, p. 16.

123Halperin, *China and the Bomb,* p.92.

124See the report in the People's Daily on "Soviet Unreasonable Demands," in Gittings, *Survey of the Sino-Soviet Dispute,* p. 106.

125See Philip Bridgham, "The P'eng Te-Huai Affair," in *Party Leadership and Revolutionary Power in China,* ed. John W. Lewis (Cambridge: Cambridge University Press, 1970), Chap. 6, pp.203-235, especially p. 217.

126Rostow, *Diffusion of Power,* p.32.

127See, e.g., "Chinese Statement of August 3, 1963," in Gittings, *Survey of the Sino-Soviet Dispute,* p.105.

128"Soviet Government Statement of August 3, 1963," in Gittings, *Survey of the Sino-Soviet Dispute,* p.191.

129"Chinese Government Statement of August 15, 1963," on proposals for Nuclear Non-Proliferation, in Gittings, *Survey of the Sino-Soviet Dispute,* p.91.

130Drummond and Coblentz, *Duel at the Brink,* pp. 85-86.

131Harold Macmillan, *Riding the Storm* (New York: Harper and Row, 1971), p. 169.

132For an account see John Newhouse, *De Gaulle and the Anglo-Saxons* (New York: Viking Press, 1970), pp. 14-16.

133*Ibid.,* p. 12.

134For a discussion of France's nuclear research program before deGaulle, see Lawrence Scheineman, *Atomic Energy Policy in France under the Fourth Republic* (Princeton, N.J.: Princeton University Press, 1965).

135Thomas Wiegele, "The Origins of the MLF Concept 1957-1960," *Orbis,* XII (Summer 1968): 469-86.

136Newhouse, *De Gaulle and the Anglo-Saxons,* pp. 23ff.

137*Ibid.,* p. 27.

138Although this memorandum has never been made public, Newhouse quotes the above passage in his book. See *Ibid.,*p. 70.

139*Ibid.,*p. 27

140Dulles seems to have conceded on the idea of "advance authorization," or a French input into the decision to use nuclear weapons, only for those weapons to be employed in Europe, *ibid.,* p.82.

141For an account of the background and development of the Nassau agreement, see Richard Neustadt, *Alliance Politics* (New York: Columbia University Press, 1970), pp. 30-55.

142Newhouse, *De Gaulle and the Anglo-Saxons,* p. 246.

143The slow demise of the MLF idea is extensively dealt with in Philip Geyelin, *Lyndon Johnson and the World* (New York:Praeger Publishers, 1966), Chap. 7.

144See George Ball's assessment in George Ball, *The Discipline of Power* (Boston: Little Brown, 1968) pp.207-208.

145For a general discussion of this problem within NATO, see Dieter Mahncke, *Nukleare Mitwirkung* (Berlin: Walter de Gruyter, 1972), passim.

146William Foster, "New Directions in Arms Control," *Foreign Affairs,* 63 (1965): 587-601 at p.600.

147See Chapter IV.

148For a good discussion of this point, see Seyom Brown, *New Forces in World Politics* (Washington, D.C.: Brookings Institution, 1974), Chaps. 6 and 11.

149See discussion below.

150For rough statistics on the trends in economic assistance in the Sixties, see Rostow, *Diffusion of Power,* p.421.

151Roger Kanet, "The Soviet Union and the Colonial Question," in *The Soviet Union and the Developing Nations,* ed. Roger Kanet (Baltimore, Md.: Johns Hopkins University Press, 1974), p. 15.

152John Foster Dulles, "The Cost of Peace," *Department of State Bulletin,* 34 (June 18, 1956): 99-1001 at p. 999.

153See, e.g. Cecil Crabb, *The Elephants and the Grass* (New York: Praeger Publishers, 1964), pp. 14-15, 170.

154For an assortment of such unfavorable epithets, see Alexander Dallin, *Soviet Foreign Policy After Stalin,* pp.292-93

155Kanet, "The Soviet Union and the Colonial Question," p.20.

156Ishwer Ojha, "The Kremlin and Third World Leadership: Closing the Circle?" in *Soviet Policy in Developing Countries,* ed. Raymond Duncan (Waltham, Mass.: Ginn Blaisdell, 1970), pp. 9-27. especially pp. 11-12.

157*Ibid.*

158*Ibid.*

159For a collection of the most important speeches at Bandung, see George McTurnan Kahin, *The Asian-African Conference* (Ithaca, N.Y.: Cornell University Press, 1955).

160For a history of the Afro-Asian movement antedating Bandung, see G.H. Jansen, *Afro-Asia and Non-Alignment* (London: Faber and Faber, 1966).

161Brzezinski, *Soviet Bloc*, p. 221.

162*Ibid.*, p. 366.

163Sorensen, *Kennedy*.p. 596.

164*Ibid.*

165Walt Rostow and Max Milliken, *A Proposal—Key to an Effective Foreign Policy* (New York: Harper Brothers, 1957), p.1. For a history of this influential pamphlet, see Rostow, *Diffusion of Power*, pp. 88-91.

166Walt Rostow, "The Great Transition: Tasks of the First and Second Postwar Generations," *Department of State Bulletin*, 56 (March 27, 1967), p.494.

167*Ibid.*, p. 495.

168Daniel Bell, *The End of Ideology* (Glencoe, Ill.: Free Press, 1960).

169Brown, *Faces of Power*, p. 199.

170See, e.g. Kennedy's attempt to influence Peruvian and Guyanian internal policy and the abandoment of the criterion of "liberal democracy" as a precondition for aid by the Johnson administration.(Not to speak of various "covert operations" later revealed). For a critical discussion of these points, see Robert Packenham, *Liberal America and the Third World* (Princeton, N.J.: Princeton University Press, 1973), Chap. 2, pp.59-110. This is not to overlook the more blatant U.S. involvements, e.g., in Cuba, as later Senate investigations were to show.

171Dallin, *Soviet Foreign Policy After Stalin*, p. 304.

172R.A. Yellon, "Shifts in Soviet Policy toward Developing Areas 1964-1968," in *Soviet Policy in Developing Countries*, ed. by Raymond Duncan, p 227.

173*Ibid.*, pp.233-34.

174Crabb, *The Elephants and the Grass*, p. 150.

175Richard Löwenthal, "On National Democracy," *Survey*, No. 47 (April 1963): 119-33.

176See Yellon, "Shifts in Soviet Policy,"pp.235-36.

177Ojha, "The Kremlin and Third World Leadership," p. 18.

178Uri Ra'anan, "Moscow and the Third World," *Problems of Communism*, 14 No. 1 (January-February 1965): 21-31.

179This distinction was reintroduced by Suslov at the February, 1964 meeting of the Central Committee of the CPSU. See Yellon, "Shifts in Soviet Policy," p. 283.

180Leonid Brezhnev, "For Greater Unity of Communists. For a Fresh Upsurge of the Anti-Imperialist Struggle," speech delivered at the International Meeting of Communist and Workers' Parties, Moscow, June 7, 1969, in L.I. Brezhnev, *Following Lenin's Course* (Moscow: Progress Publishers, 1972), pp.156-202.

181*Pravda,* October 27, 1965, as quoted by Yellon, "Shifts in Soviet Policy,"p. 251.

182See Justus van der Kroef, "The Soviet Union and Southeast Asia," in *The Soviet Union and the Developing Nations,* pp. 79-118.

183*Pravda,* June 28, 1968, as quoted in W.W. Kulski, *The Soviet Union in World Affairs* (Syracuse, N.Y.: Syracuse University Press, 1973), p.27.

184Kulski, *The Soviet Union in World Affairs,* p. 27;.

185For a treatment of this metaphor as an important decision-premise of the Johnson administration see Brown, *Faces of Power,* p. 320 ff.

186Richard Nixon, "Asia After Vietnam," *Foreign Affairs,* 47 (October 1967): 111-125.

187*Ibid.,* pp.111-112, 113-114.

188*Ibid.,* pp. 112-113.

189*Department of State Bulletin,* 61 (November 24, 1969): 440.

190Nixon, "Asia After Vietnam,"p. 121.

191Henry Brandon, *The Retreat of American Power* (Garden City, N.Y.:Doubleday, 1973),pp.19-20.

192Richard Nixon, *U.S. Foreign Policy for the 1970's: Building for Peace. A Report to Congress* (Washington, D.C.: Government Printing Office, 1971), p.6.

193Brandon, *The Retreat of American Power,* p. 31.

194*Ibid.,* p. 33.

195Henry Kissinger, *A World Restored* (New York:Grosset and Dunlop, 1964),p. 320.

196Henry Kissinger, *Nuclear Weapons and Foreign Policy* (New York:W.W. Norton, 1969),p. 249.

197Henry Kissinger, "Central Issues of American Foreign Policy," in Henry Kissinger, *American Foreign Policy* (New York: W.W.Norton, n.d.)pp.93-94.

198Richard Nixon, *U.S. Foreign Policy for the 1970's,*p.6.

199*Ibid.*, p. 157.

200Richard Nixon, *The Public Papers of the Presidents of the United States* (Washington, D.C.:Government Printing Office, 1970), Vol. 1969, p. 3.

201Nixon, *U.S. Foreign Policy for the 1970's,*p. 6.

202James Dornan, "The Nixon Doctrine and the Primacy of Detente," *Intercollegiate Review,* 9 (Spring 1974): 77-96. For a critical view of the five-power conception of world politics, see Stanley Hoffmann, "Will the Balance Balance at Home," *Foreign Policy,* No. 7 (Summer 1972): 60-86; Zbigniew Brzezinski, "The Balance of Power Delusion," *Foreign Policy,* No. 7 (Summer 1972): 54-59; Stanley Hoffmann, "Weighing the Balance of Power," *Foreign Affairs,* 50 (July 1972): 613-43; Robert Osgood, "Introduction: The Nixon Doctrine and Strategy," in Robert Osgood, et al., *Retreat from Empire* (Baltimore, Md.: Johns Hopkins University Press, 1973), pp.1-28.

203Kissinger, "Central Issues of American Foreign Policy," pp.57, 60-61. For a critique of the view that Kissinger wants to revive the Metternichean system see also Stephen Graubard, *Kissinger, Portrait of a Mind* (New York: W.W. Norton, 1973), e.g., p.10 et passim. See also Kissinger's own rejection of this thesis in his interview with Oriana Fallaci, "Kissinger," *New Republic,* December 16, 1972, p.21.

204Kissinger, *A World Restored,* p.1.

205Frank Burd, "World Order as Final Cause in the Foreign Policy of Henry Kissinger," paper prepared for the 1975 Annual Meeting of the International Studies Association, Washington, D.C., February 21, 1975, p.1 (mimeographed).

206*Ibid.*, p.20.

207See the statement of January 29, 1969, quoted in Marvin and Bernard Kalb, *Kissinger* (Boston: Little, Brown, 1974), p.107.

208*Ibid.*, p.103.

209*Ibid.*, p.104.

210*Ibid.*, p.106.

211*Ibid.*, p.219ff.

212*Ibid.*, p.235.

213David Landau, *Kissinger: The Uses of Power* (Boston: Houghton Mifflin, 1972), p.107.

214Kalb, *Kissinger,* p.213.

215For a text of the Basic Principles, see Richard Nixon, *The Public Papers of the Presidents of the United States* (Washington, D.C.: Government Printing Office, 1972), pp.633-35.

216Dan Caldwell, "The Ambiguities of Detente", paper presented to the symposium on the Theory and Practice of Henry Kissinger's Statemanship, College Park, Maryland, September 25-27, 1975, p.43 (mimeographed).

217These principles read:
Second. The USA and the USSR attach major importance to preventing the development of situations capable of causing a dangerous exacerbation of their relations. Therefore, they will do their utmost to avoid military confrontations and to prevent the outbreak of nuclear war. They will always exercise restraint in their mutual relations, and they will be prepared to negotiate and settle differences by peaceful means. Discussions and negotiations on outstanding issues will be conducted in a spirit of reciprocity, mutual accommodation, and mutual benefit."

"Both sides recognize that efforts to obtain unilateral advantage at the expense of the other, directly or indirectly, are inconsistent with these objectives. The prerequisites for maintaining and strengthening peaceful relations between the USA and the USSR are the recognition of the security interests of the parties based on the principle of equality and the renunciation of the use or threat of force."

"*Third.* The USA and the USSR have a special responsibility, as do other countries which are permanent members of the United Nations Security Council, to do everything in their power so that conflicts or situations will not arise which would serve to increase international tensions. Accordingly, they will seek to promote conditions in which all countries will live in peace and security and will not be subject to outside interference in their internal affairs."

218Kalb, *Kissinger,* p.332-33.

Conclusion

1See on this point the fundamental discussion of Richard Falk, "The Domains of Law and Justice," *International Journal,* 31 (1975-1976): 1-13; Oran Young, "Peace and Justice as Components of World Order," *Millenium,* 4 (1975): 1-9.

2This point has been emphatically made by Richard Falk, "The State System under Siege," in Richard Falk, *A Global Approach to National Policy* (Cambridge, Mass.:Harvard University Press, 1975), pp.13-28; see also Richard Falk, *A Study of Future Worlds* (New York:Free Press, 1975).

3Oran Young, "Peace and Justice as Components of World Order," p.4ff.

4Falk, "The Domains of Law and Justice," pp.5-6.

5"Advantage" need not necessarily refer solely to economic welfare but might include a variety of values.

6David Hume, *Hume's Moral and Political Philosophy,* ed. by Henry Aiken (Darien, Conn.: Hafner, 1970), pp.135-136.

7Falk, "The Domains of Law and Justice,"p.6.

8See the discussion of Seyom Brown in *New Forces in World Politics* (Washington, D.C.:Brookings Institution, 1974).

9Hedley Bull, "Order and Justice in International Society," *Political Studies,* 19 (1971): 269-283.

10See, e.g., Raymond Vernon, *Sovereignty at Bay* (New York:Basic Books, 1971).

11Karl Popper, *The Poverty of Historicism* (New York:Harper Torchbooks, 1961),passim.

12A.L. Louch, *Explanation and Human Action* (Berkeley, Calif.:University of California Press, 1969), p. 216.

13Anatol Rapoport, *Strategy and Conscience,* p.100.

Bibliography

Aside from relying on Congressional Hearings, this study used extensively the following collection of documents for the time period under discussion:

American Association for the Advancement of Slavic Studies, *Current Digest of the Soviet Press*. Columbus, Ohio: 1949ff.

----*Current Soviet Policies: The Documentary Record of the Communist Party Congress* (XX-XXIII). New York: Praeger.

Council on Foreign Relations, New York. *Documents on American Foreign Relations*, vols. 1951-1972. New York: Harper Brothers.

----*The Foreign Relations of the United States*. Washington, D.C.: Government Printing Office.

Department of Defense. *The Pentagon Papers*. Senator Gravel's edition. Boston, Mass.:Beacon Press, 1975.

LaFeber, Walter. *Eastern Europe and the Soviet Union*. vol. 2 of Arthur Schlesinger, ed., *The Dynamics of World Power*. New York:Chelsea House and McGraw Hill, 1973.

The President's Office. *The Public Papers of the Presidents of the United States*. (Roosevelt to Nixon). Washington, D.C.: Government Printing Office.

World Peace Foundation. *Documents on American Foreign Relations 1945-1951*. Princeton, N.J.:Princeton University Press.

Memoirs of leading decision makers are listed in the systematic part of the bibliography.

Books

Abel, Elie. *The Cuban Missile Crisis*. Philadelphia: Lippincott, 1966.

Acheson, Dean. *Present at the Creation*. New York: Signet Books, 1970.

Adenauer, Konrad. *Erinnerungen*. 3 vols. Stuttgart: Deutsche Verlagsanstalt, 1965.

Albert, Hans, ed. *Theorie and Realität*. Tübingen: Mohr, 1964.

Alliluyeva, Svetlana. *Twenty Letters to a Friend*. New York: Harper and Row, 1967.

Allison, Graham. *Essence of Decision*. Boston: Little, Brown, 1971.

Alperovitz, Gar. *Hiroshima and Potsdam*. London: Secker and Warburg, 1965.

d'Amato, Anthony. *The Concept of Custom in International Law*. Ithaca, N.Y.: Cornell University Press, 1971.

Anderson, Charles; von der Mehden, Fred; and Young, Crawford. *Issues in Political Development*. Englewood Cliffs, N.J.: Prentice-Hall, 1967.

Apter, David. *Ideology and Discontent*. New York: Free Press, 1964.

Aristotle. *On Interpretation*. Transl. by J.L. Ackrill. Oxford: Clarendon, 1963.

Aristotle, *Rhetoric*. Transl. by John H. Freese. Cambridge, Mass.: Harvard University Press, 1967.

Aristotle. *Politics*. Transl. by H. Rackenham. Cambridge, Mass.:Harvard University Press, 1967.

Aristotle. *Poetics*. Transl. by Ingram Bywater. Oxford: Clarendon, 1962.

Armstrong, John. *The Soviet Bureaucratic Elite*. New York: Praeger Publishers, 1959.

Aron, Raymond. *The Imperial Republic*. Englewood Cliffs, N.J.: Prentice-Hall, 1974.

Aspaturian, Vernon, ed. *Process and Power in Soviet Foreign Policy*. Boston: Little, Brown, 1971.

Augustinus, Aurelius. *The City of God*. Transl. by George McCracken Cambridge, Mass.:Harvard University Press, 1957.

Bachrach, Peter, ed. *Political Elites in a Democracy*. New York: Aldine, 1971.

Bachrach, Peter. *The Theory of Democratic Elitism*. Boston: Little, Brown, 1967.

Ball, George. *The Discipline of Power*. Boston: Little, Brown, 1968.

Banks, Arthur, and Textor, Robert. *A Cross-Polity Survey*. Cambridge, Mass.: M.I.T. Press, 1963.

Barkun, Michael. *Law Without Sanction*. New Haven: Yale University Press, 1968.

Beaufre, André. *An Introduction to Strategy*. London: Faber and Faber, 1965.

Bechhoefer, Bernhard. *Postwar Negotiations for Arms Control*. Washington, D.C.: Brookings Institution, 1961.

Bell, Coral. *Negotiations from Strength*. New York: Alfred A. Knopf, 1963.

Bell, Daniel. *The End of Ideology*. Glencoe, Ill.: Free Press, 1960.

Berger, Peter, and Luckmann, Thomas. *The Social Construction of Reality*. Garden City, N.Y.: Doubleday, 1967.

Berkowitz, Leonard. *Aggression*. New York: McGraw-Hill, 1962.

Bickel, Alexander. *The Least Dangerous Branch*. Indianapolis, Ind.: Bobbs
268

Merrlll, 1962.

Black, Cyril, et al. *Neutralization and World Politics.* Princeton, N.J.: Princeton University Press, 1972.

Blechman, Barry. *The Changing Soviet Navy.* Washington, D.C.: Brookings Institution, 1973.

Bloomfield, Lincoln, ed. *International Military Forces.* 2nd ed. Boston: Little, Brown, 1964.

Blum, John M. *From the Morgenthau Diaries.* 3 vols. Boston: Houghton Mifflin, 1967.

Blumer, Herbert. *Symbolic Interactionism.* Englewood Cliffs, N.J.: Prentice-Hall, 1969.

Bohlen, Charles. *Transformation of American Foreign Policy.* New York: W.W. Norton, 1969.

Bohlen, Charles. *Witness to History: 1919-1969.* New York: W.W. Norton, 1973.

Boulding, Kenneth. *Conflict and Defense.* New York: Harper and Row, 1962.

Brandon, Henry. *The Retreat of American Power.* Garden City, N.Y.: Doubleday, 1973.

Brezhnev, Leonid. *Following Lenin's Course.* Moscow: Progress Publishers, 1972.

Brodbeck, May, ed. *Readings in the Philosophy of the Social Sciences.* New York: Macmillan, 1968.

Brodie, Bernard, *The Absolute Weapon.* New York: Harcourt, Brace, 1946.

Brodie, Bernard. *Strategy in the Missile Age.* Princeton, N.J.: Princeton University Press, 1965.

Brodie, Bernard. *War and Politics.* New York: Macmillan, 1973.

Broom, Leonard, and Selznik, Philip. *Sociology.* New York: Harper and Row, 1963.

Brown, Seyom. *The Faces of Power.* New York: Columbia University Press, 1968.

Brown, Seyom. *New Forces in World Politics.* Washington, D.C.: Brookings Institution, 1974.

Brzezinski, Zbigniew. *The Soviet Bloc.* Cambridge, Mass.: Harvard University Press, 1971.

Bundy, W. McGeorge. *The Pattern of Responsibility.* Boston: Houghton Mifflin, 1952.

Burnham, James. *The Coming Defeat of Communism.* New York: John Day, 1950.

Burns, Arthur Lee. *Of Powers and Their Politics.* Englewood Cliffs, N.J.: Prentice-Hall, 1968.

Campbell, Thomas. *Masquerade Peace.* Tallahassee, Fla.: Florida State University Press, 1973.

Cassirer, Ernest. *Language and Myth.* New York: Harper, 1946.

Chapman, John. *Atlas: The Story of a Missile.* New York: Harper Brothers, 1960.

Churchill, Winston. *The Hinge of Fate.* Boston: Houghton-Mifflin, 1950.

Cicero, Tullius. *De re publica.* Trans. by George McCracken. Cambridge, Mass.:Harvard University Press, 1961.

Clark, Grenville, and Sohn, Louis. *World Peace Through World Law.* 2nd ed. Cambridge, Mass.: Harvard University Press, 1966.

Claude, Inis. *Power and International Relations.* New York: Random House, 1962.

Claude, Inis. *Swords into Plowshares.* New York: Random House, 1964.

Claude, Inis. *The Changing United Nations.* New York: Random House, 1964.

Cochrane, Charles. *Christianity and Classical Culture.* New York: Oxford University Press, 1949.

Cohn, Norman. *The Pursuit of the Millenium.* London: Paladin, 1970.

Coser, Lewis. *The Function of Social Conflict.* Glencoe: Free Press, 1956.

Coser, Lewis. *Continuities in the Study of Social Conflict.* New York: Free Press, 1967.

Crabb, Cecil. *The Elephants and the Grass.* New York: Praeger Publishers, 1964.

Crick, Bernard. *In Defense of Politics.* Middlesex, England: Penguin Books, 1964.

Cyert, Richard, and March, James. *A Behavioral Theory of the Firm.* Englewood Cliffs, N.J.: Prentice-Hall, 1963.

Dahl, Robert. *Who Governs?* New Haven: Yale University Press, 1961.

Dahrendorf, Ralf. *Class and Class Conflicts in Industrial Society.* Stanford, Calif.: Stanford University Press, 1959.

Dahrendorf, Ralf. *Pfade aus Utopia.* München: Piper, 1967.

Dallin, David. *Soviet Foreign Policy After Stalin.* Philadelphia: Lippincott, 1961.

Daniels, Jonathan. *The Man of Independence.* Philadelphia: Lippincott, 1950.

Dedijer, Vladimir. *Tito.* New York: Simon and Schuster, 1953.

Dedijer, Vladimir. *The Battle Stalin Lost.* New York: Viking Press, 1971.

Deutsch, Karl, and Hoffmann, Stanley, eds. *The Relevance of International Law.* Cambridge, Mass.: Schenkman Publishing Co., 1968.

Dinerstein, Herbert. *War and the Soviet Union.* Rev. ed. New York: Praeger Publishers, 1962.

Djilas, Milovan. *Conversations with Stalin.* New York: Harcourt, Brace, 1962.

Dobney, Frederick, ed. *Selected Papers of Will Clayton.* Baltimore, Md.: Johns Hopkins Unversity Press, 1971.

Donovan, Robert. *Eisenhower: The Inside Story.* New York: Harper, 1956.

Drummond, Roscoe, and Coblentz, Gaston. *Duel at the Brink.* Garden City, N.Y.: Doubleday, 1960.

Dulles, John Foster. *War or Peace.* New York: Macmillan, 1950.

Duncan, Raymond. *Soviet Policy in Developing Countries.* Waltham, Mass.: Ginn Blaisdell, 1970.

Durkheim, Emile. *Suicide.* Glencoe, Ill.: Free Press, 1952.

Eckstein, Harry, and Apter, David, eds. *Comparative Politics.* Glencoe, Ill.: Free Press, 1963.

Edelman, Murray. *The Symbolic Uses of Politics.* Urbana, Ill.: University of Illinois Press, 1967.

Edelman, Murray. *Politics as Symbolic Action.* Chicago: Markham, 1971.

Eden, Anthony. *Full Circle.* Boston: Houghton Mifflin, 1960.

Eisenhower, Dwight. *Mandate for Change.* Garden City, N.Y.: Doubleday, 1963.

Ello, Paul. *Czechoslovakia's Blueprint for Freedom.* Washington, D.C.: Acropolis Press, 1968.

Enthoven, Alain, and Smith, Wayne. *How Much Is Enough?* New York: Harper and Row, 1971.

Erikson, Erik. *Young Man Luther.* New York: W.W. Norton, 1958.

Falk, Richard. *Legal Order in a Violent World.* Princeton N.J.: Princeton University Press, 1968.

Falk, Richard, ed. *The Vietnam War and International Law*. Princeton, N.J.: Princeton University Press, 1968.

Falk, Richard. *This Endangered Planet*. New York: Random House, 1971.

Falk, Richard. *A Global Approach to National Policy*. Cambridge, Mass.: Harvard University Press, 1975.

Falk, Richard, and Mendlovitz, Saul, eds. *The Strategy of World Order*. Vol. II, *International Law*. New York: World Law Fund, 1966.

Fann, K.T. *Die Philosophie Ludwig Wittgensteins*. München: List, 1971.

Farrell, Barry E., ed. *Yugoslavia and the Soviet Union, 1948-1956*. Hamden, Conn.: Shoe String Press, 1956.

Farrell, Barry E., ed. *Approaches to Comparative and International Politics*. Evanston, Ill.: Northwestern University Press, 1966.

Farris, Robert, ed. *Handbook of Modern Sociology*. Chicago: Rand McNally, 1964.

Feis, Herbert. *Churchill, Roosevelt, Stalin*. Princeton, N.J.: Princeton University Press, 1970.

Feis, Herbert. *From Trust to Terror*. New York: W.W. Norton, 1970.

Fisher, Louis. *Russia's Road from Peace to War*. New York: Harper and Row, 1969.

Fleming, D.F. *The Cold War and Its Origins, 1917-1960*. 2 vols. Garden City, N.Y.: Doubleday, 1961.

Fontaine, André. *Histoire de la Guerre Froide*. Paris: Fayard, 1965-1967.

Fox, William R. T. *The Superpowers*. New York: Harcourt, Brace, 1944.

Franklin, Bruce, ed. *The Essential Stalin*. Garden City, N.Y.: Doubleday, 1972

Freeland, Richard. *The Truman Doctrine and the Origins of McCarthyism*. New York: Schocken, 1974.

Friedrich, Carl, ed. *The Philosophy of Kant*. New York: Modern Library, Random House, 1949.

Frohlich, Norman; Oppenheimer, Joe; and Young, Oran. *Political Leadership and Collective Goods*. Princeton, N.J.: Princeton University Press, 1971.

Fuller, R. Buckminster. *Operating Manual for Spaceship Earth*. Carbondale, Ill.: Southern Illinois University Press, 1972.

Gardner, Lloyd C. *Architects of Illusion*. Chicago: Quadrangle, 1970.

Gardner, Robert. *Sterling-Dollar Diplomacy: Anglo-American Collaboration in the Reconstruction of Multilateral Trade*. Oxford: Clarendon Press, 1956.
272

Garthoff, Raymond. *The Soviet Image of Future War.* Washington, D.C.: Public Affairs Press, 1959.

Garthoff, Raymond. *Soviet Strategy in the Nuclear Age.* New York: Praeger Publishers, 1962.

Garthoff, Raymond, ed. *Sino-Soviet Military Relations.* New York: Praeger Publishers, 1966.

Garthoff, Raymond. *Soviet Military Policy.* New York: Praeger Publishers, 1966.

de Gaulle, Charles. *War Memoirs; Salvation.* New York: Simon and Schuster, 1959.

George, Alexander, and Smoke, Richard. *Deterrence in American Foreign Policy.* New York: Columbia University Press, 1974.

Gerhardt, Uta. *Rollenanalyse als kritische Soziologie.* Neuwied-Berlin: Luchterhand, 1971.

Gerson, Louis. *John Foster Dulles.* New York: Cooper Square Publishers, 1967.

Geyelin, Philip. *Lyndon Johnson and the World.* New York: Praeger Publishers, 1966.

Gibbon, Edward. *The Decline and Fall of the Roman Empire.* New York: Harcourt, Brace, 1960.

Gittings, John. *Survey of the Sino-Soviet Dispute.* New York: Oxford University Press, 1968.

Gittings, John. *The World and China 1922-1972.* New York: Harper and Row, 1974.

Goffman, Erving. *Interaction Ritual.* Garden City, N.Y.: Doubleday, 1967.

Goffman, Erving. *Strategic Interaction.* Philadelphia: University of Pennsylvania Press, 1969.

Goldman, Eric. *The Tragedy of Lyndon Johnson.* New York: Alfred A. Knopf, 1969.

Gottlieb, Gidon. *The Logic of Choice.* London: Allen and Unwin, 1968.

Graubard, Stephen. *Kissinger; Portrait of a Mind.* New York: W.W. Norton, 1973.

Gruber, Karl. *Zwischen Befreiung und Freiheit.* Vienna: Ullstein, 1953.

Halle, Louis J. *The Cold War as History.* New York: Harper and Row, 1967.

Halperin, Morton. *China and the Bomb.* New York: Praeger Publishers, 1965.

273

Hart, H.L.A. *The Concept of Law*. Oxford: Clarendon Press, 1961.

Head, Richard G., and Rokke, Ervin J., eds. *American Defense Policy*. Baltimore, Md.: Johns Hopkins University Press, 1973.

Hegel, G.W. *Vorlesungen uber die Philosophie der Weltgeschichte*. Hamburg: Felix Meiner, 1955.

Hempel, Carl. *Aspects of Scientific Explanation and Other Essays in the Philosophy of Science*. New York: Free Press, 1965.

Henkin, Louis. *How Nations Behave*. New York: Praeger Publishers, 1968.

Herman, Charles, ed. *Crisis in Foreign Policy*. Indianapolis, Inc.: Bobbs Merrill, 1969.

Herodotus. *Histories*. Trans. by Aubrey de Selincourt. Baltimore, Md.: Penguin, 1971.

Herz, John. *International Politics in the Atomic Age*. New York: Columbia University Press, 1959.

Herz, Martin. *The Beginnings of the Cold War*. Bloomington, Ind.: Indiana University Press, 1966.

Hinsley, F.H. *Power and the Pursuit of Peace.* Cambridge: Cambridge University Press, 1967.

Hinton, Harold. *Communist China in World Politics*. Boston: Houghton Mifflin, 1966.

Hobbes, Thomas. *Leviathan*. Ed. by W. C. Hobson Smith. Oxford: Clarendon, 1962.

Hoffman, Erick, ed. *The Conduct of Soviet Foreign Policy*. Chicago: Aldine, 1971.

Hoffmann, Stanley. *The State of War*. New York: Praeger Publishers, 1965.

Hoffmann, Stanley. *Gulliver's Troubles*. New York: McGraw-Hill, 1968.

Holborn, Louis, ed. *War and Peace Aims of the United Nations*. Boston: World Peace Foundation, 1943-48.

Hoopes, Townsend. *The Devil and John Foster Dulles*. Boston: Little, Brown, 1973.

Horelick, Arnold, and Rush, Myron. *Strategic Power and Soviet Foreign Policy*. Chicago: University of Chicago Press, 1968.

Hoselitz, Bert F., ed. *Economics and the Idea of Mankind*. New York: Columbia University Press, 1965.

Hughes, Emmet John. *The Ordeal of Power*. New York: Atheneum, 1963.

Hume, David. *Hume's Moral and Political Philosophy*. Edited by Henry Aiken.
274

Darien, Conn.:Hafner, 1970.

Huntington, Samuel. *The Common Defense*. New York: Columbia University Press, 1961.

Hutmacher, Joseph, and Susman, Warren, eds. *The Origins of the Cold War*. Waltham, Mass.: Ginn and Co., 1970.

Iklé, Fred. *How Nations Negotiate*. New York: Praeger Publishers, 1964.

Jacobs, Dan, ed. *The New Communist Manifesto*. New York: Harper Torch Books, 1965.

Jacobsen, C.C. *Strategy and Soviet Foreign Policy*. Glasgow: Robert Macleanhouse and Co., 1973.

Jansen, G.H. *Afro-Asians and Non-Alignment*. London:Faber and Faber, 1966.

Jellinek, Georg. *Die Lehre von den Staatenverbindungen*. Berlin:Haering, 1882.

Jervis, Robert. *The Logic of Images in International Relations*. Princeton, N.J.: Princeton University Press, 1970.

Johnson, Raymond D., ed. *Negotiating with the Russians*. Boston: World Peace Foundation, 1951.

Jones, Joseph. *The Fifteen Weeks*. New York: Viking Press, 1955.

de Jouvenel, Bertrand. *The Art of Conjecture*. New York:Basic Books, 1967.

Junne, Gerd. *Spieltheorie in der Internationalen Politik*. Düsseldorf: Bertelsmann, 1971.

Jüttner, Alfred. *Die Deutsche Frage*. Cologne: Heymanns Verlag, 1971.

Kahin, George McTurnan. *The Asian-African Conference*. Ithaca, N.Y.: Cornell University Press, 1955.

Kalb, Bernard, and Kalb, Marvin. *Kissinger*. Boston: Little, Brown, 1974.

Kanet, Robert, ed. *The Soviet Union and the Developing Nations*. Baltimore, Md.: Johns Hopkins University Press, 1974.

Kaplan, Morton. *System and Process in International Politics*. New York:John Wiley, 1957.

Kaplan, Morton, and Katzenbach, Nicholas B. *The Political Foundations of International Law*. New York: John Wiley, 1961.

Kaplan, Morton. *Macropolitics*. Chicago:Aldine, 1969.

Kaplan, Morton, ed. *Great Issues of International Politics*. Chicago:Aldine, .1970.

Kaplan, Morton. *On Historical and Political Knowing.* Chicago:University of Chicago Press, 1971.

Kaufmann, William. *The McNamara Strategy.* New York:Harper and Row, 1964.

Keesing, Archives. *The Sino-Soviet Dispute.* Research Report No. 3. New York: Charles Scribner's Sons, 1969.

Kelsen, Hans. *Principles of International Law.* New York: Rinehart, 1952.

Kennan, George. *Russia, the Atom and the West.* New York:Harper, 1958.

Kennan, George. *Russia and the West under Lenin and Stalin.* New York: Mentor, 1960.

Kennan, George. *Memoirs.* 2 vols. Boston:Little, Brown; New York: Bantam Books, 1967.

Kennedy, John F. *The Strategy of Peace.* Edited by Allen Nevius. New York:Harper Brothers, 1960.

Kennedy, Robert. *Thirteen Days.* New York:W.W. Norton, 1971.

Khrushchev, Nikita. *Khrushchev Remembers.* Edited and translated by Strobe Talbott. Boston: Little, Brown, 1970.

Kissinger, Henry. *Nuclear Weapons and Foreign Policy.* New York:Harper, 1957.

Kissinger, Henry. *A World Restored.* New York:Grossett and Dunlop, 1964.

Kissinger, Henry, ed. *Problems of National Strategy.* New York: Praeger Publishers, 1965.

Kissinger, Henry. *American Foreign Policy.* New York:W.W. Norton, 1974.

Kolko, Gabriel. *The Limits of Power.* 1943-45. New York:Vintage Books, 1968.

Kolko, Gabriel. *The Limits of Power, 1945-54.* New York: Harper and Row, 1972.

Kolkowicz, Roman, et. al. *The Soviet Union and Arms Control: A Superpower Dilemma.* Baltimore, Md.:Johns Hopkins University Press, 1970.

Krakau, Knud. *Missionsbewusstsein und Völkerrechtsdoktrin in den Vereinigten Staaten.* Frankfurt: Metzger, 1968.

Kramish, Arnold. *Atomic Energy in the Soviet Union.* Stanford, Calif.: Stanford University Press, 1959.

Krock, Arthur. *Memoirs.* New York:Funk & Wagnalls, 1968.

Kulski, W.W. *The Soviet Union in World Affairs.* Syracuse, N.Y.:Syracuse

University Press, 1973.

LaFeber, Walter. *The Origins of the Cold War, 1941-1947.* New York: John Wiley, 1971.

LaFeber, Walter. *America, Russia and the Cold War.* New York:John Wiley, 1972.

Lakatosh, Imre, and Musgrave, Alan, eds. *Criticism and the Growth of Knowledge.* Cambridge:Cambridge University Press, 1970.

Landau, David. *Kissinger: The Uses of Power.* Boston: Houghton Mifflin, 1972.

Lauterpacht, Sir Hersch. *The Function of Law in the International Community.* Oxford: Clarendon Press, 1933.

Lee, Asher, ed. *Soviet Air and Rocket Forces.* New York: Praeger Publishers, 1959.

Lee, Asher. *The Soviet Air Force.* London: Gerold Duckworth, 1961.

Lenin, V.I. *The Highest Stage of Capitalism.* New York:International Publishers, 1939.

Leonhard, Wolfgang. *Child of the Revolution.* Chicago:H. Regnery Co., 1958.

Lepawski, Albert, ed. *The Search for World Order.* New York:Appleton Century Crofts, 1971.

Lewis, John, ed. *Party Leadership and Revolutionary Power in China.* Cambridge: Cambridge University Press, 1970.

Lichtheim, George. *Imperialism.* New York: Praeger Publishers, 1971.

Lieberman, Joseph. *The Scorpion and the Tarantula.* Boston:Houghton Mifflin, 1970.

Lindblom, Charles E. *The Intelligence of Democracy.* New York:Free Press, 1965.

Lindblom Charles, and Baybrooke, David. *A Strategy of Decision.* New York:The Free Press, 1963.

Linden, Carl. *Khrushchev and the Soviet Leadership.* Baltimore, Md.:Johns Hopkins University Press, 1966.

Lippmann, Walter. *U.S. Foreign Policy: The Shield of the Republic.* New York: Pocket Books, 1943.

Livius, Titus. *Annals.* Transl. by B.O. Foster. Cambridge, Mass.: Harvard University Press, 1960.

Louch, A.L. *Explanation and Human Action.* Berkeley, Calif.: University of California Press, 1969.

277

Lyon, Peter. *Eisenhower:Portrait of a Hero*. Boston:Little, Brown, 1974.

Macmillan, Harold. *Riding the Storm*. New York:Harper and Row, 1971.

Maddox, Robert J. *The New Left and the Origins of the Cold War*. Princeton, N.J.:Princeton University Press, 1973.

Mahncke, Dieter. *Nukleare Mitwirkung*. Berlin: Walter de Gruyter, 1972.

Mannheim, Karl. *Wissenssoziologie*. Edited by Kurt Wolff. Berlin:Luchterhand, 1966.

March, James, ed. *A Handbook of Organizations*. Chicago: Rand McNally, 1960.

May, Ernest. *"Lessons" of the Past*. New York: Oxford University Press, 1973.

McDougall, Myres, and Associates. *Studies in the World Public Order*. New Haven: Yale University Press, 1960.

McHugh, Peter. *Defining the Situation, The Organization of Meaning in Social Interaction*. New York: Bobbs Merrill, 1968.

McNeill, William. *America, Britain and Russia: Their Cooperation and Conflict, 1941-1946*. New York: Johnson Reprint Corp., 1970.

Mead, George H. *Mind, Self and Society*. Edited by Charles W. Morris. Chicago: University of Chicago Press, 1959.

Millis, Walter, ed. *The Forrestal Diaries*. New York: Viking Press, 1951.

Millis, Walter; Mansfield, Harvey; and Stein, Harold. *Arms and the State*. New York:Twentieth Century Fund, 1958.

Molotov, V.M. *Problems of Foreign Policy*. Moscow: Foreign Language Publishing House, 1949.

Morris, Charles. *Signs, Language and Behavior*. New York:Brazillier, 1946.

Murphy, Robert. *Diplomat Among Warriors*. Garden City, N.Y.:Doubleday, 1964.

Murray, Henry. *Myth and Mythmaking*. New York:Columbia University Press, 1970.

Neustadt, Richard. *Alliance Politics*. New York:Columbia University Press, 1970.

Newhouse, John. *DeGaulle and the Anglo-Saxons*. New York:Viking Press, 1970.

Newhouse, John. *Cold Dawn*. New York:Holt, Rinehart and Winston, 1973.

Oakeshott, Michael. *Rationalism in Politics*. New York:Basic Books, 1962.

Olson, Mancur. *The Logic of Collective Action.* New York:Schocken, 1969.

Osgood, Robert. *Ideals and Self Interest in American Foreign Policy.* Chicago:University of Chicago Press, 1953.

Osgood, Robert. *NATO, the Entangling Alliance.* Chicago:University of Chicago Press, 1962.

Osgood, Robert, et al. *Retreat from Empire?* Baltimore, Md.: The Johns Hopkins University Press, 1973.

Packenham, Robert. *Liberal America and the Third World.* Princeton, N.J..Princeton University Press, 1973.

Paige, Glenn D. *The Korean Decision.* New York:Free Press, 1968.

Parsons, Talcott. *The Social System.* Glencoe, Ill.:Free Press, 1951.

Patterson, Thomas G. *Containment and the Cold War.* Reading, Mass.: Addison, Wesley, 1973.

Pitkin, Hanna. *Wittgenstein on Justice.* Berkeley:University of California Press, 1972.

Plamenatz, John. *The English Utilitarians.* Oxford:Blackwell, 1958.

Polybios. *Histories.* Trans. by W.R. Paton. Cambridge, Mass.: Harvard University Press, 1960.

Ploss, Sidney. *Conflict and Decision-Making in Soviet Russia.* Princeton, N.J.: Princeton University Press, 1965.

Plato. *Republic.* Trans. by B. Jowett, vol. ii, Oxford: Clarendon, 1953.

Plato. *Statesman.* Trans. by B. Jowett, vol. iii, Oxford: Clarendon, 1953.

Plato. *Laws.* Trans. by B. Jowett, vol. iv. Oxford: Clarendon, 1953.

Popper, Karl. *The Poverty of Historicism.* New York:Harper Torch Books, 1961.

Popper, Karl. *Conjectures and Refutations.* New York:Harper and Row, 1968.

Popper, Karl. The Logic of Scientific Discovery. New York:Harper and Row, 1968.

Popper, Karl. *Objective Knowledge.* Oxford:Clarendon Press, 1972.

Quester, George. *Nuclear Diplomacy.* New York:Dunellen, 1970.

Range, Willard. *Franklin D. Roosevelt's World Order.* Athens, Ga.:University of Georgia Press, 1959.

Rapoport, Anatol. *Fights, Games and Debates.* Ann Arbor: University of Michigan Press, 1960.

279

Rapoport, Anatol. *Strategy and Conscience.* New York:Schocken, 1969.

Reale, Eugenio. *Avec Jacques Duclos.* Paris: Librarie Plon, 1958.

Richardson, Lewis. *Arms and Insecurity.* Pittsburgh, Pa.:Boxwood, 1960.

Richardson, Lewis. *Statistics of Deadly Quarrels.* Chicago:Quadrangle, 1960.

Rogowski, Ronald, and Wasserspring, Lois. *Does Political Development Exist?* Beverly Hills, Calif.:Sage, 1971.

Romulo, Carlos. *The Meaning of Bandung.* Chapel Hill, N.C.:University of North Carolina Press, 1956.

Roosevelt, Elliot. *As He Saw It.* New York:Duell, Sloan and Pearce, 1946.

Rosenau, James, ed. *International Politics and Foreign Policy.* New York:Free Press, 1969.

Rosenau, James; Davis, Vincent; and East, Maurice, eds. *The Analysis of International Politics.* New York:Free Press, 1972.

Rostow, Walt W. *The United States in the World Arena.* New York:Harper and Brothers, 1960.

Rostow, Walt W. *The Diffusion of Power.* New York:Macmillan, 1972.

Rostow, Walt W., and Milliken, Max. *A Proposal-Key to an Effective Foreign Policy.* New York:Harper Brothers, 1957.

Rousseau, Jean Jacques. *The Political Writings of J.J. Rousseau.* Edited by C.E. Vaughn. Cambridge: Cambridge University Press, 1915.

Rubinstein, Alvin. *The Soviets in International Organizations.* Princeton, N.J.:Princeton University Press, 1964.

Rubinstein, Alvin, and Ginsburg, George, eds. *Soviet and American Policies in the United Nations.* New York:New York University Press, 1971.

'Russet, Bruce, ed. *Economic Theories of International Politics.* Chicago:Markham, 1968.

Scheineman, Lawrence. *Atomic Energy Policy in France Under the Fourth Republic.* Princeton, N.J.:Princeton University Press, 1965.

Schelling, Thomas. *The Strategy of Conflict.* New York:Oxford University Press, 1963.

Schelling, Thomas. *Arms and Influence.* New Haven:Yale University Press, 1965.

Schlesinger, Arthur. *A Thousand Days.* New York:Fawcett Crest, 1965.

Schneir, Walter, and Schneir, Miriam. *Invitation to an Inquest.* Garden City, N.Y.:Doubleday, 1965.

Senghaas, Dieter. *Kritische Friedensforschung*. Frankfurt am Main:Suhrkamp, 1972.

Sherwood, Robert. *Roosevelt and Hopkins*. New York:Harper and Brothers, 1948.

Schilling, Warner; Hammond, Paul; and Snyder, Glenn. *Strategy, Politics and National Budgets*. New York:Columbia University Press, 1962.

Shulman, Marshal. *Stalin's Foreign Policy Reappraised*. Cambridge Mass.:Harvard University Press, 1963.

Shulman, Marshal. *Beyond the Cold War*. New Haven:Yale University Press, 1966.

Simmel, George. *Conflict*. Translated by Kurt H. Wolf. New York:Free Press, 1955.

Simon, Herbert. *Administrative Behavior*. New York:Macmillan, 1948.

Simon, Herbert. *Models of Man*. New York:John Wiley, 1957.

Simon, Herbert, and March, James. *Organizations*. New York:John Wiley, 1958.

Singer, J. David. *Deterrence, Arms Control and Disarmament*. Columbus, Ohio: Ohio State University Press, 1962.

Skilling, Gordon. *Interest Groups in Soviet Politics*. Princeton, N.J.:Princeton University Press, 1971.

Smith, Clagett G., ed. *Conflict Resolution: Contributions of the Behavioral Sciences*. Notre Dame, Ind.:Notre Dame University Press, 1971.

Smith, Walter Bedell. *My Three Years in Moscow*. Philadelphia:Lippincott, 1950.

Snyder, Glenn. *Deterrence and Defense*. Princeton, N.J.:Princeton University Press, 1961.

Sorel, Georges. *Reflections on Violence*. Translated by T.E. Hulme and J. Roth. New York: Collier, 1961.

Sorensen, Theodore. *Decision-Making in the White House*. New York:Columbia University Press, 1963.

Sorensen, Theodore. *Kennedy*. New York:Bantam Books, 1965.

Stalin, Joseph. *Works*. 3 vols. Moscow:Foreign Language Publishing House, 1954.

Stebbins, Robert. *The United States in World Affairs*. New York:Simon and Schuster, 1958.

Stettinius, Edward. *Roosevelt and the Russians: The Yalta Conference*. Garden City, N.Y.:Doubleday, 1949.

281

Stimpson, Henry L., and Bundy, McGeorge, eds. *On Active Service in Peace and War.* New York:Harper and Brothers, 1948.

Stoessinger, John, *et al. Financing the United Nations System.* Washington, D.C.: Brookings Institution, 1964.

Stromberg, John L. *The Internal Mechanism of the Defense Budget Process, Fiscal 1953-1968.* Santa Monica, Calif.:Rand Corp., September 1970.

Thucydides. *The Peloponnesian War.* Trans. by Sir Richard Livingston,. New York: Oxford University Press, 1956.

Timasheff, Nicholas. *War and Revolution.* New York:Sheed and Ward, 1965.

Tokaev, G.A. *Stalin Means War.* London:Genge Weidenfield and Nicholson, 1951.

Toland, John. *The Rising Sun.* New York:Random House, 1970.

Tournoux, Jean Raymond. *Secrets d'Etat.* Paris:Librarie Plon, 1960.

Troeltsch, Ernst. *The Social Teaching of the Christian Churches.* 2 vols. New York:Macmillan, 1949.

Truman, Harry S. *Memoirs.* 2 vols. Garden City, N.Y.:Doubleday, 1954.

Tucker, Robert C. *Philosophy and Myth in Karl Marx.* Cambridge:Cambridge University Press, 1961.

Tucker, Robert C. *The Marxian Revolutionary Idea.* New York:W.W. Norton, 1970.

Tucker, Robert C. *The Soviet Political Mind.* New York:W.W. Norton, 1971.

Tucker, Robert W. *The Radical Left and American Foreign Policy.* Baltimore, Md.:The Johns Hopkins University Press, 1971.

Tudor, Henry. *Political Myth.* New York:Praeger Publishers, 1972.

Ulam, Adam. *Titoism and the Cominform.* Cambridge, Mass.:Harvard University Press, 1950.

Ulam, Adam. *The Rivals.* New York: Viking Press, 1971.

Ulam, Adam. *Stalin:The Man and His Era.* New York:Viking Press, 1973.

Vandenberg, Arthur, Jr., ed. *The Private Papers of Senator Vandenberg.* Boston:Houghton Mifflin, 1952.

Voegelin, Eric. *New Science of Politics.* Chicago:University of Chicago Press, 1952.

Voegelin, Eric. *Order and History.* Vol. II: *The World of the Polis.* Baton Rouge:University of Louisiana Press, 1956.

282

Wagar, Warren. *Building the City of Man.* New York:Grossman Publishers, 1971.

Walton, Richard. *Cold War and Counterrevolution: The Foreign Policy of John F. Kennedy.* Baltimore, Md.:Penguin Books, 1972.

Waltz, Kenneth. *Man, The State and War.* New York:Columbia University Press, 1954.

Weber, Max. *Aufsätze zur Wissenschaftslehre.* Edited by Johannes Winckelmann. Tübingen: Mohr, 1973.

Wechsler, Herbert. *Principles, Politics and Fundamental Law.* Cambridge, Mass.:Harvard University Press, 1961.

Wells, Sumner. *Seven Decisions that Shaped History.* New York: Harper, 1950.

Werth, Alexander. *Russia at War.* New York:Viking Press, 1966.

Wildavski, Aaron. *The Politics of the Budgetary Process.* Boston:Little, Brown, 1964.

Williams, William A. *The Tragedy of American Diplomacy.* New York:Dell Books, 1962.

Wittgenstein, Ludwig. *Philosphische Untersuchungen.* Translated by G.E.M. Anscombe. New York:Macmillan, 1953.

Wohlstetter, Albert. *Selection and Use of Strategic Air Bases.* Santa Barbara, Calif.:Rand Corp., 1954. (Declassified, 1962).

Wolfe, Thomas. *Soviet Strategy at the Cross Roads.* Cambridge, Mass.:Harvard University Press, 1964.

Wolfe, Thomas. *Soviet Power and Europe.* Baltimore, Md.:The Johns Hopkins University Press, 1970.

Wolfers, Arnold. *Discord and Collaboration.* Baltimore, Md.:The Johns Hopkins University Press, 1962.

Young, Oran. *The Intermediaries.* Princeton, N.J.:Princeton University Press, 1967.

Young, Oran. *The Politics of Force.* Princeton, N.J.:Princeton University Press, 1968.

Zagoria, Donald. *The Sino-Soviet Conflict, 1956-61.* Princeton, N.J.:Princeton University Press, 1963.

Zhdanov, Andrei. *Essays on Literature, Philosophy and Music.* New York:Intern Publishers, 1950.'

Zimmerman, William. *Soviet Perspectives on International Relations.* Princeton, N.J.:Princeton University Press, 1969.

Articles

Alker, Hayward. "Dimensions of Conflict in the General Assembly." *American Political Science Review*, 58 (September 1964): 642-58.

Augenstein, B.W. "The Chinese and French Programs for the Development of National Nuclear Forces." *Orbis*, XI (Fall 1967):642-58.

Bachrach, Peter, and Baratz, Morton. "Decision and Non-Decision." *American Political Science Review*, 52 (1963): 632-42.

Ball, George W. "Top Secret: The Prophecy of the President Rejected." *Atlantic Monthly*, 230 (July 1972): 35-39.

Barkun, Michael. "International Norms: An Interdisciplinary Approach." *Background*, 8, No. 2: 121-29.

Bell, Daniel. "Twelve Models of Prediction." *Daedalus* (Summer 1964): 845-80.

Blumer, Herbert. "Society as Symbolic Interaction." In Herbert Blumer, *Symbolic Interactionism*. Englewood Cliffs, N.J.: Prentice-Hall, 1969.

Boulding, Kenneth. "Organization and Conflict." *Journal of Conflict Resolution*, I (1957): 122-34.

Bridgham, Philip. "The P'eng Te Huai Affair," in John Lewis, *Party Leadership and Revolutionary Power in China*, pp. 203-235. Cambridge: Cambridge University Press, 1970.

Brzezinski, Zbigniew. "The Balance of Power Delusion." *Foreign Policy*, No. 7 (Summer 1972): 54-59.

Buchan, Alastair. "The Multilateral Force," in *Problems of National Strategy*, pp. 285-86. Edited by Henry Kissinger. New York: Praeger Publishers, 1965.

Bull, Headly. "Order and Justice in International Society." *Political Studies*, 19 (1971): 269-83.

Bullitt, William. "How We Won the War and Lost the Peace." *Life* 25, Part 1 (August 30, 1948): 94.

Burin, Frederic. "The Communist Doctrine and the Inevitability of War." *American Political Science Review*, 57 (1963): 334-54.

Burns, Arthur. "Military Technological Models and World Order." *International Journal*, 42, No. 4 (Fall 1969): 790-800.

Chase, John. "Unconditional Surrender Reconsidered." *Political Science Quarterly*, 70 (1955): 258-79.

Chroust, AntonHermann. "Law: Reason, Legalism and the Judicial Process." *Ethics*, LXXIV (October 1963): 1-18.

Coser, Lewis. "The Termination of Conflict." *Journal of Conflict Resolution*, V

(1961): 347-53.

Coser, Lewis. "Peaceful Settlements and the Dysfunction of Secrecy." *Journal of Conflict Resolution*, VII, No. 3 (1963): 246-53.

Dahl, Robert. "A Critique of the Ruling Elite Model." *American Political Science Review*, 52 (1958): 463-70.

Dinerstein, Herbert. "The Soviet Union and the Communist World." *Survey*, 19 (Spring 1973): 140-50.

Dornan, James. "The Nixon Doctrine and the Primacy of Detente." *Intercollegiate Review*, 9 (Spring 1974): 77-96.

Dulles, John Foster. "The Cost of Peace." *Department of State Bulletin*, 34 (June 18, 1956): 999-1001.

Dulles, John Foster. "A Policy of Boldness." *Life*, 32 (May 19, 1952): 52-55.

Falk, Richard. "International Jurisdiction: Horizontal and Vertical Conceptions of Legal Order." *Temple Law Quarterly*, 32 (1959): 295-320.

Falk, Richard. "The Relations of Law to Culture, Power and Justice." *Ethics*, LXXII (1961-62): 12-27.

Falk, Richard. "The Domains of Law and Justice." *International Journal*, XXXI, No. 1 (1975-76): 1-13.

Fallaci, Oriana. "Kissinger." *New Republic*, December 16, 1972, p. 21.

Feis, Herbert. "The Conflict Over Trade Ideologies." *Foreign Affairs*, 25 (January 1947): 225-36.

Fink, Clinton. "Some Conceptual Difficulties in the Theory of Social Conflict." *Journal of Conflict Resolution*, XII (1968): 413-60.

Fisher, Roger. "Perceiving the World Through Bipolar Glasses." *Daedalus*, 93 (1964): 910-15.

Ford, Harold. "The Eruption of Sino-Soviet Politico-Military Problems 1957-1960." In *Sino-Soviet Military Relations*. Edited by Raymond Garthoff. New York: Praeger Publishers, 1966.

Foster, William. "New Directions in Arms Control." *Foreign Affairs*, 43 (July 1965): 587-601.

Galay, Nikolai. "New Trends in Soviet Military Doctrine." *Bulletin, Institute for the Study of the USSR*, 3, No. 6 [June 1956]: 2-12.

Gallois, Pierre. "U.S. Strategy and the Defense of Europe." In *Problems of National Strategy*, pp. 228-312. Edited by Henry Kissinger. New York: Praeger Publishers, 1965.

Galtung, Johann. "A Structural Theory of Imperialism." *Journal of Peace Research*, 8 (1971): 81-117.

Gilpin, Robert. "The Politics of Transnational Economic Relations." *International Organization,* 25(Summer 1971): 398-414.

Glackin, James. "How Secrecy Played Executioner." *Bulletin of the Atomic Scientist,* XXXI, No. 6: 14-16.

Gray, Collin S. "What RAND Hath Wrought." *Foreign Policy,* No. 4 (Fall 1971): 111-29.

Halperin, Morton. "The Gaither Committee and the Policy Process." *World Politics,* 13, No. 3 (April 1961): 360-84.

Halperin, Morton. "Why Bureaucrats Play Games." *Foreign Policy,* No. 2 (1971): 70-90.

Halperin, Morton. "The Decision to Deploy the ABM: Bureaucratic and Domestic Politics in the Johnson Administration." *World Politics,* 25 (1972): 62-95.

Hamburger, Harry. "Separable Games." *Behavioral Science,* 14(1969): 121-32.

Harasanyi, J.C. "On the Rationality Postulates Underlying the Theory of Cooperative Games." *Journal of Conflict Resolution,* 5 (1961): 179-96.

Harris, Jonathan. "Historicus on Stalin." *Soviet Union,* Pt. 1 (1974): 54:73.

Hays, David G. "Language and Interpersonal Relationships." *Daedalus,* (Summer 1973): 203-216.

Herring, George. "Lend and Lease to Russia and the Origins of the Cold War, 1944-45." *Journal of American History,* 56 (June 1969): 93-114.

Hoffmann, Stanley. "Report of the Confernece on Conditions of World Order." *Daedalus.* 95(1966): 455-78.

Hoffmann, Stanley. "Weighing the Balance of Power." *Foreign Affairs,* 50(July 1972): 613-43.

Hoffmann, Stanley. "Will the Balance Balance at Home?" *Foreign Policy,* No. 7 (Summer 1972): 60-85.

Hoffmann, Stanley. "After the Creation, the Watch and the Arrow." *International Journal,* 28 (Spring 1973): 175-84.

Historicus. "Stalin on Revolution." *Foreign Affairs,* 27 (January 1949): 363-89.

Jaffee, Philip. "The Cold War Revisionists and What They Omit." *Survey,* 19 (Fall 1973): 123-43.

Kanet, Roger. "The Soviet Union and the Colonial Question." In Roger Kanet, *The Soviet Union and the Developing Nations.* Baltimore, Md.:Johns Hopkins University Press, 1974.

Kautsky, John. "Myth, Self-fulfilling Prophecy, and Symbolic Reassurance in the East-West Conflict." *Journal of Conflict Resolution,* 9(1968):1-18.
286

Kelman, Herbert C. "Compliance, Identification and Internationalization." *Journal of Conflict Resolution,* II (1958): 51-60.

Kennan, George. "Polycentrism and Western Policy." *Foreign Affairs,* 42 (July 1964): 171-83.

Kissinger, Henry. "Coalition Diplomacy in the Nuclear Age." *Foreign Affairs,* 42 (July 1964): 525-45.

van der Kroef, Julius. "The Soviet Union and South East Asia." in Roger Kanet, *The Soviet Union and the Developing Nations,* pp.79-118. Baltimore, Md.: Johns Hopkins University Press, 1974.

Ladner, Robert. "Strategic Interaction and Conflict." *Journal of Conflict Resolution,* XVII (1973): 175-84.

Leonhard, Wolfgang. "The Domestic Politics of the New Soviet Foreign Policy." *Foreign Affairs,* 52 (October 1973):59-74.

Levi, Werner. "On the Cause of Peace." *Journal of Conflict Resolution,* VIII, No. 1 (1964): p. 23-36.

Löwenthal, Richard. "On National Democracy." *Survey,* No. 47 (April 1963): 119-33.

Mack, Raymond. "The Components of Social Conflict." *Social Problems,* 22 (1965): 388-97.

McDougall, Laswell et al. "The World Constitutive Process of Authoritative Decision." *Journal of Legal Education,* 19 (1967): No. 3, pp. 253-300, and No. 4, pp.403-437.

Masters, Roger. "World Politics as a Primitive Political System." *World Politics,* 16 (1964): 595-619.

Mastny, Vojtech. "Stalin and the Prospects of a Separate Peace in World War II." *American Historical Review,* 77 (1972): 1365-88.

Milburn, Thomas E. "What Constitutes Effective Deterrence?" *Journal of Conflict Resolution,* II (June 1959): 138-45.

Mosley, Peter. "The Dismemberment of Germay." *Foreign Affairs,* 28 (April 1950): 437-98.

Nixon, Richard. "Asia After Vietnam." *Foreign Affairs,* 46 (October 1967): 111-125.

Ojha, Ishwer. "The Kremlin and Third World Leadership—Closing the Circle?" In *Soviet Policy in Developing Countries.* Edited by Raymond Ducan. Waltham, Mass.: Ginn Blaisdell, 1970.

Osgood, Charles E. "Questioning Some Unquestioned Assumptions About National Defense." *Journal of Arms Control,* I (January 1963): 14-26.

Paterson, Thomas G. "The Abortive Loan to Russia and the Origins of the Cold

War, 1943-46." *Journal of American History,* 56 (June 1969): 70-92.

Pipes, Richard. "Operational Principles of Soviet Foreign Policy." *Survey,* 19 (Spring 1973): 41-61.

Powers, Richard. "Who Fathered Containment." *International Studies Quarterly,* 15 (1971): 526-43.

Ra'anan, Uri. "Moscow and the Third World." *Problems of Communism,* 14(January-February 1965): 21-31.

Raskin, M.F. "Political Anxiety and Nuclear Reality." *American Journal of Psychiatry,* CXX (March 1964): 831-36.

Richardson, J.S. "Cold War Revisionism: A Critique." *World Politics,* 24 (1972): 579-612.

Rostow, Walt W. "The Third Round." *Foreign Affairs,* 42 No. 1 (October 1963): 1-10.

Rostow, Walt W. "The Great Transition." *Department of State Bulletin,* 56 (March 27, 1967): 495-506.

Russet, Bruce. "Pearl Harbor, Deterrence Theory and Decision Theory." *Journal of Peace Research,* 4 (1967): 89-106.

Scharpf, Fritz W. "Judicial Review and the Political Questions Doctrine." *Yale Law Journal,* 75 (March 1966): 517-98.

Schilling Warner. "The H Bomb Decision." *Political Science Quarterly,* 76 (1961): 24-47.

Sellen, Robert W. "Old Assumptions versus New Realities: Lyndon Johnson and Foreign Policy." *International Journal,* 28 (Spring 1973): 206-29.

Shepley, James. "How Dulles Averted War." *Life,* 40 (January 16,1956): 77-80.

Smolinski, Leo, and Wiles, Peter. "The Soviet Planning Pendulum." *Problems of Communism,* XII (November-December 1963): 21-33.

Starobin, Joseph. "Origins of the Cold War: The Communist Dimension." *Foreign Affairs,* 48 (July 1969): 681-96.

Wiegele, Thomas. "The Origins of the MLF Concept 1957-1960." *Orbis,* XII (Summer 1968): 469-86.

Wilson, Warner. "Reciprocation and Other Techniques for Inducing Cooperation in the Prisoners' Dilemma Game." *Journal of Conflict Resolution,* 15. No. 2 (June 1971): 167-96.

Wohlstetter, Albert. "The Delicate Balance of Terror." *Foreign Affairs,* 37, No. 2 (January 1959): 211-34.

Yellon, R.A. "Shifts in Soviet Policy in Developing Countries." In *Soviet Policy in Developing Countries.* Edited by Raymond Duncan, Waltham,

Mass.: Ginn Blaisdell, 1970.

Young, Oran. "International Law and Social Science." *American Journal of International Law*, 66 (1972): 60-77.

Young, Oran. "Peace and Justice as Components of World Order." *Millennium*, 4, No. 1 (1975): 1-9.

Monographs and Unpublished Materials

Burd, Frank. "World Order as a Final Cause in the Foreign Policy of Henry Kissinger." Paper prepared for the Annual Meeting of the International Studies Association. Washington, D.C., February 21, 1975. (Mimeographed).

Caldwell, Dan. "The Ambiguities of Detente." Paper prepared for the symposium on the Theory and Practice of Henry Kissinger's Statesmanship. College Park, Md., September 25-27, 1975. (Mimeographed).

Cohen, Samuel. "SALT and the Test Ban: Parallels and Prospects." California Arms Control and Foreign Policy Seminar, May 1973.

Diesing, Paul. "Decision-Making." State University of New York at Buffalo. (Mimeographed: no further data given.)

Diesing, Paul. "Notes on a Cognitive Process Model of Bargaining." Working Paper No. 7. State University of New York at Buffalo. (Mimeographed).

Diesing, Paul. "Types of Bargaining Theory." Working Paper No. 5. State University of New York at Buffalo (Mimeographed, no further data).

Ellsberg, Daniel. "The Crude Analysis of Strategic Choices." Santa Monica, Calif.: Rand Corp., December 15, 1960.

Falk, Richard. "What is Wrong with Henry Kissinger's Foreign Policy." Policy Memorandum No. 39. Princeton University, Center of International Studies, July 1974.

Hunter, Douglas E. "Development of a Decision Making Model in Nuclear Deterrence Theory." Ph.D. dissertation, University of Southern California, 1973.

Kinnard, Leo. "Strategic Innovation and the Eisenhower Administration." Ph.D. dissertation, Princeton University, 1973.

Lockhart, Charles. "The Formulation of Interaction Strategies in International Crisis." Ph.D. dissertation, State University of New York at Buffalo, 1971.

Marshall, A.W. "Bureaucratic Behavior and the Strategic Arms Competition." Southern California Arms Control and Foreign Policy Seminar, 1971.

Monks, Alfred. "Soviet Military Doctrine: 1964 to Armed Forces Day 1969." Ph.D. dissertation, University of Pennsylvania, 1970.

Rosen, Steven. "The Ideal Type of War." Ph.D. dissertation, University of Syracuse, 1972.

Snyder, Glenn. "Prisoner's Dilemma and Chicken Models in International Politics," Working Paper No. 4. University of New York at Buffalo, no date. (Mimeographed).

York, Herbert. 'SALT I and the Future of Arms Control and Disarmament." California Arms Control and Foreign Policy Seminar, May 1973.

Young, Oran. "On International Order." Princeton University, Center of International Studies, 1971. (Mimeographed).

Index